*Lost T'ai-chi Classics
from the
Late Ch'ing Dynasty*

SUNY Series in Chinese Philosophy and Culture
David L. Hall and Roger T. Ames, editors

Lost T'ai-chi Classics
from the
Late Ch'ing Dynasty

Douglas Wile

State University of New York Press

Published by
State University of New York Press, Albany

For information, address State University of New York Press,
State University Plaza, Albany, N.Y. 12246

Production by Dana Foote
Marketing by Bernadette LaManna

Library of Congress Cataloging-in-Publication Data

Wile, Douglas.
    Lost T'ai-chi classics from the late Ch'ing dynasty / Douglas
Wile.
        p. cm. — (SUNY series in Chinese philosophy and culture)
    Includes bibliographical references and index.
    ISBN 0-7914-2653-X (hc:alk. paper). — ISBN 0-7914-2654-8 (pbk. :
alk. paper).
    1. T'ai-chi ch'üan. I. Title. II. Series
GV504.W46 1996   96–17699
613.7'148—dc20   CIP

10 9 8 7 6 5 4 3 2 1

CONTENTS

Contents

PREFACE

Visitors to this museum may wish to consult the Table of Contents as a kind of floor plan before proceeding. Some might wish to visit every room in the museum and others might have more specialized interests. We look forward to welcoming three kinds of visitors: t'ai-chi ch'üan practitioners, martial arts historians, and scholars of late imperial China. The exhibit on the ground floor, "Social and Historical Background of T'ai-ch'i Ch'üan in the Nineteenth Century," should appeal to practitioners and scholars alike. The second floor features a critical retrospective of the previously received classics, which is aimed primarily at practitioners and martial arts historians. The third floor offers a collection of newly discovered nineteenth-century masterpieces published for the first time in the last decade. This show is essential viewing for all practitioners and martial arts history enthusiasts. The fourth-floor exhibit, "Significance of the New Texts," was specifically mounted for the enjoyment of students of t'ai-chi literature and history. Appendix 1 offers the full original Chinese texts drawn from sources that might otherwise be very difficult to locate. Appendix 2 serves as the research and restoration department, where the curious can observe the behind-the-scenes methods that produced the various exhibitions. All of the museum's exhibits are unified by the theme of t'ai-chi ch'üan in the formative nineteenth century, but the individual collections are designed so that visitors can begin on any floor that initially interests them and move to any other floor for further exploration.

ACKNOWLEDGMENTS

The following individuals have my sincerest gratitude: Bill Eastman, Dana Foote, and Wendy Nelson of SUNY Press for acquisition, production, and editing; Greg Bissell and the late Wu Ta-yeh for a constant stream of articles, ideas, and encouragement; Zhang Xiaoqin of the Chinese Martial Arts Research Institute, Beijing, for her capable diplomatic and detective work and the PSC-CUNY Research Foundation for funding my research in China during the summer of 1993; Bill Brown for masterful translation editing; Michael Cherney and Huang Dong for word-processing wizardry; and finally Janet Christie Wile for reinventing the organization and style.

NOTE ON TRANSLITERATION
OF CHINESE WORDS

The Wade-Giles system of transliteration has been adopted for this book as it is still the standard for library cataloguing. Mass media conversion to the *Hanyü pinyin* system in recent years has made many words, particularly place and personal names, more familiar to readers in *pinyin* romanization. Therefore, with the exception of familiar place names, chiefly major cities (e.g., Beijing, Nanjing) and provinces (e.g., Henan, Shanxi), all other transliterations follow the Wade-Giles system.

NOTE ON ILLUSTRATIONS

The gazetteer maps and drawings reproduced in this volume are our only visual record of the world of the shapers of t'ai-chi ch'üan in the nineteenth century. From Kuang-p'ing Prefecture in southern Hopei, to Yung-nien County, and down to the streets and landmarks of Kuang-p'ing City, they provide a concrete frame for the Wu, Li, and Yang families. The delicate condition of the original string-bound gazetteers makes rare books curators understandably reluctant to expose their treasures to the harsh light of photoreproduction. Fortunately, nearly the entire corpus of Ch'ing gazetteers is available on microfilm. This is highly convenient for most research purposes, but from the point of view of photocopying one is prevented from taking steps to neutralize unwanted shadows and is at the mercy of temperamental microfilm copiers. Nevertheless, and in spite of substandard graphic quality, these vintage illustrations convey some of the atmosphere of the period and may provide valuable clues for other researchers.

INTRODUCTION

Millions of Westerners today have been exposed to media images of elderly Chinese practicing t'ai-chi ch'üan in China's urban parks. Hundreds of thousands of Westerners have taken at least one class in the art themselves and tens of thousands practice on a daily basis for physical and mental health, or as a serious self-defense system. Indeed, t'ai-chi ch'üan—the internal, or soft-style, martial art—might well be considered China's cultural ambassador to the world. Touching the lives of more Westerners, and perhaps more deeply, than books, films, museums, or college courses, t'ai-chi ch'üan is often the entrée to Chinese philosophy, medicine, meditation, and even language. The role of Asian martial arts in contemporary Western culture has attracted the attention of medical and social scientists, and Asian martial arts history has established itself as a branch of Asian Studies. For the tens of millions of practitioners in China today, t'ai-chi ch'üan fills the spiritual vacuum left by the collapse of socialist idealism, and t'ai-chi history has become a major intellectual battleground between myth-centered traditionalists and human-centered rationalists. The time is ripe, then, for a new stage of scholarship in the West to evaluate recently released premodern primary writings and advance new interpretations of t'ai-chi's origins and development.

The question of t'ai-chi ch'üan's origins is hugely controversial. However, when adjusted for stylistic and ideological partisanship and analyzed strictly on the basis of scholarly methodology, the various accounts differ according to their emphasis on the following conceptual tracers: postures and form, training techniques and combat strategies, and philosophy and legend.

If traced as a distinctive form with specific postures and names, then t'ai-chi's history may be said to begin with Ming general Ch'i Chi-kuang's 戚繼光 (1528–87) *Ch'üan-ching* 拳經 (Classic of pugilism), twenty-nine of whose postures are borrowed for the Ch'en Village art of Henan, possibly as early as Ch'en Wang-t'ing in the seventeenth century, and certainly no later than Ch'en Ch'ang-hsing (1771–1853) and Ch'en Ch'ing-p'ing (1795–1868) in the early nineteenth. From Ch'en Ch'ang-hsing the transmission passed to Yang Lu-ch'an (1799–1872) of Yung-nien County, Hebei, creator of the Yang style, and from Lu-ch'an's son Pan-hou to Ch'üan-yu (1834–1902) and his son Wu Chien-ch'üan (1870–1942), creator of the Wu style. Wu Yü-hsiang (1812?–1880?) studied with Lu-ch'an and Ch'en Ch'ing-p'ing and passed his Wu (Hao) style to his nephew Li I-yü (1832–92). Li in turn transmitted his art to Hao Wei-chen (1842–1920), who taught Sun Lu-t'ang (1861–1932), the creator of the Sun style. The paucity of pre-twentieth-century theoretical writings in Ch'en Village prior to the twentieth century and the difficulty of dating and authenticating genealogies and form manuals there leaves the door open for questions of which Ch'en created the art or whether it was transmitted from the outside. When specifically t'ai-chi theoretical texts do appear, it is with Wu Yü-hsiang in the nineteenth century, and his editor and mouthpiece Li I-yü attributes them not to Ch'en Village but to an accidental manuscript find in Wu-yang County, Henan, and to a mysterious master, Wang Tsung-yüeh. Attempts to construct a linear one-dimensional transmission based on form alone is somewhat successful for the late nineteenth and twentieth centuries, but prior to that is frustrated by inadequate and falsified documentary records.

If we ignore the external form and focus exclusively on a distinctive theory of internal training and soft-style strategy, then the line begins with Huang Tsung-hsi's (1610–95) "Wang Cheng-nan mu-chih ming" 王征南墓志銘 (Epitaph for Wang Cheng-nan) and Huang's son, Pai-chia's, "Nei-chia ch'üan-fa" 內家拳法 (Methods of the internal school of pugilism), which describe a strategy based on "stillness overcoming movement" and "reversing the principles of Shaolin." The Internal School form, as described by Huang Pai-chia, bears little resemblance to t'ai-chi forms, and it is not until a century later that we have a similar statement of soft-style principles. Furthermore, although Pai-chia traces the Internal School transmission from his teacher Wang Lai-hsien (Cheng-nan) all the way back to "Chang San-feng of the Sung," he says that he himself abandoned the art and thus suspended the transmission. After the Huangs in the late seventeenth century, the next documentary evidence of soft-style theory is Ch'ang Nai-chou in the late eighteenth century. Once again Ch'ang's form is radically different from any known t'ai-chi form, yet the emphasis on slow movements during training, sticking to the opponent, and concentrating and circulating the *ch'i*, as well as numerous verbatim parallels with the t'ai-chi classics, suggests a long-lost relative and very possibly a missing link. Finally, in tracing the theoretical lineage of t'ai-chi ch'üan we come to the t'ai-chi classics themselves, containing probably a pre-nineteenth-century core, edited and augmented by Wu Yü-hsiang and reedited by Li I-yü. Thus, tracing the history of t'ai-chi ch'üan at the level of theory and principles shows considerable intellectual continuity but no historical lineage to connect the literary dots. An unbroken master–disciple transmission might not in fact be necessary if we consider that soft-style theory is permanently embedded in the culture and perennially available to any art, or that it is a universal kinesthetic possibility that can be rediscovered at any time through praxis.

If we trace the evolution of the art at the level of general philosophical principles and semihistorical Taoist figures, then there is no need for documentary evidence of the marriage of these principles with martial arts or of the participation of these figures in martial arts. Such transmission lineages often begin with the putative founder of Taoism, Lao Tzu, in the Eastern Chou (770–221 B.C.E.) and include reclusive poet Hsü Hsüan-p'ing of the T'ang (618–907) and alchemist Chang San-feng of the Sung (960–1279), Yüan (1271–1368) or Ming (1368–1644). Using these legendary figures as root and trunk, more historical branches can be grafted on in places such as Ch'en Village, Chao-pao Village, the Wu-tang Mountains, or with figures such as Sung Shu-ming of the late Ch'ing. The motivation for constructing such mythologies may be as parochial as aggrandizing one's own lineage or as patriotic as exalting the whole of Chinese culture.

The historical, the theoretical, and the mythological approaches may supplement each other to some degree, but ultimately the modern intellectual historian will want names, places, and dates and will insist on evidence of principles and practice coming together. It is precisely a lack of reliable documentary evidence—primary (the writings of masters and theoreticians) and secondary (biographies and histories)—that has plagued researchers since serious efforts at tracing t'ai-chi's origins began in the 1930s. In fact, not since Wu Yü-hsiang's manuscripts edited by Li I-yü and Li's own writings came to light in the 1930s have we had significant new nineteenth-century source materials. However, in the recent Deng era climate of "openness" and "modernization," families and collectors of t'ai-chi texts have felt safe to come forward with literary treasures that have survived the antifeudal book burnings of the Cultural Revolution and nearly a century and a half of tumultuous history. These texts released between 1985 and 1993 represent the writings of Wu Yü-hsiang's older brothers, Ch'eng-ch'ing and Ju-ch'ing, Yü-hsiang's nephew, Li I-Yü, and Yang Lu-ch'an's son Pan-hou.

The recorded history of t'ai-chi ch'üan may be divided into four phases: legendary, Ch'en Village, Yung-nien, and Beijing and beyond. Scholarly research has hitherto focused on the Ch'en Village phase, for which unimpeachable documentary records are scant, and neglected the Yung-nien phase, which includes the Wu, Li, Hao, and Yang families. This is probably because the center of the Yung-nien discussion has been Wu Yü-hsiang, about whom reliable biographical information is almost nonexistent, and Yang Lu-ch'an, who left no writings (probably because of his illiteracy), and accounts of whose background and activities are anecdotal and wildly contradictory. The occasion of the revelation of new Ch'eng-ch'ing, Ju-ch'ing, Li I-yü, and Yang Pan-hou material is the perfect time to reopen the Yung-nien file. This book, then, seeks to accomplish three goals. First, it presents a translation of the new material for the sake of the theoretical and technical teachings it offers to the practitioner. Second, it seeks to reexamine the previously received classics and outstanding problems in t'ai-chi history in light of these new works. Third, it attempts to make use of nineteenth-century historical documents, modern scholarship on the period, and parallels with other late-nineteenth-century non-Western societies to illuminate the social and historical background of the pre-modern shapers of t'ai-chi ch'üan and to place it in the context of late-Ch'ing intellectual history. T'ai-chi practitioners will find a new infusion of primary texts—classics, if you will—and sinologists will glimpse a neglected facet of late imperial history.

SOCIAL AND HISTORICAL BACKGROUND OF T'AI-CHI CH'ÜAN IN THE NINETEENTH CENTURY

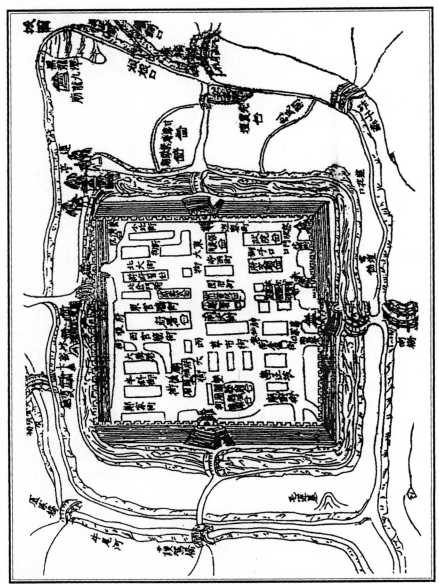

Map of Kang-p'ing City showing the Lien-t'ing (Lotus pavillion) restored by Wu Ju-ch'ing at the upper right, Tung ta chieh (East grand street) dividing the eastern half of the city north and south where the Wu family lived, and the Nan-kuan (South gate) where the Yang family lived south of the city walls. From the *Yung-nien Gazetteer*.

The Wu brothers came of age at the turn of the nineteenth century, a time when Manchu overthrow, defeat at the hands of the West, and large-scale peasant rebellion were all unthinkable. As the Wu brothers entered middle age, the Opium Wars and Taiping Rebellion shook the foundations of the dynasty and caused the near collapse of the world as they knew it. It was in the midst of this crisis that Yang Lu-ch'an returned to Yung-nien from Ch'en Village, Wu Yü-hsiang studied with Ch'en Ch'ing-p'ing, and Wu Ch'eng-ch'ing reportedly found the classics in Wu-yang. These momentous events for the evolution of t'ai-chi ch'üan did not take place on mist-wrapped mountains. Modern intellectual historians are able to place the ancient Greek Olympics in the context of classical ideals of physical beauty and health and admiration for feats of strength and endurance. Nineteenth-century romantics' rage for swimming can likewise be seen in light of their reaction against crass industrialism and bourgeois conformity, their desire to commune with the gods and goddesses of woods and water, and their flirting with the mystery and danger of the sea. However, the tendency to treat the story of t'ai-chi ch'üan in an historical vacuum has been correctly identified by Wu Wen-han:

> In the past, students of the development of t'ai-chi ch'üan have ignored historical, economic, and political conditions and have focused narrowly on the art itself and a small number of masters.[1]

Anything earlier than the Republican period (1911–49) tends to slip into the mist of "ancient China," and we often overlook the fact that Yang Lu-ch'an and the Wu brothers were of the same generation as Darwin and Marx, and that the Li brothers were contemporaries of Einstein, Freud, and Gandhi. Railroads, telegraph, and missionary schools were already part of the Chinese landscape, and Chinese armies (and rebels) sometimes carried modern Western rifles. How often have we stopped to reflect that Yang Lu-ch'an was probably in Beijing in 1860 when British and French troops stormed the capital and the Manchu Emperor took flight. It is our proposition, then, that this watershed period in the evolution of the art and theory of t'ai-chi ch'üan did not take place in spite of larger social and historical events but somehow in response to them. Although the "classics"

3

and early writings, the focus of our study here, have a timeless, art-for-art's-sake tone, this should not prevent us from asking who were the Ch'ens, Yangs, Wus, and Lis, why did they involve themselves in the martial arts, and why did they create this kind of martial art? This section will begin to describe in a very general way the world of the Wus, Yangs, and Lis and what can be gathered from actual historical documents of their family backgrounds.

China and the Nations

The century that bounds the lives of Wu Ch'eng-ching (b. 1800), Li I-yü (d. 1892), and the Yung-nien t'ai-chi circle began in one world and ended in another. For China, whose cultural self-image was still one of centrality and superiority, to confront a swarm of new barbarians "from across the sea" while old barbarians from the north still sat on the dragon throne was a complex political and psychological ordeal. The Manchu tiger, now old and enfeebled herself, still jealously guarded the bones of China's old carcass from the strong young jackals at the gates. However, by the early 1800s, fired by industrialism, science, democracy, evangelical Christianity, and, above all, a belief in the divine right of trade, the West, led by Great Britain, would not be barred from China. Britain's reliance on opium smuggling to offset an unfavorable balance of trade, and the general incompatibility of the political and economic instruments of interface, led to the Opium War of 1839, which after China's easy defeat exposed the military weakness of the dynasty. The Treaty of Nanking, signed in 1842, and subsequent "unequal treaties" wrested from China Hong Kong, five Treaty Ports, the International Settlement, extraterritoriality, a war indemnity, a 5 percent tariff limit, most-favored-nation protection, and missionary access. Thus, in the first years of the 1840s, China suffered a humiliating defeat and substantial loss of sovereignty.

Still not satisfied with Chinese concessions, the British and French attacked again in 1856, seizing Canton in 1858 and Beijing in 1860. Better channels of communication were then developed following the Treaty of Tientsin, which paved the way for Western diplomats to reside in Beijing, the establishment of the Tsung-li ya-men to handle negotiations, and even the opening of a Ch'ing embassy in London in 1877. The scent of blood from the wounded empire excited the ambitions of rapidly modernizing Japan, who seized the Ryukyu Islands in 1872, followed by expeditions against Korea and Formosa. The Russian czar won access to the eastern coast of Manchuria in 1860, and in 1880 a dispute over the Ili region in Turkestan brought Russian ships to menace the port of Ningbo. French colonial expansion in Indo-China led to the Sino-French War in 1883, culminating in France's attack on Taiwan and the bombardment of the Fuzhou shipyards. Although Li I-yü died just two years before the Sino-Japanese War of 1894, the century ended with China's most humiliating defeat, the loss of Taiwan and Korea, and the international race to "carve up the Chinese melon."

The economic effects of foreign penetration touched even more lives than did "gunboat diplomacy" and "unequal treaties." Opium trafficking created a huge underground economy, draining silver from the country, corrupting officialdom, and devastating the lives of millions from all classes. Importation of foreign factory goods undercut domestic Chinese handicrafts, an essential supplement to peasant income. Cash cropping and the rapid expansion of commercialism created new wealth for the few who benefited from cooperation with the West, but led to inflation and rising taxes that further increased the misery of the peasantry and nascent proletariat. Revenues diverted from public works into military defense led to a neglect of dikes, canals, and granaries and exposed the populace to the ravages of flood, drought, and famine.

The shapers of modern t'ai-chi ch'üan thus witnessed repeated military defeat and reduction of the empire to semicolonial status. T'ai-chi ch'üan as we know it today rose from the ashes of a collapsing empire. With roots that clearly reach back farther than the nineteenth century, t'ai-chi's association with national revival did not become explicit until the twentieth. China's anti-imperialist struggles began in the nineteenth century, yet t'ai-chi writings from this period do not yet show self-conscious patriotic sentiments. Succeeding sections of this chapter will explore t'ai-chi ch'üan as a cultural response to China's political predicament.

Rebellion at Home

T'ai-chi ch'üan as we know it today was born not only in a period of national crisis, but at the geographic epicenter of the most intense sectarian rebellions in China's history. Subjected to nearly annual drought or flood, the provinces of the North China Plain—Hebei and Henan, Shandong and Shanxi—were traditional hotbeds of sectarian rebellion going all the way back to the Red Eyebrows and Yellow Turbans of the Han (206 B.C.E.–220 C.E.), Huang Chao's rebellion during the T'ang (618–907), and the rebel-heroes of the Sung (960–1127) immortalized in the novel *Water Margin*. During the late Yüan (1271–1368) and through the

Ming (1368–1644) and Ch'ing (1644–1911) the White Lotus Sect was a rallying point for popular unrest, and Hsü Hung-ju's rebellion at the end of the Ming was one of the first to combine a millenarian movement with martial arts elements borrowed from the Cudgel and Whip Society. This volatile mix of religious heterodoxy and martial arts flared again in Wang Lun's rebellion of 1774, the Eight Trigrams of 1813, and the antiforeign Boxer Uprising of 1898–1900.

The Wu brothers' hometown, Yung-nien, was located in the middle of the Eight Trigrams Sect's base area, southern Hebei/northern Henan, and the brothers were young boys when a force of Eight Trigrams guerrillas broke into Beijing's Forbidden City itself. Martial arts scholar Chao Hsi-min, who believes that Wu Yü-hsiang wrote the "classics" himself, contends that t'ai-chi theory is simply borrowed from Eight Trigram's sectarian teachings.[2] Other millenarian movements that swept over Yung-nien in the nineteenth century included the Celestial Principle Society, the Celestial Bamboo Sect, and the Prebirth Sect, all of which were prone to turn from magical salvation to militant rebellion in times of crisis.

Passing over regional rebellions in other parts of the empire, the most entrenched and long-lived antidynastic movement in North China during the nineteenth century was the Nien Rebellion. Originating in the area north of the Huai River in Anhui Province, it spread to Shandong, Henan, and Hebei between the years 1852 (when Ch'eng-ch'ing was appointed magistrate in Wu-yang) and 1868 (when Ju-ch'ing declined Tso Tsung-t'ang's invitation to join his counterinsurgency campaign). Although scholars disagree over whether to classify the Niens as bandits, rebels, or revolutionaries, their military strategy shifted from entrenchment in walled communities (originally established to repulse bandits) to reliance on mobile cavalry units. The rusty Manchu Bannermen were no match for the resourceful Nien, and they were suppressed only by the regional Chinese armies of Tseng Kuo-fan (1811–72), Li Hung-chang (1823–1901), and Tso Tsung-t'ang (1812–85).

Although originating in South China among the Hakka minority of Guangdong in 1850, the Taiping Rebellion cannot be overlooked here, because at its height it controlled the rich Yangtze River basin, established a rival capital and dynasty in Nanjing, and was turned back only at Tianjin in 1864. Creatively borrowing from missionary tracts, the movement's leader, Hung Hsiu-ch'üan, proclaimed himself the younger brother of Jesus and preached a message of anti-Confucian and anti-Manchu utopianism. In 1853, the Taiping Northern Expedition overran Ssu-shui, where Ch'ang Nai-chou's descendants still lived, but after crossing the Yellow River were repelled, according to the *Yung-nien Gazetteer*, at Huai-ch'ing

Prefecture (the location of Ch'en Village), and thus Yung-nien was spared. Again the rebellion was successfully suppressed only by regional and mercenary armies when the foreign powers decided to prop up the dynasty by supplying munitions, advisors, commanders, and even troops on the ground. The proliferation of reprints and anthologies of Ming military strategists (Ch'i Chi-kuang, T'ang Shun-chih, Ho Liang-ch'en, Mao Yüan-i, et al.) during the late Ch'ing dynasty attests to gentry-class anxiety over military defense.

The persistence of rebellion during the nineteenth century puts into historical perspective the Wu brothers' participation in militia training, counterinsurgency, community fortification, and contacts with regional military leaders, Tseng Kuo-fan and Tso Tsung-t'ang. Late Ch'ing gazetteer maps show approximately forty garrisons, stockades, and walled villages in the immediate vicinity of Kuang-p'ing Prefectural City, with those located south of the city, facing the direction of greatest anticipated threat, outnumbering those to the north by a ratio of three to one. As far as defense of the prefectural city itself is concerned, the *Kuang-p'ing Gazetteer* describes Ju-ch'ing's role in these words: "He established the militia in the city, arranged for its budget and weapons, and trained them night and day into a powerful force. That the city held against repeated Taiping and Nien rebel attacks was all due to Ju-ch'ing's efforts."[3]

The North China Plain

Yung-nien County, located virtually at the intersection of the north-south axis of Hebei and Henan and the east-west axis of Shandong and Shanxi is at the heart of what William Skinner calls the "North China macroregion." Continuously populated by humans for half a million years, this alluvial flood plain of the Yellow River stretches flat for hundreds of miles in every direction. Flatness means flooding, and flooding means enrichment by loess (silt) and devastation by water. Continental climate produces cold, dry winters and hot, humid summers. Lacking irrigation, North China was at the mercy of the late-summer rainy season, which, depending on annual vagaries, could bring floods or drought. In spite of these natural hazards, the region's economy in the nineteenth century was still dependent on subsistence grains—wheat, soy, millet, and sorghum—and population density had risen to approximately five hundred souls per square mile, of whom more than 90 percent were peasants. In 1875, according to the *Yung-nien Gazetteer*, the population of the county was 55,344 households, or 232,420 individuals. Although one of the original cradles of

Chinese civilization and the seat of the imperial capital for almost a thousand years, the North China plain was backward in transportation, commercialization, urbanization, and landlordism, the latter being a symptom of poverty and unattractive real estate prospects.

Environmental and economic conditions produced a number of social phenomena of special relevance to the development of martial arts. Exacerbated by female infanticide and polygamy, North China boasted a surplus of unmarried and unemployed males approaching perhaps 20 percent of the population. These "marginal men" were prime candidates for the ranks of bandits, smugglers, beggars, gamblers, sectarian rebels, kidnappers, tax revolters, vigilantes, family feuders, and refugees. As such, they practiced a "predatory" strategy for survival by illegally expanding their resources at others' expense. Some of this was a redistributive form of "social banditry" aimed at hoarders and corrupt landlords and officials, and some was mere opportunism. The reaction to vertical violence coming from those at the bottom was a "protective strategy" by those at the top. This included village militia, private vigilantes, and crop watching. The final phase of this protective response, sometimes called "coercive closure," involved withdrawing into armed forts and severely restricting access by outsiders. To vertical violence operating along class or sectarian lines must be added the equally pervasive pattern of horizontal violence that took the form of interlineage or intervillage feuds motivated by revenge or sometimes simply profit. Becoming a traditional way of life for generations in some locales, feuds involved not only clan members themselves but mercenaries and "adopted sons" hired or raised to fight in the front ranks or to be handed over as compensation for casualties on the other side. Still other regions were plagued by ethnic conflicts, particularly in the mid nineteenth century between Hans and Muslims, as in Yunnan in the southwest, Gansu/Shaanxi in the northwest, and the nearly permanent state of *jihad* in Xinjiang in the far west.

Living in the path of repeated waves of northern invasion, the people of the North China plain developed a justly deserved reputation for their martial spirit. The *Yung-nien Gazetteer*, Chüan 24, "Military Affairs" states: "From the Spring and Autumn Period [770–476 B.C.E.] down through the Yüan [1271–1368] and Ming [1368–1644] Yung-nien has been a battleground." Whether channeled into soldiering or "social banditry," the martial spirit is as much a part of the cultural landscape of northern China as it is for the southern United States. Although records for military-exam passers are not as complete as for civil exams, and data are somewhat inconsistent in different sources, nevertheless conclusions are dramatic and inescapable. For the hundred-odd times the military metropolitan examinations were held during the two and a half centuries of Ch'ing rule, and averaging totals in different sources and reducing them to ratios, the number of top three placers (*chuang-yüan* 狀元, *pang-yen* 榜眼, *t'an-hua* 探花) for Hebei is approximately three times that for Shandong, and the two together boasted more winners than the remaining sixteen provinces combined. Thus Hebei not only led the nation by a huge margin, but nearly tripled the total of its nearest rival, Shandong, which itself was head and shoulders above the rest. That major style founders, Wu Yü-hsiang, Yang Lu-ch'an, Hao Wei-chen, Wu Chien-ch'üan, and Sun Lu-t'ang, all hailed from Hebei, China's most fertile breeding ground for martial arts, must be more than coincidence.

On the other side of the fence, martial arts were also a feature of sectarian and secret-society activities in North China during the nineteenth century. The Boxers (*I-ho-ch'üan* 義合拳) were only the most notorious example, but techniques of invulnerability, such as Armor of the Golden Bell (*chin-chung-chao* 金鐘罩) and of possession, such as Spirit Boxing (*shen-ch'üan* 神拳) have been traced in North China to the early 1800s. So pervasive was martial arts culture that Joseph Esherick, in commenting on one of the forerunners of the Boxers, concludes:

> More than anything, the Song Jing-shi rebellion illustrates the extent to which martial artists and sectarians had entered the mainstream of peasant life in western Shandong. The participation of martial artists on both rebel and governmental sides bespeaks the prominence of such people in the social fabric of the region.[4]

The stereotype of the effete Confucian literati has long made it difficult to explain the intense involvement in martial arts of the Wu and Li families of Yung-nien. The extraordinarily violent nineteenth century and the martial tradition of the North China plain go a long way to clarifying the picture.

Elite Culture

Confucius had said that those who work with their minds rule and those who work with their hands are ruled. Although landlords constituted perhaps 5 percent of the population of 300 million in late Ch'ing China, degree-holding literati were only about 250,000, or less than 0.1 percent, and there were only about 25,000 upper-level degree holders qualified for important posts in the imperial bureaucracy. Mastery of about ten thousand characters, memorization of the Confucian canon, and essay composition in the "eight-legged" style were the core of the examination system curriculum. Preparation for, travel to, and participation in endless rounds of local, provincial, and national examinations was the life of the literati. The metropolitan exam, the grueling literary Olympics of the system, was held every three years in Beijing. Ch'eng-ch'ing was fifty-two years old when he finally earned his metropolitan degree after eighteen years since his provincial exam, and Ju Ch'ing was thirty-eight with a fifteen-year interval. Moreover, Ju-ch'ing was the only successful *chin-shih* from Yung-nien County in the fifteen years between 1835 and 1850, and he passed in the regular triannual exam. Ch'eng-ch'ing, who won his degree during a specially scheduled exam in 1852, was the only winner from Yung-nien between 1851 and 1859. Thus both men were well into their middle years before "graduating" and winning their first government posts, and this was by no means atypical. Given the content of the exams—largely literary and philosophical—and the slowness of the process, one can see the difficulty of producing men of practical abilities who could respond to new challenges.

With office holding often the sole, and certainly the surest, path to wealth and status, holding public office for private gain came to be the norm. This was done by skimming tax revenues as they passed through one's hands on their way to the imperial treasury and by extorting money from peasants and merchants; "profits" were then invested in land, which was rented to peasants at exorbitant rates. Although these practices were customary and thoroughly institutionalized, the honest official remained an ideal. Ju-ch'ing's biographies praise him extravagantly for prosecuting a case of shortchanging on grain rations for prisoners, accurately reporting on criminal investigations, and refusing bribes.

Elite dominance was maintained, then, first through control of material resources—land, commercial wealth, and military power—but also through social networks. These included clan or kin groups on the local level and might reach all the way up to political cliques in the national ministries and even the imperial court. Personal qualities could also be a significant factor in the elite equation where technical expertise or leadership abilities served to further distinguish an individual and make him useful, particularly in times of national crisis. Much has been made of "symbolic capital" in defining elite status in China, and this includes all the degrees, titles, honors, and ranks, as well as the cultural refinements and lifestyle, of the gentry class. Among the credential-conscious Confucian elite, so coveted were degrees as status symbols during the late Ch'ing, and so desperate was the government to raise revenues, that one-third of all degrees were secured through purchase. Even worse, two-thirds of office holders had qualified to sink their fangs into the miserable peasantry by the "irregular route" of purchase.

Traditional gentry disdain for commerce began to break down during the nineteenth century as trade with the West and indigenous industrialization rapidly expanded. Degree and office holding were still prestigious, but the supply of posts never equaled demand and high public profile brought exposure to intrigue. Land owning was still considered the most secure investment, but new opportunities for wealth through commerce motivated many gentry families to diversify. A typical strategy was to channel some sons into the examination track and others into business. Looking at families, then, rather than individuals, we begin to see in the nineteenth century a fusion of literati and commercial interests within the gentry class. Yü-hsiang's remaining in Yung-nien while his older brothers pursued national careers may in part be explained by the youngest son's obligation to care for his widowed mother, but economic diversification may also have been a factor.

Elite activity may be conveniently divided into official (*kuan* 官), public (*kung* 公), and private (*ssu* 私) spheres. Official functions were those associated with office holding, which because of the "rule of avoidance" barring service in one's native place, meant being posted in distant provinces or in the national capital. Beset by foreign incursions and domestic rebellion, and ossified by ritual and corruption, the official sphere during the period in question occasioned the highest degree of frustration in the life of elites. By contrast, the public sphere experienced exuberant expansion during the same period as local gentry rose to fill the gap left by thinly spread officials in providing education, relief work, and militia defense. With disaster-prone North China's nearly annual crop of refugees, charitable relief was a traditional part of gentry obligations there, but following the wholesale devastation of the Taiping Rebellion (caused as much by government and regional soldiers as by rebels) the task of organizing reconstruction was added to their voluntary functions. Everything from soup kitchens to the repair of city walls fell into the sphere of public activities. The private sphere included business, on the one hand (land management, real estate, manufacturing, or commerce), and self-development, on the other. Attainment in poetry, music, calligraphy, and painting, or even art, antiques, or rare book collecting, could significantly enhance one's status among gentry peers and further distinguish one from the unwashed masses. Private pursuits among less conventional literati might also include scholarly research in medicine, mathematics, or astronomy.

The above outline of gentry-class life during the nineteenth century demonstrates the degree to which the Wu family of Yung-nien were not only typical but highly successful exploiters of the various options opened up by the age. Wu family matriarch, Madame Wu, an award-winning widow, nurtured her three sons into the ranks of upper gentry, two of them earning the coveted *chin-shih* degree. Moreover, in addition to their success in the examination system and distinguished service to the nation, they were leaders in the public sphere through education, public works, gazetteer editing, and militia training, and in the private sphere through business, scholarship, and martial arts. It is only the last of these pursuits—martial arts—that remains somewhat mysterious. Not only are the extant Wu family biographies completely devoid of any reference to martial arts, but the *Yung-nien Gazetteer* has only one lone biography of a martial artist. Notwithstanding elite reticence about being associated with the martial arts, the Yung-nien records must be contrasted with the *Ssu-shui Gazetteer*, which records not only the martial arts activities of scholar Ch'ang Nai-chou but the biographies of many professional martial artists in the section entitled "Notable Personalities" (*ren-wu* 人物).

Late Ch'ing Intellectual Trends

The Wu and Li families' orientation to nineteenth-century intellectual trends is potentially the most fruitful area of investigation for understanding their devotion to t'ai-chi ch'üan. If their motivation were simply "self-defense," we might be more likely to find them clamoring for military modernization, and thus their involvement in t'ai-chi ch'üan must be seen as articulating with some current of thought at the time. This section will attempt to sketch at least the major trends in late Ch'ing thought as the broad context out of which a better understanding of the shaping of t'ai-chi ch'üan as a cultural artifact in the hands of Wu Yü-hsiang and Li I-yü must ultimately come.

Dynastic decline during the late Ming, accompanied by nearly successful peasant rebellion and Manchu conquest, forced intellectuals into a period of intense soul-searching as the alien dynasty closed its grip on China in the mid seventeenth century. The question of loyalty to the Ming—resistance versus accommodation—was the first order of the day. As all hope of restoration faded, attention turned to analyzing the reasons for the failure of the previous dynasty. Philosophically, the Idealist School of Wang Yang-ming (1472–1529) was blamed for focusing on inner life to the neglect of the nuts and bolts of good government. Some, like Huang

Tsung-hsi (1610–85), Wang Fu-chih (1619–85), and Ku Yen-wu (1613–82), sought solutions to fundamental problems of despotism, corruption, and empty erudition. The process of reevaluating the past, and certainly that of protesting the present, was hampered by Manchu censorship and persecution of dissent. Huang, Wang, and Ku were all active in armed resistance, and all refused to serve the alien dynasty before turning to historical, philosophical, and scientific studies. The Manchu state confirmed the orthodoxy of Chu Hsi's (1130–1200) School of Reason, while unofficial scholarly circles were dominated by the Han Learning movement, which turned away from subjectivism and metaphysics to historical and exegetical studies. At the same time, the Eastern Chekiang School, stemming from Huang Tsung-hsi, stressed the importance of empirically based unofficial histories as a counterpoise to self-serving official histories. Another trend promoted by independent minds like Yen Yüan (1635–1704), Li Kung (1659–1733), and Tai Chen (1724–77) argued that universal principles did not exist outside of the material world and that moral progress was a matter not of self-purification but of praxis in the mundane world.

The generation of thinkers that closed out the eighteenth century were able to write critically, but strictly within the native tradition and insulated from Western influence. There is a gap in philosophical discourse between Tai Chen and the radical reformers of the 1890s, like K'ang Yu-wei, Liang Ch'i-ch'ao, and T'an Ssu-t'ung. The generation in between, that of the Wu brothers and Li I-yü, produced two poles: the eremitism of Li Hsi-yüeh's (c.1800–c.1860) Yu-lung Sect and Wei Yüan's (1794–1856) insistence on Western studies, both of whose major works, *Chang San-feng Ch'üan-chi* 張三豐全集 (The Complete Works of Chang San-feng) and *Hai-kuo t'u-chih* 海國圖志 (Illustrated Gazetteer of the Maritime Countries), were published in 1844. The progressive thinkers of Wu's generation, though constitutionally incapable of acknowledging any value in Western intellectual or religious life, accepted the necessity of adopting Western military technology in order to preserve traditional Confucian culture. Reformers like Feng Kuei-fen (1809–87) and Hsüeh Fu-ch'eng (1838–94) could upbraid their countrymen for ineptitude and arrogance and praise the West for intelligence and competence, even while asserting the fundamental superiority of Chinese culture. Meanwhile, Tseng Kuo-fan (1811–72) and Li Hung-chang (1823–1901) seemed to combine personal Confucian virtues and statesmanship with a willingness to adopt Western methods for immediate utility. Wang T'ao (1828–97) begins to anticipate the radical reformers of the generation of the second half of the nineteenth century by suggesting that national renovation go deeper than guns and steamships to the actual educational system and institutions of government. It was not until the post-Taiping generation that a handful of radical thinkers could begin to conceive of China as politically one among equal nations and Confucianism as one of many equal world religions.

In a general way, I think we would not be amiss in saying that the Wu brothers' thinking was aligned with the Self-Strengthening Movement of the mid to late nineteenth century. There is ample evidence in the gazetteers that Ju-ch'ing enjoyed a relationship of mutual admiration with model self-strengtheners Tseng Kuo-fan and Tso Tsung-t'ang. The *Yung-nien Gazetteer* praises the Wu brothers' local hero Shen Tuan-min as one whose life exemplified the words of the *I ching*, "ceaseless self-strengthening." In a biography of Hao Ch'eng-tsung 郝承宗, the *Gazetteer* approvingly says: "There were some in his village who practiced the Catholic religion. He ordered them to disband." This is in keeping with the Self-Strengthening attitude that China might learn from the West in matters of weaponry, and even administration, but certainly not religion. Faith in the sufficiency and superiority of Chinese culture, if the Chinese themselves would but live up to it, must be seen as underlying the Wu brothers' involvement in practicing and promoting t'ai-chi ch'üan in the late nineteenth century.

Most elites of the Wu brothers' generation were too preoccupied with careerism, class dominance, and national defense to launch any bold new intellectual projects. Moreover, they were forced to respond to the challenge of Western and Taiping ideas and the Japanese model of reform with one hand tied behind their backs—fear of offending their ultraconservative Manchu rulers. The West and Japan might be useful in undermining Manchu power, but there was the danger of simply changing alien masters. Nevertheless, available biographical data indicate that the Wu brothers' Confucian sense of social responsibility had a high degree of articulation with national trends towards localism, practical studies, and the search for solutions to the contemporary crisis in traditional sources. By the late 1850s the Wu brothers had withdrawn from the official sphere and plunged into every aspect of local revival. The two and a half centuries of the Manchu dynasty saw a number of cycles of patriotic scholar-officials shifting their attention from the national to the local scene. Given the court's show of impotence and honest officials' frustration with pervasive corruption and conservatism, one can understand the Wu brothers' decision to return to their roots, to publish the writings of the older generation of progressive Yung-nien scholars, and through education, to raise up a new generation of able and committed talent. Echoes of the Han Learning movement, with its emphasis on relevance, can be heard in this passage from Ju-ch'ing's biography in the *Kuang-p'ing Gazetteer:* "He detested superficiality and devoted himself to practical studies, bringing about a great reform in the intellectual climate of the locale." Similarly, Ch'eng-ch'ing's preface to Yen Pin's 閻斌 *Yün-ch'uang i-ts'ao* 芸窗易草 (Random notes on the *I-ching* from the rue window), excerpted in the same gazetteer, praises the author for discovering the practical principles hidden in the hexagrams and text of the *I ching*. Underlying this trend to localism and practical studies is the assumption that new challenges were not qualitatively different from old and that solutions could be found in models of resistance to Manchu conquest or in Han Learning interpretations of the classics. Again, Ju-ch'ing's publication of Sun Hsia-feng's 孫夏峰 *Chi-fu jen-wu k'ao* 畿輔人物考 (A study of famous men from the capital region) and *Ssu-shu chin-chih* 四書近指 (Lessons for today from the Four Books) typifies this approach. It parallels on an intellectual level the military regionalism of Li Hung-chang and Tseng Kuo-fan and prefigures the more radical local salvation strategies of the 1890s.

Ku Liu-hsin in a note on sources following his biographical sketch of Li I-yü in *T'ai-chi ch'üan yen-chiu* lists several biographies of Li and Wu family members. These might be useful in reconstructing the intellectual lives of the Yung-nien gentry, but they have not been located. In his *Ta-ch'ing chi-fu shu-cheng*, Hsü Shih-ch'ang, following his biographies of Ju-ch'ing and Ch'eng-ch'ing, lists a number of works written by the brothers. These, together with their writings mentioned in the gazetteers, would obviously be invaluable sources for our purposes here if they have survived and could be found. Hsü's more detailed biographies in his *Ta-ch'ing chi-fu hsien-che chuan* provide some interesting internal and comparative clues. Ch'eng-ch'ing's biography mentions his interest in "Lao tzu and Taoist occultism" and the writings of Mei Wen-t'ing (1633–1721), Chiang Fan (1761–1831), Chiao Hsün (1763–1820), and Juan Yüan (1764–1849). A survey of all the biographies in Hsü's collection shows that an interest in Taoism was rare indeed. Of course, no reference is made to martial arts, and brother Yü-hsiang does not merit a biography at all. As for the four Ch'ing thinkers, what they have in common is that in approaching the native tradition they attempted to uncover the true Confucian essence buried beneath Buddhist and Taoist influence, and in approaching the West they tried to assert the priority and superiority of Chinese science and mathematics. The movement to exhume evidence of China's superiority to the West may be related to the Wu and Li brothers' creation of a superior fighting art based on the quintessential Chinese principle of softness overcoming hardness. In this way, when the "Treatise" says, "There are many other styles of martial arts, but they are nothing more than the strong bullying the weak," we cannot rule out the possibility that Wu was thinking of the West as much as other schools of Chinese martial arts. The appeal to Chang San-feng and Wang Tsung-yüeh may also be an attempt to give the art deeper roots and make it seem less like a contemporary creation. It is indeed ironic that although it is a synthesis of many traditional elements in the culture—martial arts, *ch'i-kung*, Taoist philosophy, medicine, and military strategy—t'ai-chi ch'üan stands as one of the most creative, lasting, and internationally influential contributions of the Ch'ing period.

Reexamining the Biography of Wu Yü-hsiang

To martial arts enthusiasts Wu Yü-hsiang is student of Yang Lu-ch'an and Ch'en Ch'ing-p'ing, discoverer of the Wang Tsung-yüeh classics, writer of classics in his own right, and founder of the Wu (Hao) style of t'ai-chi ch'üan. To gazetteer editors, however, he is merely the brother of Ch'eng-ch'ing and Ju-ch'ing; to official historians he does not exist. This irony demonstrates that despite the academic and political successes of Ch'eng-ch'ing and Ju-ch'ing in their day, they have been forgotten by history, whereas Yü-hsiang, obscure in his own day, is known throughout the world wherever the story of t'ai-chi ch'üan is told. Unfortunately for martial arts history, this means that we have standard reliable sources for Ch'eng-ch'ing and Ju-ch'ing but only anecdotal information for Yü-hsiang. Li's "Short Preface" is extremely stingy, and grandson Lai-hsü's "Biography" only slightly better; dates are lacking, both obfuscate the relationship between Wu and Yang Lu-ch'an, and neither mentions the source of the Wang Tsung-yüeh classics. In truth, Wu Yü-hsiang, although his historicity is indubitable, is only slightly less shadowy than Chang San-feng and Wang Tsung-yüeh.

The cultural biases of the local gazetteers are apparent in both what they include and what they omit. Yang Lu-ch'an, for example, arguably Yung-nien's most famous native son from today's vantage point, merits not a single word. Highest priority is given to examination success, official appointment, meritorious service to the state, charitable activity, and awards. Merchants and peasants are largely invisible, and the economic life of scholar-officials is vague and nonspecific. Women enter only through the back door marked "faithful widows." Given the Wu brothers' participation in the writing and editing of the *Yung-nien Gazetteer* (Ch'eng-ch'ing was one of the principal editors and Ju-ch'ing a contributor), we should not be surprised to see them emerge from its pages as the model Confucian family.

Biographies of Yü-hsiang written in the twentieth century invariably refer to the Wus as a wealthy scholar family, but they are not unanimous in explaining the source of the wealth. T'ang, Hsü, and Ku mention only Wu family ownership of the building rented to Ch'en Te-hu of Ch'en

Village, who operated it as the T'ai-ho Pharmacy.[5] Contemporary Wu (Hao) style exponent Hao Yin-ju states, "The Wu family was wealthy, possessing vast lands and real property. The T'ai-ho Pharmacy was rented from them."[6] Hsüeh Nai-yin gives the most detailed account: "The Wu family was rich and operated two tea dealing shops, one each on East and West Streets in Kuang-p'ing Prefectural City. Later they combined the tea dealing business in the East Street shop and rented the West Street shop to Ch'en Te-hu as a pharmacy."[7] Chou Ming adds, "Pharmacy real estate was an old occupation of the Wu family."[8] Although these various accounts are not mutually contradictory, it is unfortunate that in no instance is any source cited for the information.

Looking at the Yung-nien County and Kuang-p'ing Prefecture gazetteers, we read that Yü-hsiang's grandfather Ta-yung impoverished the family through charitable contributions to other families in distress, that his father, Lieh, died at only thirty-three years of age, and that his widowed mother sold her jewelry to hire tutors for her sons. In this way, the Wu family fortune must have been made (or remade) in one generation—Wu Yü-hsiang's own. If wealth was not inherited in Yü-hsiang's generation, there can be only two sources: Yü-hsiang's business acumen and/or Ch'eng-ch'ing's and Ju-ch'ing's official posts. Although it is not impossible that Yü-hsiang made a fortune in tea dealing and real estate, it should be remembered that North China had the lowest rate of commercialization and landlordism of any nonborder region in the empire. In relation to office holding, it should be remembered that salaries alone did not begin to cover expenses (the Yung-nien magistrate's salary was only 45 ounces of silver), but that great wealth could be accumulated in a short time through customary tax skimming and bribe taking. Gazetteer biographers' portrayal of Ju-ch'ing's incorruptibility leaves a lot of unanswered questions regarding the source of Wu family wealth.

Research on the Wu family of Yung-nien conducted by T'ang Hao and Hsü Chen in the 1930s, summarized in Ku Liu-hsin's 1963 *T'ai-chi ch'üan yen-chiu* and 1982 *T'ai-chi ch'üan shu*, and repeated in most subsequent accounts, contains the following bare bones:

1. As boys, Wu Yü-hsiang and his brothers studied the martial art handed down in their family (in more recent sources usually identified as Hung Boxing 洪拳).
2. Yü-hsiang, a martial arts amateur, was impressed with Yang Lu-ch'an, who, returning to his native Yung-nien after more than thirty years as a bond servant in Ch'en Village, stayed in Ch'en Te-hu's pharmacy rented from the Wu family.

3. Wu studied with Yang and arranged for him to go to Beijing, where Yang and his sons were employed as instructors in the Manchu garrisons.
4. On his way to visit his brother, Ch'eng-ch'ing, newly appointed magistrate in Wu-yang, Henan, Yü-hsiang passed through Ch'en Village, where he studied for a short time with Ch'en Ch'ing-p'ing.
5. Proceeding to Wu-yang, Yü-hsiang was shown the Wang Tsung-yüeh manuscript that Ch'eng-ch'ing found in a salt shop.
6. Returning to Yung-nien, Yü-hsiang edited and supplemented Wang's writings and created a style of t'ai-chi ch'üan synthesizing Lu-ch'an, Ch'ing-p'ing, Wang's indications, and his own insights.
7. As a member of the upper gentry, Yü-hsiang had no interest in being a professional martial arts master, and so his only students were his nephews Li I-yü and Li Ch'i-hsüan.

Alternatives to the above account have focused mainly on Yang Lu-ch'an's status and the circumstances of his sojourn in Ch'en Village. Some have claimed that he was a scholar and/or that he traveled to Ch'en Village as an adult and stole the secrets of t'ai-chi ch'üan by spying. More recently, other versions have attempted to explain how Yü-hsiang as an outsider was able to win Ch'ing-p'ing's confidence or even to assert that he received the Wang texts from Ch'ing-p'ing. These new interpretations, emanating largely from Chao-pao Village and other Neo-Chang San-fengists, take advantage of key loopholes in existing sources, filling them with speculation presented as fact without advancing any new primary sources. However, triangulating from information in the gazetteers and Hsü Shih-ch'ang's biographies allows us to amplify and question some aspects of the standard picture.

The notion that the Wu brothers studied some family art is nowhere stated in available documents, and I believe it is based on hearsay from the Hao family or supposition stemming from previous generations' military careers. Grandfather Ta-yung, however, according to his biographies in the gazetteers, turned to literary studies, determined to steer the family onto the civil track, and explicitly forbade his sons Lieh and Hsü to engage in martial arts. Moreover, we are told that Yü-hsiang's father, Lieh, destroyed his health mourning his mother's passing, pursued studies outside the county, and died at thirty-three while his oldest son was not more than ten. It seems likely that the Wu brothers had some background in the martial arts before they met Yang Lu-ch'an, but, as can be seen, the family transmission theory is not without its problems.

As to the discovery of the salt shop manuscript, the "Short Preface" and "Biography of My Late Grandfather" do not state that Yü-hsiang went to Wu-yang, but only that he traveled to Chao-pao Village. Even the "Post-script" of Li I-yü says only, "This manual was obtained in a salt shop in Wu-yang," and does not state that Yü-hsiang traveled there personally. I believe that T'ang Hao may have speculatively connected the given dots in order to form a logical picture. Widening the data base, however, to include contemporaneous biographies and historical facts makes the story of Yü-hsiang's journey to Wu-yang far less plausible. Ch'eng-ch'ing passed his metropolitan exam in 1852 and was appointed magistrate in Wu-yang County, Henan, the same year. In 1851, the previous year, Ju-ch'ing, as vice director in the Ministry of Justice assigned to Sichuan, was sent on an investigation to Gansu. Thereafter he spent some years in Beijing, returning to Yung-nien no later than 1860, as the gazetteer attests. This means that in 1852 it is very likely that Yü-hsiang was the only son at home with a widowed mother then in her seventies. Under these circumstances it is difficult to explain why he would have undertaken a journey to Wu-yang at the outbreak of the Nien Rebellion and on the eve of the Taiping North-ern Expedition. We need more than "business" to explain why Yü-hsiang was on the road when every other rich man in the region was pulling up the drawbridge.

Although reliable biographical data on the Wu family provides no more than marginal references to Yü-hsiang, extrapolating from material on other members allows us to raise some additional questions about re-ceived wisdom. For example, the birth and death dates for Yü-hsiang given by T'ang and Ku in their *T'ai-chi ch'üan yen-chiu*, and repeated by every other martial arts scholar without exception, are 1812 and 1880. The *Yung-nien Gazetteer*, written while the brothers were still alive, gives precise birth and death dates only for grandfather Ta-yung, so there must be some other source for the T'ang/Ku's dates, yet they do not mention examining gravestones or family genealogies. Calculating from his mother's marriage at nineteen and her widowhood at twenty-nine, it is difficult to account for a twelve-year gap between Ch'eng-ch'ing's birth in 1800 and Yü-hsiang's in 1812, even allowing for the statement that she was pregnant at the time of her husband's death and actually gave birth after his passing (遺腹生子). Furthermore, based on data in her biography, Yü-hsiang's daughter was married at eighteen and widowed at twenty-five and had been a faithful widow for twenty-one years in 1877. Therefore, she must have been born in 1830, which means that Yü-hsiang, if born in 1812, could have been no more than eighteen at the time of her birth, two years before the traditional "capping ceremony" generally associated with man-hood and marriage for gentry-class males. All of this points to an earlier birth date for Yü-hsiang. Yü-hsiang's own grandson, Lai-hsü, in writing his grandfather's biography, was unable to provide either birth or death dates, and thus one must wonder at others' ingenuity.

What was the relationship between the Wu and Yang families? Generally accepted accounts today explain the Wu/Yang connection through the T'ai-ho Pharmacy in Yung-nien and Lu-ch'an's introduction to the Manchu princes through Ju-ch'ing's contacts in the capital. The idea that Lu-ch'an's son, Pan-hou, pursued literary studies for a time under Yü-hsiang is also often repeated. There is nothing implausible here, but scholars have struggled a bit with the fact that Li I-yü's "Short Preface" refers to Yang Lu-ch'an only as "a certain Yang" and says that Yang was very circumspect in teaching, forcing Wu to seek the secrets himself in Ch'en Village. At first glance, given that Yü-hsiang himself is nothing but a name in the *Yung-nien Gazetteer,* it is not surprising that a poor peasant like Yang is left out altogether. However, on closer examination, in the section of the *Gazetteer* entitled "Men of Special Talent" (*Ts'ai-i* 材藝), we find the biography of a Wang Fu-sheng of whom it is said: "He was a native of Kao-ku Village who excelled at the martial arts. His students numbered in the thousands. He was devoted to good works and righteousness." If Lu-ch'an's relationship with the Wu family was so close, and if his fame in Beijing boxing circles really earned him the epithet "Yang the Invincible," why is it not he instead of Wang Fu-sheng, or he along with Wang, whom the *Gazetteer* touts as Yung-nien's pride?

Approaches to Understanding
Wu and Li Involvement in T'ai-chi Ch'üan

Nineteenth-century China, "late imperial China," is one of the most intensively studied periods in Chinese history. In the past, peoples who challenged China militarily (northern warriors) did not also do so intellectually, and those who challenged China intellectually (Indian Buddhism) did not also do so militarily. The nineteenth century, however, saw a total assault on Chinese culture. China's "response to the West," "semi-colonialism," "millenarian rebellion," and "the fall of the last dynasty" have been studied by sinologists in and out of China in great detail, yet nothing in the scholarly literature can explain the involvement of the Wu and Li families in t'ai-chi ch'üan. The Wu family was in so many ways both ideal and typical. They fit the Confucian ideal of scholarship, service to the state and people, filial piety, and faithful widowhood. They also match the typical pattern of the age down to some of the smallest details. Mary Rankin could have been writing about Madame Wu's endowment of a school for poor scholars when she observed, "Continuing annual operations [of charity schools] required more automatic sources of income. The time honored method was to acquire an endowment of agricultural land."[9] Drawing an examination-degree graph of the family over the generations shows that they also conform to the typical curve described by Esherick and Rankin: "Upper degree holders usually come in the middle of a cycle of rise and decline."[10] The division of labor noted among the Wu brothers could also be a case study proving Rankin's generalization: "Despite numerous local variations, merchants and gentry can no longer be considered two separate classes in the nineteenth century—particularly if one looks at the career pattern of entire families as opposed to isolated individuals."[11] Ju-ch'ing's editing of the works of anticollaborationist Shen Tuan-min also falls within Esherick and Rankin's purview when they describe the private sphere of late Ch'ing elites as including "affinial ties, poetry clubs, and historically oriented scholarship with links back to dead heroes of anti-Manchu resistance."[12]

There is nothing explicit in premodern Wu family biographies alluding to martial arts, and Western scholarship of the period offers no insight into how a gentry family could become so intensely involved in shaping and projecting an art like t'ai-chi ch'üan. James Hayes, for example, in his "Specialists and Written Materials in the Village World," delineates twelve categories of written documents commonly found in the Chinese village, but there is no category in his scheme that would remotely embrace the t'ai-chi manuals or classics.[13] Esherick and Rankin, in noting the extracurricular high-culture pursuits of the gentry, observe:

> Cultural mastery thus overlapped, but did not duplicate, the skills required for examination success. In both local and wider avenues the ability to write poetry was, for instance, a mark of elite refinement that was not directly oriented toward acquiring an official degree.[14]

Again, there is nothing specific, or even a theoretical niche, in this analysis that could explain or advance our understanding of the Wu and Li brothers' devotion to t'ai-chi ch'üan. Omission of any reference to martial arts in their official biographies is consistent with our understanding of conventional norms of propriety, but we have no idea whether they operated in secret or with whom they felt free to share their interest in martial arts. Outside of official documents, there may have been considerable dissonance between propriety and practice during this period.

Edward McCord, writing specifically on elite participation in local defense, and focusing on one family in southwestern Guizhou who enhanced their status and fortune in the process, says, "In 1810 Liu Yanshan and his four sons led local residents in constructing a stone fortress and then began to train local residents as militiamen."[15] Many scholars in recent decades have attempted to destereotype our image of Chinese elites as corrupt and effete by pointing out their volunteerism and activism during this period of crisis. However, while everyone takes note of their leadership in local defense and militia training, no one has explained how men whose lives were oriented toward classical exegesis and essay composition suddenly qualified as drill sergeants. How did they acquire sufficient competence in weapons, military engineering, and strategy to command the respect and cooperation of tough peasants, remembering that even military examination graduates seldom rose far in the army because men would only follow proven leaders who had come up through the ranks.[16] When martial arts are mentioned in the work of modern scholars of the late imperial period, it is in the context of sectarianism and rebellion. For example, Susan Naquin, in her article "Transmission of White Lotus Sectarianism," says:

> Sectarian martial arts were probably also greeted with suspicion, if for different reasons. Fighting skills were associated as much with criminal activity as with good health. Furthermore, to train groups of men privately in boxing and fencing was to encroach on the jealously guarded Manchu military monopoly.[17]

This statement not only gives us no clue into elite participation in martial arts, but is difficult to reconcile with Han martial arts masters such as Yang Lu-ch'an in the Manchu garrisons and local masters like Wang Fu-sheng with followers in the thousands. Similarly, Joseph Esherick's *The Origins of the Boxer Uprising* helps us to understand the geographic and social milieu of North China and the practice of martial arts in secret societies and even crop-watching associations, but again nothing that would explain elite involvement in a martial art with unique characteristics.

If neither Western social science nor Chinese martial arts research can answer the fundamental question of why men like Wu Yü-hsiang and Li I-yü involved themselves in t'ai-chi ch'üan, it may be that the question has never been posed. What was the conscious political or unconscious psychological motivation? We have tried in the preceding chapters to hang the backdrop of macrohistory behind the flat facts of gazetteer biography in order to develop at least a two-dimensional picture of t'ai-chi ch'üan in the nineteenth century. In what follows we will speculatively stretch for the third dimension—inner motivation—in order to illuminate both the origins of the art and another aspect of the intellectual milieu of late Ch'ing China. The method here is purely heuristic: to present a number of possible perspectives, some mutually complementary, some mutually contradictory, as a basis for further research and reflection.

Taking the classics and new material at face value and on their own terms, what we have is simply a prescription for a superior martial art. The "Treatise" states, "This art has many rivals . . . , but they are all based on native ability and have nothing to do with the real science of power." Even Li's "Short Preface" simply presents a picture of individuals—Wang Tsung-yüeh, Wu Yü-hsiang, Ch'en Ch'ing-p'ing, Yang Lu-ch'an, and Li I-yü himself—devoted to mastering an art of self-defense with absolutely no personal or historical context. The new material is similarly self-contained, transpersonal, and ahistorical—in other words: technical. The question of why is utterly absent at this stage, and even a formula as abstract as "to establish health and avoid humiliation" does not appear until the twentieth century. Why were certain members of the intellectual and political elite so bent on discovering, mastering, and elaborating the ultimate martial art at a time when gunboats, cannons, and rifles were determining the fate of the nation? Reading the classics and new material in a vacuum, one would assume that t'ai-chi ch'üan for t'ai-chi ch'üan's sake was the only thing in their lives, or at least the most important thing. Was it? No serious intellectual historian could accept a simple yes as the answer to this question.

Juxtaposing China's political and cultural crisis during the nineteenth century with a coterie of elites perfecting a subtle system of personal self-defense forces us to consider the possibility of escapism. While missionary universities sprang up in China, rails and telegraph startled the spirits of "wind and water," Chinese students traveled to Europe and America, and Chinese sharpshooters (*ch'iang-shou* 槍手) sold their services to the highest bidder, were the Wus and Lis simply burying their heads in the sand and escaping into a nostalgic and antiquarian hobby? Judging from available biographical data, by the late 1850s the Wus and Lis had all retired from official posts and confined themselves to public and private concerns on the local level. Although available accounts are couched in traditional formulas of filial piety, we do not know what else prompted them to withdraw from national politics and sit out the period known as the T'ung-chih Restoration (1862–74). Where did they stand in relation to the ultraconservative Empress Dowager, the accommodationist Prince Kung, the Purist Party, the Self-Strengtheners, or the advocates of Western Learning? Were they unwilling to lend further support to propping up the Manchu regime? Or were they optimistically convinced that rebellion was pacified, the West appeased, and they could return to local and personal interests?

Ju-ch'ing had his share of brushes with corruption and court slander and may have become disgusted enough to make the decision not to serve. The long biography of late Ming anti-Manchu martyr Shen Tuan-min, together with Ju-ch'ing's "Postscript" to Shen's *Complete Works* in the *Yung-nien Gazetteer* certainly glorify the spirit of principled passive resistance.

The Wu and Li families' preoccupation with martial arts may have been a very timely response to a practical need for personal self-defense and to develop skills necessary for militia training. Three hundred years earlier, Ch'i Chi-kuang in introducing his "Classic of Pugilism" (*Ch'üan-ching* 拳經) stated that barehanded forms had little direct application to warfare but were valuable for basic training. Given the absence of themes of health, enlightenment, and even national self-strengthening in the Wu and Li material, they may have been addressing the need for wealthy individuals to develop personal fighting skills during a period when anti-Confucian, antilandlord movements were afoot and to use this martial charisma to train militia in the defense of fortified towns and crops. Far from being escapist, then, t'ai-chi ch'üan may have been a very practical component of self-strengthening, a supplement to the moral education of the examination curriculum, and a revival of "charioteering and archery" originally part of the Confucian "Six Arts."

In terms of traditional Chinese philosophical categories, and not rooted in the particularities of history, we might say that t'ai-chi ch'üan for the Wus and Lis was an attempt to resolve tensions resulting from the Confucian/Taoist polarity. As degree holders, officials, public works managers, and filial sons, the Wu brothers by training and career were typical Confucians. However, Hsü Shih-ch'ang's biography of Ch'eng-ch'ing states that he was deeply interested in Taoist philosophy and occultism. This is borne out by Ch'eng-ch'ing's "Postscript," featuring explicit parallels between the *Lao tzu* and t'ai-chi classics. The oft-repeated aphorism that a Chinese gentleman is a Confucianist at the office and a Taoist at home seems appropriate in relation to Wu and Li activities. T'ai-chi ch'üan accomplishes the harmonization of Confucian and Taoist tendencies by being externally active but internally quiescent. The times demanded that men of learning not only serve society but save the nation. T'ai-chi may have allowed them to satisfy Taoist yearnings for self-cultivation without withdrawing to the mountains.

Another traditional dichotomy in Chinese thought is the civil (*wen* 文) versus the martial (*wu* 武). China is often seen as a unique example of a society where for more than two thousand years the military was decisively subordinated to civil authority. In this vast agrarian empire ruled by a tiny grammatocracy, lack of military preparedness repeatedly led to conquest by numerically inferior mounted warriors from the north. When the martial and civil could not be compounded within the "Wall," it often fell to barbarian dynasties—Liao, Chin, Yüan, Ch'ing—to bring the martial spirit to Beijing and rule with Confucian trappings. Having dismounted and ensconced themselves in Chinese palaces, the barbarians by the nineteenth century could not cope with peasant rebellion, let alone Western gunboats. Once again the civil prevailed and China could not put down her own rebellions without Western military assistance.

The civil/martial dichotomy was also transferred to the sphere of self-cultivation, where it came to be used to differentiate sitting meditation from *ch'i-kung* generally, or, in special contexts, gentle techniques of mind and breath control versus more forceful approaches to practice. China's easy defeats by the Western powers and Japan encouraged many Chinese intellectuals to think in terms of restoring the balance of the civil and the martial. This was most often expressed by late-nineteenth-century "self-strengtheners" as "essence and application" (*t'i-yung* 體用), meaning that Chinese tradition would remain the cultural essence, while Western technology could be adopted for self-defense. Rebalancing the civil and the martial, East and West, was the most pressing challenge facing the generation of the Wu and Li brothers. T'ai-chi ch'üan may have represented for them a way of infusing a martial art with the most subtle spiritual values of the culture and thus synthesizing the civil and the martial. As a ritual or psycho-physical performance of this synthesis, t'ai-chi ch'üan could serve as a vehicle for promoting transformation without arousing Manchu fears of sedition.

Huang Tsung-hsi in the seventeenth century used both pen and sword to fight his enemies in the corrupt late-Ming regime and to resist Manchu invasion. Loyalty and service are paramount Confucian values, but in the ambiguous world of the Ming-Ch'ing transition principled men like Huang Tsung-hsi could find heroes only in figures like Wang Cheng-nan, who fought the Manchu conquest, would not collaborate, and continued to serve the people as a righteous knight-errant, righting wrongs with an art based on the Taoist principle of "using stillness to overcome movement." Following the collapse of Han resistance, Huang tells us, "Wang abstained from meat for the rest of his life to express his commitment." This reference has been widely hailed as expressing Huang's patriotism, and it may be that the opening words of the "Epitaph for Wang Cheng-nan," providing the philosophical, mythological, and genealogical frame for the Internal School art, is a coded strategy for surviving the Manchu occupation:

> The Shaolin Temple is famous for its fighting monks. However, their art stresses only offense, which allows an opponent

to take advantage of this for a counter-attack. Then there is
the so called Internal School that uses stillness to control movement and can easily throw an opponent. Therefore we call
Shaolin the External School. The Internal School originated
with Chang San-feng of the Sung dynasty. San-feng was a
Taoist immortality seeker of the Wu-tang Mountains. Emperor
Hui-tsung summoned him, but the roads were impassable and
he could not proceed. That night in a dream he received a
martial art from the God of War and the next morning single-
handedly killed more than a hundred bandits.

Interpreting the "Epitaph" in this way, Chang San-feng represents
the spirit of the Chinese people, which communes with Hsüan-wu, the
god of war. The "internal" (*nei* 內) and "external" (*wai* 外) designations
imply Chinese versus Manchu; "stillness" represents the Chinese strategy,
and "movement" the Manchu mode; "Chang San-feng" is a Chinese de-
fender, and the "hundred bandits" are Manchu invaders. Since Huang
was not given to superstition or mythological thinking, it is difficult to
read this as anything but political allegory.

For Wu Yü-hsiang to have resurrected the spirit of Chang San-feng at
a time when China once again was under threat cannot be coincidence.
Like Huang Tsung-hsi, Wu was caught between a dynasty unworthy of
support and a peasant rebellion few gentry-class members could identify
with. What is unique about t'ai-chi ch'üan as a martial art is precisely what
has allowed China as a nation to endure: to assimilate and sinicize conquerors, to wait in stillness for their energies to peak and decline and then
to swallow them. A foreign dynasty could never represent or defend China's
interests, especially not one too corrupt to command the people's loyalty
and too afraid of popular rebellion to arm them. If it is true, as T'ang
Hao's later research suggests, that Wu Yü-hsiang himself first floated the
story of Chang San-feng's authorship of t'ai-chi ch'üan, whom could Wu
have gotten this notion from if not Huang Tsung-hsi, and what could it be
if not a coded message? Tracing the arc of Chang San-feng sightings from
the Ming/Ch'ing cataclysm to the twilight of Manchu rule through the
Republican period of anti-Japanese resistance and the post-Mao spiritual
vacuum and cultural identity crisis, Chang's banner is unfurled whenever
the Chinese state or national psyche are under siege.

T'ai-chi ch'üan in the nineteenth century may be seen as a psychological defense against Western cultural imperialism, a clinging to chivalry
in the face of modernity. Joseph Alter has studied the role of wrestling in
postcolonial Indian culture and makes the following observation:

The notion of a fit and healthy body being an ideological construct is a fairly common theme in discourse of nationalism
and power. . . . If one considers Gandhi's adherence to yogic
principles it is indeed difficult to draw any line between the
physical, mental, and the political. . . . The wrestler's way of
life is seen as a form of protest against self-indulgence and
public immorality. By disciplining his body the wrestler is seeking to implement ethical national reform. . . . Shastri and others
believe fundamentally that the body is the site of national
reform, that nationalism must be embodied to have any real
effect.[18]

Among the generation of Wu Yü-hsiang and Li I-yü there were few advocates of wholesale Westernization; moderate reform went under the slogan
"Chinese studies as the cultural essence; Western studies for practical application." What distinguishes this from personal escapism is the attempt to
create a space where purely Chinese values and worldview could survive.
Thus, as China's political body was losing control (sovereignty), t'ai-chi
ch'üan became a way to maintain a measure of autonomy in the practitioner's body. It must have been clear to China's elites in the second half
of the nineteenth century that the West could not be beaten at their own
game. They were thus thrown back on their own bodies, the microcosm
where traditional Taoist self-cultivation sought to discover and become
attuned to the *tao*. This was to pursue a Chinese brand of strength.

Looking at t'ai-chi ch'üan not just as a martial art but as a social phenomenon forces us to consider the question of gender. Traditional China
was a male-dominant society: It was males who assumed responsibility for
China's welfare, and t'ai-chi ch'üan was a male invention. This art emphasizing the soft, yielding, empty, internal—the "feminine," if you will—was
not invented by women. Could t'ai-chi ch'üan represent, in part, an attempt
by colonized males to regain a sense of power and charisma, to hold their
heads up in a world where they could not compete on the terms dictated
by the West and the West's precocious disciple, Japan? Men made to feel
inferior in relation to other groups of men will inevitably engage in some
form of compensatory behavior in order to preserve face and hence control
over their own women. Perhaps the t'ai-chi training hall, like the pub or
playing field in the West, was a space where male psyches, wounded in the
real world, could indulge in collective fantasies of power.

Late-eighteenth and early-nineteenth-century European romanticism
suggests some interesting parallels with the t'ai-chi movement in nineteenth-
century China. Romanticism advocates returning the body to nature; t'ai-

chi advocates returning to nature in the body. The romantics felt suffocated by civilization, which in nineteenth-century Europe meant industrialism, science, bourgeois mediocrity, and morality, and they withdrew to nature and classical culture. Nature is the setting in which man is beautiful and powerful, the stage on which Greek mythology is acted out. The Chinese literati in the nineteenth century faced an external but similar culture shock, and the effect, of course, was even more alienating. Disaffected young European aristocrats created a romantic subculture and took refuge in the arts as a realm of personal perfectability. The shapers of t'ai-chi ch'üan also project a vision of personal perfectability, or mastery, through the martial arts. As opposed to all other pursuits in their lives, which were overtly familial or political, t'ai-chi was an individual and interior quest. The almost religious solace that men like Goethe, Byron, Swinburne, Flaubert, Valéry, Poe, and Brooke found in swimming, a subset of Chinese intellectuals found in t'ai-chi ch'üan. It may be no coincidence that Cheng Man-ch'ing called t'ai-chi ch'üan "swimming on dry land." Both feature physical effort against a mythological backdrop: for one it was Greek mythology and for the other Taoist hagiography.

It has often been noted that the oversupply of degree holders in late Ch'ing China contributed to a proliferation of private cultural pursuits. This cannot, however, explain the devotion of the Wu brothers to the art of t'ai-chi ch'üan, as they had served in high posts and were still very much in demand, even in retirement. As the body-politic and the body-cultural were coming apart at the seams, there can be no doubt that the Wu brothers and their contemporaries sensed that the "Mandate" was slipping from the Manchus. The powerful body-mind integrative ability of t'ai-chi ch'üan is well known in the West, but in the context of nineteenth-century China, it may have had a social and political dimension. Jonathan Benthall and Ted Polhemus, editors of *The Body As a Medium of Expression*, state:

> These and other theorists have tackled the vast question of the possibility of consonance between all layerings of experience— the physical, the psychological, the social, and the cosmic. [Mary] Douglas has suggested that the achievement of consonance between different realms of experience is a source of profound satisfaction.[19]

At a time when the diseased social body could not be brought into consonance, perhaps the framers of t'ai-chi ch'üan in the nineteenth century sought to harmonize at least the physical and the cosmic layers as a protective reflex against total cultural disintegration. This process may be further illuminated by Roger Ames's definition of ritual: "What distinguishes ritual from law or rule or principle as a source of order is that ritual practices not only inform the participants of what is proper, they are also performed by them."[20] In this way, we may see t'ai-chi ch'üan as a form of ritual, a ritual whose function in the nineteenth century was to embed the practitioner in an inviolably Chinese community and Chinese-defined cosmos. From a negative point of view, this may look to some like a perfect example of novelist Lu Hsün's "Ah Qism," the tendency for conservative Chinese to soothe their wounded pride by claiming "moral victory" over their conquerors rather than reflecting on their own inadequacies.

Rejecting Westernization and withdrawing into nativist roots might appear to be merely a reactionary reflex, but the reconstruction of fractured cultural psyche may be the healing that prepares the way for modern nation building in the twentieth century. In a bold analysis of the role of traditional art during Japan's Meiji Restoration, Steven Tanaka proposes:

> Aesthetics—primarily art and ethics—is not something "cultural" that exists separate from temporal and spatial constructions of the nation-state; rather it helps construct a certain belief in the ideals and goals of that politico-cultural unit. As such it is complicit with modernity. Our tendency to treat aesthetics as traditional, romantic, even backward, elides a fundamental contradiction that confronts non-Western cultures as they form nation-states: the building of a modern society requires that non-Western peoples forget their past in favor of alien (modern) institutions and ideas, yet that past must be celebrated to establish the commonality and goals of the nation-state as an organism distinct from others.[21]

Selective celebration of tradition thus helps to consolidate Chinese identity, and in this sense it is "complicit" with the task of modern nation building rather than antagonistic to it. Only a secure sense of national self could permit China to change and adapt to a new international environment. By consolidating and retaining firm control over the spiritual sphere, it becomes easier to compromise with modernity. If t'ai-chi ch'üan in the West today represents a reaching out from within modernity to embrace a foreign and traditional practice, in nineteenth-century China it may have been a recoiling from modernity and withdrawing into native roots, but in both cases an attempt to make modernity tolerable. Taoist self-cultivation and Confucian social commitment are usually seen as opposites, but by the turn of the nineteenth century, and especially after the May Fourth

Movement, language like "On a large scale, t'ai-chi ch'üan can strengthen the nation and the race, and on a small scale it can eliminate illness and promote longevity"[22] came to be standard. Assuming historical continuity, the Wus and Lis may have prefigured linkage of traditional health practices and nationalism.

The collaboration between Huang Pai-chia with Wang Cheng-nan and Wu Yü-hsiang with Yang Lu-ch'an is an irresistible parallel. In both cases we have a peasant-class professional martial artist collaborating with a gentry-class student who gives theoretical expression to and records the art. Elites in sophisticated societies are often fascinated with lower-class "primitive" knack-masters. Chuang tzu's butcher, P'ao Ting, and Liu Tsung-yüan's gardener, Kuo T'o-t'o, are just this sort of hero. The knack-master appears as a primitive product of nature and of the native culture, untouched by foreign or effete values. Their power is a "force of nature," as white music critics often characterize black blues and jazz musicians. In the face of external threat, China needed both to transcend class antagonisms and to infuse the literati with the martial spirit. T'ai-chi ch'üan might have served as a kind of bridge between lower-class knack-masters and the literati who supplied a legitimizing philosophical overlay.

Without Wu Yü-hsiang's resurrection of eighteenth-century soft-style theory and his recognition of these principles in the Ch'en family art of Henan, there would be no international t'ai-chi ch'üan phenomenon as we know it today. The Wus and Lis were not eremitists but highly engaged elites caught in times that tried the souls of men of Confucian conscience. Whether we conceptualize the contradictions as between Manchu and Han, East and West, Taoist and Confucian, civil and martial, or traditional and modern, t'ai-chi ch'üan in the nineteenth century must be seen as part of a personal and broader cultural process of resolving these tensions. There may have been a subconscious sense that China was about to enter a second and deeper phase of internal cultural exile and that time capsules would be needed to preserve spiritual values and national identity.

TEXTUAL TRADITION
OF THE T'AI-CHI CLASSICS

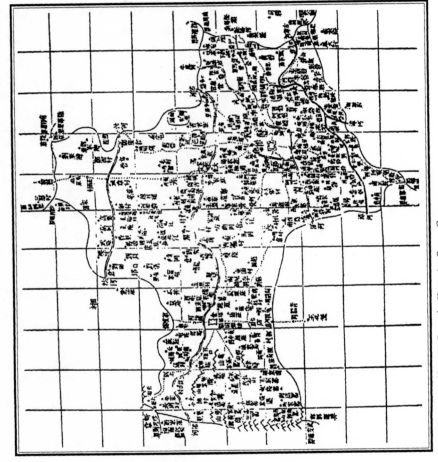

Map of Yung-ning County. From the *Yung-nien County Gazetteer*.

In order to put the pedigree of these new late Ch'ing t'ai-chi texts into perspective, it is useful to first review the background of the hitherto received "classics." The prevailing concept of the t'ai-chi classics, in both China and the West, has been shaped by the five core texts transmitted in the Yang family lineage, the earliest to be published and disseminated. It was the "manuals" (p'u 譜) that Yang Lu-ch'an presumably brought with him to the capital that Kuan Pai-i 關百益 published in 1912 (the first year of the Republic) at the Beijing Physical Education Research Institute (Ching-shih t'i-yü yen-chiu-she 京師體育研究社) under the title *T'ai-chi Ch'üan Classics* (T'ai-chi ch'üan ching 太極拳經). Although the likes of Yang Shao-hou 楊少侯 and Wu Chien-ch'üan 吳鑑泉 taught at the Institute, we do not really know what manuscripts Kuan had at his disposal or what alterations he might have introduced (see Appendix, p. 189).[1] Nevertheless, this publication event placed these texts in the public arena, created a prototypical literary form, and raised them from the status of "manual" to "classic."

As illustrated in Appendix 2, pp. 176, 189, 193, the first generation of published Yang material shows a considerable lack of textual stability. Although the actual language is quite consistent, it is variously distributed in different configurations and under different titles. For example, the Kuan edition separates the "Long Boxing . . ." (長拳者) passage and makes it a freestanding titled text (as does the Wu/Li edition), while Ch'en Wei-ming's 1925 *T'ai-chi ch'üan shu* 太極拳術 combines the "With each movement . . ." (一舉動), "Long Boxing . . ." (長拳者), and "T'ai-chi is born . . ." (太極者) into one text under the title "Treatise on Tai-chi Ch'üan" 太極拳論. Yang Ch'eng-fu's 1931 *T'ai-chi ch'üan shih-yung fa* 太極拳使用法 was so idiosyncratic in its style and organization that it was soon withdrawn from circulation, but its treatment of the classics included altering two titles, combining the "With each movement . . ." and "Long Boxing . . ." passages into one text, and creating a new text from two of the "It is also said . . ." (又曰) passages. It omits entirely the "Song of Sparring" 打手歌, but presents the first fifteen texts of the *Yang Family Forty Chapters* plus the eight key characters from the Wu/Li "Secrets of Repelling" 撒放秘訣 and "Four-Character Secret Transmission" 四字秘訣 without authorship or commentary under the title "T'ai-chi yung-fa mi-chüeh" 太極用法秘訣. It was not until Ch'eng-fu's 1934 *T'ai-*

chi ch'üan t'i-yung ch'üan-shu 太極拳體用全書 that the Yang recension achieved a fairly standard form in language, titles, and number of texts.

Ch'eng-fu's *T'ai-chi ch'üan t'i-yung ch'üan-shu* remained the normative redaction of the t'ai-chi classics for the next generation of Yang disciples writing in the 1940s. Thus Wang Hsin-wu's 王新午 *T'ai-chi ch'üan fa ch'an-tsung* 太極拳法闡宗 (c.1942), Ch'en Kungs's 陳公 1943 *T'ai-chi ch'üan tao, chien, kan, san-shou ho-pien* 太極拳刀劍桿散手合編, Cheng Man-ch'ing's 鄭曼青 1946 prefaced *Cheng tzu t'ai-chi ch'üan shih-san p'ien* 鄭子太極拳十三篇, and Tung Ying-chieh's 董英桀 *T'ai-chi ch'üan shih-i* 太極拳釋義 all implicitly recognize the *T'ai-chi ch'üan t'i-yung ch'üan-shu* as the normative redaction. However, of this group, Wang, Ch'en, and Tung all add other material, often giving it equal billing with the five core texts. For example, Ch'en Kung, after presenting four of the five Yang "classics," appends seven texts attributed to a "Ch'ien-lung period (1736–1795) handwritten manuscript."[2] Six of the seven texts are colorless concoctions, and the last is actually the "Song of the Thirteen Postures" 十三勢歌 ("Do not neglect the thirteen postures . . ." 十三總勢莫輕視). Wang and Tung also add seven undistinguished texts (not the same as Ch'en's or each other's) to the classics in a sequence that appears to give all texts equal status. In addition, Tung presents twenty-four of the forty *Yang Family Forty Chapters* texts, calling them the work of "former masters."[3] Cheng Man ch'ing's version in titles, order, and language is identical with Ch'eng-fu's *T'ai-chi ch'üan t'i-yung ch'üan-shu,* not surprising in view of Cheng's probable editorship of the latter work. These two books make a clear distinction between canon and commentary. The *T'ai-chi ch'üan t'i-yung ch'üan-shu* gives them a section of their own at the very end of the book, not mixed with or interrupted by other texts, while Cheng's *Thirteen Chapters* further demarcates them with the section title "The Works of Chang San-feng."

Although Ch'eng-fu's *T'ai-chi ch'üan t'i-yung ch'üan-shu* exercised the strongest normative influence in defining the classics, as late as Sung Shih-yüan's 宋史元 1946 *T'ai-chi ch'üan yün-chen t'u-chieh* 太極拳蘊眞圖解 we find in place of "Wang Tsung-yueh's Treatise on T'ai-chi Ch'üan" ("T'ai-chi is born . . ." 太極者) a never before seen text entitled "The Classic of T'ai-chi Ch'üan" 太極拳經. Also given equal billing are a host of other texts, most unknown and some lifted from sources such as Ch'eng-fu's "Ten Points" and Ch'en Hsin's 陳鑫 *T'ai-chi ch'üan t'u-shuo* 太極拳圖說. Another work, Wu Chih-ch'ing's 吳志青 *T'ai-chi cheng-tsung* 太極正宗, undated in photo reprint but which I judge to be of the early 1940s, also seems outside the standardizing orbit. Wu presents seven texts attributed to "Wang Tsung-yüeh of the early Ch'ing"[4] that Chiang Jung-ch'iao 姜容樵 claims were shown him in manuscript form by T'ang Shih-lin 湯士林. These texts mix language from the standard classics with lines of unknown origin to form seven new synthetic works.

The Wu 吳 style of t'ai-chi ch'üan evolved from Lu-ch'an's son Pan-hou to Ch'üan Yu and from Ch'üan Yu to his son Chien-ch'üan, who standardized the form. Wu authors adopt the Yang classics and interestingly are more consistently faithful to the standard five-text format than were many in the Yang lineage itself. Hsü Chih-i's 徐致一 1927 *T'ai-chi ch'üan ch'ien-shuo* 太極拳淺說, Wu T'u-nan's 吳圖南 1928 *K'e-hsüeh hua te kuo-shu t'ai-chi ch'üan* 科學化的國術太極拳, Ch'en Chen-min 陳振民 and Ma Yüeh-liang's 馬岳樑 1935 *Wu Chien-ch'üan shih te t'ai-chi ch'üan* 吳鑑泉氏的太極拳, and Wu Kung-tsao's 吳公藻 1935 *T'ai-chi ch'üan chiang-i* 太極拳講義 all preserve the integrity of the five core Yang classics with little equal billing or admixture. Wu T'u-nan's work is the only exception, eliminating the "Song of Sparring" and adding two unknown texts.

Even as late as recent decades, a lack of stability and standardization is still evident, as is arbitrary and uncritical author attribution. For example, Li Ying-ang's 李英昂 1977 *Chang San-feng ho t'a te t'ai-chi ch'üan* 張三豐和他的太極拳 alters titles and authorship, eliminates the "Song of Sparring," and separates the "Song of the Thirteen Postures" from the core classics, adding it to a section containing Li I-yü's "Five-Character Transmission," which itself is unattributed. P'ei Hsi-jung 斐錫榮 and Feng Kuo-tung's 馮國棟 1983 *T'ai-chi ch'üan t'ui-shou yao-i* 太極拳推手要義 follows neither the Yang, Wu Chien-ch'üan, nor the Wu/Li version exclusively, presenting three of the five Yang/Wu Chien-ch'üan classics, but omitting the "Long Boxing . . ." (長拳者) passage from the "Treatise on T'ai-chi Ch'üan" and attributing two of the texts, in agreement with Wu/Li manuscripts, to Wu Yü-hsiang. Even Fu Chung-wen 傅鍾文, one of Ch'eng-fu's closest disciples, in his 1989 *Yang shih t'ai-chi ch'üan chiao-fa lien-fa* 楊式太極拳教法練法, takes liberties with Ch'eng-fu's *T'ai-chi ch'üan t'i-yung ch'üan-shu*, shifting the "Long Boxing . . ." (長拳者) passage to the "T'ai-chi is born . . ." (太極者) text and assigning authorship according to Ku Liu-hsin's indications for the roughly equivalent Wu/Li texts.

Given the various treatments of the Yang classics, it appears that while the teachings and even the language were considered normative, in practice authors felt free to display the gems in different settings with impunity. On a subtextual level one cannot help but detect a dissonance between efforts to wrap the classics in an aura of supernatural authorship and permissiveness in the treatment of the text. Such license may imply either latent skepticism concerning the authenticity or antiquity of authorship or emphasis on the oral transmission rather than the written word.

By the 1930s two new alternative recensions claiming pre-Republican origins were offered to the public. One was discovered in a Beijing bookstall by T'ang Hao and the other was revealed to Hsü Chen by Hao Wei-chen's son, Hao Shao-ju. In 1930 or 1931, T'ang Hao purchased a handwritten manuscript in the Beijing bookstalls (see Appendix 2, p. 175) consisting of the "Yin-fu Spear Manual" (*Yin-fu ch'iang-fu* 陰符槍譜) and "T'ai-chi ch'üan Manual" (*T'ai-chi ch'üan p'u* 太極拳譜) bound together in one volume along with the "Spring-Autumn Broadsword" (*Ch'un-ch'iu tao* 春秋刀). The "Spear Manual" is preceded by an anonymous preface dated 1795 containing biographical data on a certain "Master Wang of Shanxi," whom T'ang believed to be Wang Tsung-yüeh. T'ang reasoned that the two "Wangs" shared the same surname and native province, that the spear and t'ai-chi manuals were bound together, and that the language and theory of the spear manual comported closely with t'ai-chi principles.[5] T'ang accepted Wang Tsung-yüeh as an historical figure and this manuscript as authentic, taking it as his ur-text. Of the fourteen editions of the classics reviewed by T'ang in the early 1930s and analyzed in his *Wang Tsung-yüeh t'ai-chi ch'üan ching* 王宗岳太極拳經, only the Ma T'ung-wen edition, dated 1867 (see Appendix 2, p. 170), was unequivocally not of Yang origin. T'ang explained the differences between the Ma and Yang editions as Yang disciples' alterations and thus minimized the historical significance of the differences. Since at this point he believed the bookstall manuscript to be genuine, he already had his ur-text in hand.

Hsü Chen, writing in his 1936 *T'ai-chi ch'üan k'ao-hsin lu* 太極拳考信錄, casts the first stone of suspicion at T'ang's "bookstall classics," noting the similarity between the "bookstall" and the Yang redactions and traces of Wu Yü-hsiang's hand. He thus denied any direct or even disciplic Wang authorship, a view that T'ang Hao came to himself on later reflection.[6] Hsü, after receiving the Li I-yü handwritten manuscripts from Hao Shao-ju, began to emphasize the role of Wu Yü-hsiang in the transmission of the classics. Wu's name as author at the end of the "Essentials of Sparring" 打手要言 indicates that the works cannot be exclusively Wang's and that Yang must have later received them from Wu.

The manuscript introduced to Hsü Chen by Hao Shao-ju was one of the "three old manuscripts" (*lao san pen* 老三本), or holographic manuscripts of Li I-yü's redaction of Wu Yü-hsiang's writings, the "Treatise on T'ai-chi Ch'üan" attributed to Wang Tsung-yüeh, and Li's own works (see Appendix 2, pp. 171–72). I-yü kept one copy of the classics for himself, gave one to his younger brother, Li Ch'i-hsüan 李啓軒, and one to his chief disciple, Hao Wei-chen.[7] Li's personal copy, dated 1881, contains the "Four-Character Secret Transmission" 禹襄母舅太極拳四字不傳秘訣 not included in the copy given to Hao in 1881, as well as a "Postscript to the T'ai-chi Ch'üan Manual" 太極拳譜跋, attributed to Li I-yü, explaining the discovery of the original manual in a salt shop in Wu-yang.[8] The copy given to Ch'i-hsüan is dated 1880, and the one given Hao is dated 1881. The last three texts in Li's manuscript, those written entirely by Li himself, first surfaced publicly in Sun Lu-t'ang's *T'ai-chi ch'üan hsüeh* 太極拳學. Sun was a student of Hao Wei-chen, who was Li's chief disciple. The manuscripts in Hao Shao-ju's possession also included a handwritten "copy" (*i-lu pen* 遺錄本) of the Li I-yü manuscript in an unidentified hand and a reedited version by Li Huai-yin 李槐蔭 called the "Lien-jang Hall Edition" 永年李氏廉讓堂藏本. This last was published as a book in 1935. The "copy" features three texts not found in Li I-yü's holographs: "Thirteen Broadsword," "Thirteen Spear," and "Colloquial Song of T'ai-chi Ch'üan." The "Lien-jang Hall" edition arranges the texts variously by title, author, and genre, assigning some to Wu Yü-hsiang, some to Li I-yü, and one to Li Ch'i-hsüan. The Li I-yü holographs, although themselves a collection of different material, are the oldest authenticated primary documents available to date in the history of t'ai-chi ch'üan.

Both T'ang Hao and Hsü Chen subjected the Yang, "bookstall," and Wu/Li editions to intensive analysis in an effort to tease out the original strands of Wang Tsung-yüeh's words. Hsü Chen's method begins by tracing the primitive Yang version. Isolating the interpolations of Wu Yü-hsiang and Li I-yü through comparison with the Ma T'ung-wen manuscript, and reconstructing the original order by thematic continuity, Hsü established the following core classics of Wang Tsung-yüeh:

- "Treatise on T'ai-chi Ch'üan" 太極拳論 (太極者無極而生)
- "Thirteen Postures" 十三勢 (十三勢者掤攦擠按 . . . minus 長拳者)
- "Song of the Practice of the Thirteen Postures" 十三勢行工歌訣 (十三總勢莫輕視)
- "Essentials of Sparring" 打手要言 (內固精神外示安逸彼不動己不動彼微動己先動)
- "Song of Sparring" (掤攦擠按須認眞)

The most striking feature of Hsü's reconstruction is the "Essentials of Sparring," reduced by his analysis to just two lines. Differences that developed over the course of transmission, in Hsü's view, are simply a failure on the part of redactors to distinguish classic from commentary, running them together as a continuous text. It might seem ironic that Hsü, who earlier attempted so resourcefully to prove that the Yang version predated the Wu/Li and was thus closer to Wang, also denied the authenticity of the "bookstall classics" on the grounds of their being identical with Yang editions. It is not impossible to have it both ways, however. The "bookstall manuscript" might indeed be a forgery in whole or part and the Yang classics might also be based on a pre-1880s redaction. T'ang Hao was less impressed with differences between the Yang and Wu/Li versions, mainly affecting the first two paragraphs of the "Essentials of Sparring," all of which can be explained, he felt, by Yang disciples' tampering. If the Yang texts were an earlier version of the Wang and Wu material, T'ang reasoned, why were they not given to Li I-yü and to Li Ch'i-hs'üan, who, after all, were relatives? Thus T'ang and Hsü disagree on the reasons for differences between the Yang and Li editions, but agree in the main on which texts represent Wang's original writings. Hsü accepts a few lines from the "Essentials," but T'ang is silent on the issue.

The previously received classics have been and remain the center of intense scholarly controversy. The revelation of the Wu/Li manuscripts highlighted the role of Wu and Li in the creation of what had come to be considered classics and made it more difficult to assert Chang San-feng or exclusive Wang Tsung-yüeh authorship. Nevertheless, the existence, and certainly the quality, of the classics has contributed greatly to the respect for and image of the art of t'ai-chi ch'üan. They have the force of scriptural authority and are a teaching tool, a standard for competition judging, and a core for the accumulation of countless commentaries. As much as the art itself, the classics have raised the dignity of t'ai-chi ch'üan by demonstrating the intense involvement of subtle minds and alignment with the culture's highest spiritual values. The classics closely document the marriage of meditation, medicine, and movement to form a *ch'i-kung* and the overlay of *ch'i-kung* on the body mechanics of a martial art.

ANALYSIS AND TRANSLATION
OF THE NEW TEXTS

蓮亭圖

Rendering of the Lien-t'ing (Lotus pavillion) restored by Wu Ju-ch'ing and located at the northeast corner of Kuang-p'ing City. From the *Yung-nien Gazetteer.*

The Writings of Wu Ch'eng-ch'ing

Analysis of the Texts

Wu Ch'eng-ch'ing (styles: Ch'i-yü and Ch'iu-ying) was Wu Yü-hsiang's oldest brother, born c.1800. He passed his provincial exam in 1834, earning the degree of *chü-jen* and won his *chin-shih*, or metropolitan degree, in a special exam held in 1852. In the same year he was appointed magistrate in Wu-yang County, Henan. Until the publication in 1993 of the four texts translated below, Ch'eng-ch'ing's place in t'ai-chi history was based on his nephew Li I-yü's claim that the Wang Tsung-yüeh manuals were found in a salt shop in Wu-yang. With the revelation of these four texts attributed to Ch'eng-ch'ing, however, it is clear that he was not only a t'ai-chi practitioner himself, but an active participant in the formulation of theory. Below is an introduction to and translation of the four Ch'eng-ch'ing texts.

As the title implies, the "Notes to the Original 'Treatise'" 釋原論 is an exegesis of the "Treatise" attributed to Wang Tsung-yüeh. Quoting passages from the classics (see Appendix 1, p. 127), the commentary moves quickly through a discussion of *yin* and *yang*, advance and retreat, and body mechanics and internal energetics. In an abrupt transition, the author next introduces a theory for analyzing an opponent's energy and opportunities for attack that appears nowhere in the received classics or anywhere else I am aware of. Strongly resonant with the *Classic of Swordsmanship's* (*Chien-ching* 劍經) "Take advantage of the moment when the old energy has just passed and the new energy has not yet issued," this model of "stalled," "incoming," and "retreating" energy is a significant extension of the classics' concept of "drawing the opponent in so that his energy lands on nothing" and provides a strategy for handling the stages before and after neutralization. A fourth section deals chiefly with grammatical questions in the "Treatise" text, supplying the first- or third-person referents that are left ambiguous in the literary language of the original. In doing this it also provides an interesting analytical scheme for dividing the entire

"Treatise" into passages relating to one's own posture and those relating to the opponent's strategic position. The fifth and final section emphasizes the importance of avoiding double-weightedness as the foundation for "turning," "softness," and "following."

Ch'eng-ch'ing's "Treatise on Boxing" 拳論 begins with another original contribution to the literature of t'ai-chi theory. The "three old techniques" (*lao san cho* 老三著), based on a call-and-response interplay of three of the "eight hand techniques"—roll-back, push, and elbow-stroke—is not found in the previously received classics or subsequent literature I know of. Wu Wen-han judges this passage to be the earliest recorded description of a push-hands method.[1] It may have been part of the oral tradition developed by the generation of Yü-hsiang and Lu-ch'an in Yung-nien or brought back by them from Ch'en Village or Chao-pao. When compared with the more familiar "four sides" (*ssu-cheng* 四正) or "four corners" (*ssu-yü* 四隅) styles of push-hands, it may represent an earlier, later, or simply alternate practice that lends itself to a free-flowing improvised exercise.

The "Treatise on Boxing" moves from the very concrete training and self-defense methods of the "three old techniques" to a middle passage emphasizing the need to transcend mere body mechanics and discover the "inner energy" (*nei-kung* 內功) that makes "interpreting energy" possible. The author arrives, finally, at the level of the mind, but leaves us with a paradox: The knowledge of the mind (*hsin-chih* 心知) must be prior to the knowledge of the body (*shen-chih* 身知), but the body's knowledge is superior to the mind's. Since the knowledge of the mind cannot be transmitted orally (mind to mind), but is the fruit of "enlightenment" (*hsin-wu* 心悟), we must ask if it arises spontaneously or is the culmination of practice (experience). Here Ch'eng-ch'ing fails to explicitly provide the logical link—either causal or simultaneous—between practice and knowledge. Does the mental breakthrough necessary to transform gross mechanics to "subtle movement" (*ling-tung* 靈動) come from long practice, a teacher, or theory? He does not insist, as did Wang Yang-ming (1472–1529) on a theory of "innate wisdom," but we do hear echoes in all of this of Wang's "Knowledge is the beginning of action, action is the completion of knowledge." In spite of gaps in linear logic, Wu, as an intellectual and as a practitioner, is simply calling for the need to integrate theory and practice.[2]

Wu Ch'eng-ch'ing's eight-line "Song of Sparring" 打手歌 joins a received trio of versions, including the Ch'en Village four-line, Ch'en Village six-line, and Wu/Li (same as Yang) six-line. The unique feature of this version is the inclusion of the phrases "pull-down, split, elbow-stroke, and shoulder-stroke" and "advance, retreat, gaze-left, and look-right" found in the Wu/Li "Thirteen Postures." Hsü Chen, T'ang Hao, and Ku Liu-hsin all assign authorship of the Wu/Li/Yang "Song of Sparring" and the additional language from the "Thirteen Postures" to Wang Tsung-yüeh. We do not know, however, if Ch'eng-ch'ing's version differs from the other three because it is based on an earlier version or whether it was created by him, reworking old material and adding the line "Hands and feet follow each other and waist and legs are coordinated," which does not appear in the received literature.

Last is Ch'eng-ch'ing's "Postscript," whose opening line, "The art of t'ai-chi ch'üan has been described most brilliantly by Wang Tsung-yüeh," echoes Li I-yü's "Short Preface," "I do not know who created t'ai-chi ch'üan, but the subtleties and marvels of the art have been most thoroughly described by Wang Tsung-yüeh" (see Appendix, p. 129). He goes on to use the familiar essence/application (體用) paradigm to analyze the role of softness and hardness in t'ai-chi ch'üan, linking defense with softness and offense with hardness. The remainder of the text is devoted to parallels between the t'ai-chi classics and the *Lao tzu* and *Chuang tzu*. This immediately brings to mind Ch'en Wei-ming's 1925 *T'ai-chi Ch'üan Shu* 太極拳術 list of relevant passages from the *Lao tzu* and Cheng Man-ch'ing's parallels section in his *Master Cheng's New Method of Self-Study for T'ai-chi Ch'üan* 鄭子太極拳自修新法. If authentic, Ch'eng-ch'ing's parallels would be the earliest self-conscious attempt to connect t'ai-chi theory with Taoist teachings. It would also lend confirmation to Hsü Shih-ch'ang's biography of Ch'eng-ch'ing that hinted at his Taoist leanings.

Translation of the Texts

Notes to the Original "Treatise"

Movement: "In movement it separates; in stillness it unites." Separation is the separation of *yin* and *yang;* unity is the unity of *yin* and *yang;* this is the form of *t'ai-chi.* Separation and unity refer to oneself. "My opponent does not understand me, but I understand him." This is what is meant by interpreting energy. With long study understanding comes.

Drawing in: "Draw in (the energy of your opponent), and when it lands on emptiness, unite and issue." "With only four ounces deflect a thousand pounds." To unite means to deflect. If one can understand the meaning of this word, it leads to true comprehension.

When practitioners of t'ai-chi ch'üan understand *yin* and *yang* and clearly distinguish full and empty, only then can they understand advance and retreat. Thus advance contains retreat, and retreat remains advance, for the potential of advance is concealed within retreat. This process involves transformation and unification. Body techniques include "maintaining openness at the top of the head," "raising the back and relaxing the chest," "sinking the *ch'i* to the *tan-t'ien*," and "protecting the crotch and belly." When you raise the spirit, the whole body can move freely. The two hands control the eight directions, moving as freely as a wheel without opposition. Striking the opponent when his attack is imminent but has not yet issued forth is called "striking the contained energy." Awaiting the opponent's touch in stillness and striking after his attack is already under way is called "striking the incoming energy." Striking the opponent after he has landed on emptiness and seeks to change his energy is called "striking the retreating energy." Looking at it in this way and paying close attention to study, one naturally attains spontaneity and perfect clarity.

"Weight on the left," "weight on the right," "looking up," "looking down," "advancing," and "retreating" refer to the opponent. "Empty on the left," "invisible on the right," "higher," "deeper," "more distant," and "more pressed" refer to oneself and also to the opponent. "Emptiness, invisibility, height, and depth" are what the opponent senses as I draw him in and his energy lands on nothing. "Retreating one feels increasingly pressed" refers to forcing the opponent into a position of having nowhere to hide, like reining in a horse at the brink of a precipice. Without the ability to interpret energy it is impossible to neutralize an opponent. These six phrases covering above, below, left, right, front, and back all refer to this.

"By sinking all of the weight onto one side, one can follow, but double-weightedness brings stiffness." This illustrates the meaning of the phrase "as lively as a wheel" and refers to oneself. With all the weight on one side, one can turn; with the weight divided on both sides, one is stiff. By avoiding double-weightedness, one cannot be controlled by the opponent. This describes one's own error and is the result of hardness. With softness one can follow, and by following one abandons oneself and sticks to the opponent. In this way one will not become inflexible.

Treatise on Boxing

When first learning to spar it is best to study roll-back, push, and elbow-stroke. When I use roll-back, my opponent will use elbow-stroke. When I use push, my opponent will use roll-back; and when I use elbow-stroke, my opponent will use push. This applies to both partners, round and round without end. These are called "the three old techniques." Later on one can add more high and low postures. The whole body from top to bottom responds whenever it is attacked. The body follows the energy. We are concerned with internal skill and not with the external form. This is the method of training in sparring. After it is perfected, one can draw the opponent's energy in, and when it lands on nothing, then unite and issue. In this way, your art will be realized. However, if you are unable to interpret energy, how can you understand the opponent's incoming energy and thus use your own energy to draw it in? This marvel must be grasped intuitively and cannot be expressed in words. Only when it is known in the mind can the body know it; but knowing with the body is superior to knowing with the mind. When one becomes enlightened to both the wisdom of the mind and the wisdom of the body, the energy moves most subtly. If it is only known in the mind, it cannot be applied, but when the body realizes it, one can then interpret energy. Interpreting energy is assuredly not easy.

Song of Sparring

Be serious in the practice of ward-off, roll-back, press, and push,
And in pull-down, split, elbow-stroke, and shoulder-stroke mind your
   bending and extending.
In advance, retreat, gaze-left, look-right, and central equilibrium,
You must stick, connect, adhere, and follow, distinguishing full and
   empty.
The hands and feet follow each other, and the waist and legs act in
   unison;
Drawing the opponent in so that his energy lands on nothing is a
   marvelous technique.
Let him attack with great force,
While I deflect a thousand pounds with four ounces.

Postscript

The art of t'ai-ch'i ch'üan has been described most brilliantly by Wang Tsung-yüeh. The essence of this art is softness and bending, whereas its application is hardness and straightness. Thus when we are attacked with great force, only softness and roundness can neutralize it; when the opponent's force is already neutralized, only hardness and straightness will repel him for a great distance. Therefore, it is said, "Seek the straight within the bent, concentrate your energy and then issue it."

The practice of this art is based on sinking the *ch'i* to the *tan-t'ien* and moving solely with the spirit; it has nothing to do with native physical

45

strength. Getting the best of an opponent seems to be effortless. Although allowing one to demonstrate great skill, it also contains the highest philosophical principles. The *Lao tzu* says, "If you want to get something, you must give something." This is what the original manual meant by, "If pressure is applied to the left, empty the left; if pressure is applied to the right, empty the right." The meaning here is that what the opponent takes, I give. The *Chuang tzu* says, "From the center of the circle one can respond to infinite variations." This is the idea of "the *ch'i* is like a wheel" and "move the *ch'i* as though threading a pearl with nine bends." Therefore, the emphasis on "concentrating the *ch'i* and developing softness" in this art corresponds to the teachings of the Taoists. Without several decades of dedicated practice, it cannot be perfected.

This martial art values emptiness and forbids double-weightedness. Is this not the same as the *Lao tzu's* "empty and inactive, it issues forth when activated?" Is not t'ai-chi's "the force terminates but the mind does not" the same as the *Lao tzu's* "continuously without end?" Is not t'ai-chi's "from the bent to the straight, your mind is ahead of the opponent" the same as the *Lao tzu's* "meeting it in front, you cannot see it's head; following behind, you cannot see it's rear?" Therefore I say that "wishing to behold the secret," it is nothing other than the thirteen postures.

The Writings of Wu Ju-ch'ing

Analysis of the Texts

Wu Ju-ch'ing, Yü-hsiang's second older brother, was the star of the Wu family. He passed his provincial exam at only twenty-three and in 1840 at thirty-eight earned his *chin-shih* degree and a post in the Ministry of Justice. He rose through the ranks within the Ministry of Justice in both the provinces and the capital, eventually being promoted to second-class board secretary. According to gazetteer biographies he made enemies among corrupt officials but was praised by the likes of Tseng Kuo-fan, Tso Tsung-t'ang, and even the emperor himself. Retiring from national politics in the late 1850s he played a leading role in local Yung-nien projects as varied as education, publishing, city renovation, and military training. To this long list of interests and accomplishments we must now, with the publication of this "Treatise on T'ai-chi Ch'üan" in 1986, add t'ai-chi ch'üan.

Wu Ju-ch'ings "Treatise on T'ai-chi Ch'üan" conflates phrases and passages previously seen in the Wu/Li manuscript and Ch'eng-ch'ing's "Notes to the Original 'Treatise'." Because these quotations cross the boundaries of "Treatise," "Essentials," and "Body Techniques," one would like to know whether Ju-ch'ing's source was the "salt shop" manual, or Yü-hsiang's, or even Li I-yü's, manuscripts. Judging from the juxtaposition of quoted material, it appears that at least parts of the "Essentials" and "Body Techniques" represent an earlier transmission, perhaps the same body of literature as the Wang Tsung-yüeh "Treatise." Although appearing in the Wu/ Li "Essentials" over Yü-hsiang's authorship ("Written by Wu Yü-hsiang" 禹襄並識), the eight phrases from the "Essentials" and two from the "Body Techniques" (see Appendix, p. 129) are probably not original with Yü-hsiang as it is unlikely Ju-ch'ing would quote his younger brother as if citing a classic. Conflating passages from classic works is a common compositional technique in Chinese literature, but it is remarkable here, if the piece is authentic, how in the short time between the "salt shop" discovery (1852) and the Ma T'ung-wen manuscript (1867) a slim body of material acquired the status of scripture.

Translation of the Texts

Treatise on T'ai-chi Ch'üan

This martial art is called "t'ai-chi" because it is based on *yin* and *yang,* full and empty. After one is clear about *yin* and *yang,* one can begin to understand advance and retreat. Although advance means to advance, it must contain an awareness of retreat; to retreat is still to retreat, but it conceals an awareness of the opportunity to advance. Both of these hinge on the ability to open the energy at the crown of the head. This together with raising the back and relaxing the chest allows the spirit to rise. By sinking the *ch'i* to the *tan-t'ien* and protecting the crotch and buttocks, one can move freely and with agility. Bend the elbows, for from a bent position you can extend them and control the situation to your advantage. Bend the knees, for from the bent position they can extend, and thus when issuing energy you will have power. When it comes to sparring with opponents and hands first make contact, concentrate on listening to your opponent's energy. Your task is to follow your opponent and not to do as you please. You must know your opponent and not allow him to know you. Once I understand the opponent, I can easily draw him in regardless of direction so that his energy lands on nothing. In this way, my opponent goes against the flow, whereas I go with it. Here the critical principle is to relax the shoulders. The control mechanism is in the waist and the root in the feet, but they take orders from the mind. With each movement everything moves; in stillness all is still. Above and below are united as with one *ch'i.* This is what is meant by "stand like a balance and turn as easily as a wheel." Controlling the eight directions, you will be invincible. Striking the opponent when his attack is imminent but has not yet issued forth is called "striking the contained *ch'i.*" Awaiting the opponent's touch in stillness and striking after his attack is already under way is called "striking the incoming energy." Striking the opponent after he has landed on emptiness and seeks to change his energy is called "striking the retreating energy." If you study these principles and pay attention to practice, you will naturally gain complete mastery and gradually attain spiritual illumination.

The Writings of Li I-yü

Analysis of the Texts

Li Ching-lun (style: I-yü, 1832–92) was a maternal nephew of Wu Yü-hsiang and a fellow resident of Kuang-p'ing Prefectural City. Although Wu Yü-hsiang was the compiler of the classics and had five sons of his own, we have no manuscripts in his hand and none of his sons continued his transmission. It was Li I-yü who edited and preserved Wu's manuscripts and contributed a number of seminal writings of his own. It was also Li I-Yü and his younger brother, Ch'eng-lun (style: Ch'i-hsüan), who not only transmitted the art in the family for four generations down to the present, but whose disciple Hao Wei-chen (1849–1920) and his son Hao Yüeh-ju (1877–1935) and grandson, Hao Shao-ju (1908–83), spread the Wu (Hao) style of t'ai-chi ch'üan to the whole country. The six new texts by Li I-yü made public in 1989, together with his three compositions included in the "three old manuscripts" and one additional text included in the Lien Jang Hall edition, constitute the most significant corpus of pre-twentieth-century writings after the classics themselves.

The two most striking features of the six texts in the recently published Li I-yü material are the five- and seven-character verse form, and the highly derivative nature of the content. On closer examination, however, Li's writings go considerably beyond the received classics in detail and represent a second stage of synthesis (see Appendix, pp. 130–34).

The "Wang Tsung-yüeh of Shanxi's Treatise on T'ai-chi Ch'üan," though not in consistent five- or seven-character verse form, shows an extremely high tendency for parallel couplets of four, five, six, seven, and eight characters. Of the 357 characters in the text, fully 246 are in mnemonic couplet form, each phrase carrying a high epigrammatic charge with very little filler or linking material. By contrast, what the Li texts lack in density they gain in compositional coherence. If these are authentic examples of Li's literary style, this supports the thesis that the "Essentials of Sparring" was a record of Wu's notes or oral teachings with little editorial polish.

The first piece in the new Li I-yü material, "Song of the Essence and Application of T'ai-chi Ch'üan," strings quotations from the "Treatise," "Essentials," and "Body Techniques" (Li Ch'i-hsüan version) to form a highly refined verse text of five character lines, but containing few fresh ideas or images. By contrast, the second piece, "Song of the Thirteen Postures," describes the techniques and strategies of the thirteen postures in vastly greater detail than found in the classics. This is not only the earliest interpretation of the applications of the thirteen postures, but clearer and more precise than any explanation I know of in the later literature. The third text, "The Eight-Word Transmission," continues in this vein, exploring the "eight hand techniques" in all dimensions. Each technique is first introduced with an opening image—"rising crescent moon," "tiger pouncing on a sheep," and so on—and then a line or two on body mechanics. This is followed by advice on appropriate responses to specific attacks and finally sequences of techniques to deal with counterattacks and changing situations. This text is a valuable contribution to our understanding of the original content of the "eight hand techniques" often lost in the stylization of contemporary solo form and fixed-step push-hands practice.

The fourth text," Song of the Circulation of *Ch'i*," borrows the language of the classics as a framework, fleshing it out with detail from the Taoist yoga and meditation traditions. The classics speak in very general terms about the movement of *ch'i*—"sink the *ch'i* to the *tan-t'ien*," "when *ch'i* fills the entire body there is no clumsiness," "circulate the *ch'i* as if threading a pearl with nine bends," etc.—but here Li gives us a sketch of the "macrocosmic orbit" and of the point by point circuit from the ball of the foot to the fingertip. The text moves on to an interesting discussion of breathing that matches exhalation with "closing" (*ho* 合) and "issuing" (*fa-fang* 發放) and inhalation with "opening" (*k'ai* 開) and "returning" (*kui* 歸). The correspondence of exhaling with issuing and inhaling with returning is standard, but pairing exhaling with closing and inhaling with opening contradicts the more commonly heard martial arts expression, "open with the exhalation; close with the inhalation" (*k'ai-hu ho-hsi* 開呼 合吸).[3] This conception is not unique, however, and does represent a minority school of thought that can be explained, perhaps, by point of view. The more familiar conception takes the movement of the arms— centripetal or centrifugal—as point of view, while the opposite takes the expansion or contradiction of the diaphragm and chest as point of view. What is unusual about Li's formulation here is that he mixes the two points of view, combining the "closing" of the breathing mechanism with "issuing energy" and the "opening" of the breathing mechanism with "gathering energy." One can see a resolution of this contradiction in Ch'en style use of "reverse breathing" (*ni hu-hsi* 逆呼吸) where "opening" and "issuing" are united.

The two final texts, "Song of the Free Circle" and "Ode to T'ai-chi Sparring," are songs of praise for the seamless coordination of techniques and energies that characterize the t'ai-chi virtuoso. Like writings on poetry, painting, and calligraphy, Li treats the art of t'ai-chi as an object of aesthetic contemplation and shows how exposition of t'ai-chi theory becomes a literary genre in its own right.

Translation of the Texts

Song of the Essence and Application of T'ai-chi Ch'üan

How wonderful is t'ai-chi ch'üan,
Whose movements follow nature!
Continuous like a jade bracelet,
Every movement expresses the t'ai-chi symbol.
The whole body is filled with one unbroken *ch'i*;
Above and below are without imbalance.
Place the feet with cat steps,
Moving the *ch'i* like coiling silk.
In movement, everything moves;
In stillness, all is still.
Above, the crown of the head is suspended,
And below the *ch'i* sinks to the *tan-t'ien*.
Drape the shoulders and sink the elbows;
Raise the back and relax the chest.
When the *wei-lü* is naturally vertical,
The body feels relaxed and the *ch'i* lively.
Use the mind and not strength,
Turning the body with the waist.
Everything rises from the root in the feet,
While legs and waist are perfectly aligned.
Energy issues from the spine,
Reaching the arms and fingertips.
Stretch the sinews and draw out the bones;
Relax the wrists and spread the fingertips.
There is a slight feeling of swelling in the fingers,

For wherever the *chi* goes there is a manifestation in the body.
All of this is a function of the mind,
And has nothing to do with brute force.
When full and empty are clearly distinguished,
Hard and soft follow the changing situation.
Yin and *yang* must complement each other,
As moving back and forth we shift and change.
The *chi* is aroused with the changing power relationship,
And the spirit is held within.
Movement arises from stillness,
But even in movement there is stillness.
The spirit leads the *chi* in its movement,
And the palm and wrist are connected to the waist.
Our steps adapt to the changing situation,
And hands and eyes conform to conditions.
Speed or slowness follow the opponent's movements;
With the weight on one side our movements will not be tardy.
Without either losing contact or grappling,
Every posture must anticipate the opponent.
After drawing the opponent in and neutralizing his energy,
We issue power like a bubbling well.
Let the strongest aggressor attack us,
While four ounces deflect a thousand pounds.

Song of the Thirteen Postures

The secret of the thirteen postures,
Has been known by very few.
For the sake of those destined to be masters,
I will make an exception and reveal them to you.
In applying ward-off, the arm must be round and alive;
In extending the hand, emphasize sensitivity.
If the opponent is empty, I use press;
If he is full, I drop the elbows and deflect.
By warding off diagonally upward,
My opponent will be forced to lean backward and lose his balance.
After roll-back, push, and ward-off,
Sink the shoulders and turn the waist and rib cage.
Roll-back is used to neutralize energy,
Drawing the opponent into our empty trap.
Press is used mainly as a feint,

And by sinking down the opponent is startled.
Turn and then strike straight ahead;
Far off and to the side a slope appears on the horizon.
Push must contain the element of union;
First down and then folding back.
When the upper body turns, then push forward again,
Throwing the opponent for ten feet.
Pull-down must use real power,
For a light touch is ineffective.
Approach from above, first sinking down,
Then pull down with the body moving sideways.
Split strikes with a horizontal rotation,
A swift sword slicing forehead or throat.
When the attack comes fierce and close,
Split should be our first response.
Elbow-stroke is used at close quarters;
Bend the arm and aim for chest or ribs.
If the opponent uses push against my elbow,
Then the open flower has no place to hide.
For shoulder-stroke, first seek the triangle;
Step into the crotch with eyes gazing down.
The waist and body turn together,
Sending the opponent straight to hell.
Advance and seize the central palace,
With an attack no opponent can withstand.
When closing, take half a step,
Making sure not to give the opponent an opportunity.
In retreating, carefully sweep behind you,
Seeking the seam that reveals no trace.
Pay attention to the use of the "three forwards,"
And take heed of the employment of the "seven stars."
The "central earth" never leaves its position;
Release the chest and relax the waist.
If you thoroughly grasp the thirteen postures,
Each posture will reveal its infinite marvels.

The Eight-Character Secret Transmission

The ward-off arm is extended at an angle like the crescent moon;
The front knee is slightly bent and the rear knee round.

The pounds and ounces of an opponent's strength
Are weighed in the balance of the ward-off arm.
When my opponent issues energy, I respond with block or pull-down;
When he reveals gaps, I respond with press.
Above and below, my whole body is filled with an unbroken *ch'i*,
Like a great snake coil upon coil.

The hand is like a deer looking backward;
Whether high or low, the hand moves freely.
Our spirit is completely revealed in our hands;
Our waist and legs are coordinated like a boat going with the current.
In sticking and adhering we never leave the "central earth" position;
The basis of roll-back is drawing the opponent in.
Roll-back without press is a waste of roll-back;
Press without roll-back is a foolish risk.

In press, the hand is extended like an arched bridge,
Feeling your way from an angle and always maintaining an undaunted
    spirit.
If you encounter push, respond with press, but first use roll-back;
Draw the opponent in, and when his energy lands on nothing, explore
    with one arm.
With your "arched bridge" block the opponent's shoulder and arm;
First sink, then advance without swerving.
Unless press follows roll-back, there is no drawing the opponent in,
And if roll-back is not followed up with press, it is a waste of time.

Push is employed like a tiger pouncing on a sheep;
Waist, legs, arms, and hands all perfectly coordinated.
First sink, then connect, and now push forward,
And the opponent will surely be sent flying with overpowering force.
While executing push, ward-off, roll-back, and neutralizing, pay
    attention
That the elbow not extend much beyond the knee.
As the opponent steps backward in an attempt to use pull-down against
    me,
I step in with elbow- or shoulder-stroke to hurt him.

Pull-down is like a monkey plucking peaches;
After sinking, grasp obliquely, enticing the opponent to steal.
Step backward, pulling down the wrist forcefully;

If our execution does not destabilize the opponent and is not clean, we
    are wasting our energy.
Regardless of whether we are attacked with ward-off or push,
Pull-down resolves them like melting ice.
In using pull-down, guard against the opponent's elbow- or shoulder-
    stroke,
Always protecting the "central palace" against wanton blows.

Split strikes out with horizontal force like a surprise shot;
Avoid the "central gate" and take the spiral path.
With a single hand sweeping the opponent's neck,
I am like a speeding horse destroying all in its path.
It takes split to counter split,
But if my opponent treats me with decorum, then I respond with
    decorum.
The shoulders follow the turning of the waist like a dragon twisting its
    body;
At all cost avoid being clumsy or unnatural.

Elbow-stroke is like a bull lowering its head;
The flowers freely open one after another.
This technique can be used effectively at close quarters against an
    attempt to use pull-down,
Or at long range to chagrin the opponent.
When the opponent adopts block or pull-down, then use this technique
    appropriately;
An elbow aimed at the opponent's ribs can take a life.
In using elbow-stroke be most wary of "play guitar,"
For if you encounter it, turn the body and protect the throat.
Step in with shoulder-stroke like a swimming dragon;

In executing shoulder-stroke, you should step directly into your
    opponent's crotch.
Push up at an angle from below, quickly rotating the body,
And strike the opponent's chest with your shoulder without mercy.
Be careful that your leg is able to support you,
Lest your opponent have room to escape.
Most often shoulder-stroke is a transformation of pull-down,
So that if the opponent evades my pull-down, then the technique comes
    into play.

Song of the Circulation of Ch'i

The *ch'i* is like the waters of the Yangtze,
As it flows eastward wave upon wave;
Arising from the" bubbling well" point in the ball of the foot,
It travels up the spine in the back.
Arriving at the *ni-wan* in the center of the brain,
It returns to the *yin-t'ang* between the brows.
The mind leads the *ch'i*,
And never leaves it for an instant.
For example, if you want to raise your right hand,
The mind-*ch'i* first reaches the armpit.
Then following the kinetic energy,
You will feel the mind-*ch'i* in the pit of the elbow.
Turning over your hand,
The *ch'i* will arrive at the *nei-kuan* point on the inside of the arm above
    the wrist.
If the right hand extends outward in push,
The palm will slightly protrude,
As the *ch'i* travels to the *yin* side of the hand,
And finally reaches the tips of the five fingers.
It is the same with one or two hands,
And the feet and hands are no different.
If I reveal one side to you,
You should be able to complete the other three for yourself.
If you practice in this way,
Your whole body will be connected as if with a single thread.
The mind leads the *ch'i*,
And the whole body moves as one.
In movement, everything moves;
In stillness, all is still.
In speed, all is fast;
In slowness, all is slow.
Exhale, concentrate your energy, and repel the opponent;
Inhale, expand your energy, and return it to the *tan-t'ien*.
Circulate the *ch'i* as if threading a pearl with nine bends,
So that the whole body is thoroughly penetrated.
But strictly avoid moving the *ch'i* too rapidly,
So that it jumps from the spine to the fingertips.
It must touch every point step by step,
And pass through each and every gate.

It is essential that it move by the proper measure,
And that the internal and external follow what is natural.
If the mind and strength are harmonized,
Then after long practice, the *ch'i* will naturally pass through the gates.
In this way, after many years,
You will become an *arhat* of steel.

The mind and *ch'i* are rulers,
And the bones and flesh are ministers.
The waist and legs are commanders;
The hands are vanguards,
And the eyes and skin are spies.
The ruler gives orders and the ministers act;
The commanders give orders and the ruler acts.
The spies must immediately report to the commander,
And the commander issues orders to the troops.
Ruler and follower work together;
Above and below act in harmony,
And the whole body is one flow of *ch'i*.

Song of the Free Circle

Within the circle *Ch'ien* (heaven) and *K'un* (earth) are great;
In all their splendor the sun and the moon are eternal.
Yin and *yang* ceaselessly change,
While hard and soft rise and fall.
Perfect, indeed, is roundness,
For the free circle is without separation or excessive force.
The feet follow the advancing hands,
While the waist and legs play the leading role.
Above and below in absolute harmony,
Motion is expressed in the two hands.
Forward, backward, left, and right,
Responding to opportunities with perfect composure.
Extend your hand to touch your opponent's chest;
The power of the free circle is invincible.
Shake your opponent's root,
With your mighty *ch'i*.
If the opponent raises a hand to challenge me,
I use pull-down or push, never separating from his motion.
When the opponent uses push,
I go with the downward movement and then rise up.

In rising, though, I must not forget pull-down,
For the opponent will be quick to block me.
When left and right are without error,
Your superiority will be apparent.
Of all of t'ai-chi's marvels,
The art of the free circle is the king.

Ode to T'ai-chi Sparring

Our founder has handed down a truly marvelous art;
Hard, soft, full, and empty change with the situation.
Diligently seek the truth in the teachings,
And deeply examine the internal, external, gross, and fine.
When the opponent approaches I draw him in;
When he retreats I pursue him.
If your emptiness does not conceal fullness, it is not effective emptiness;
If your fullness does not contain emptiness, it is foolish risk taking.
Within emptiness, adapt to changing situations;
Seek perfection in the principle of roundness.
When the opponent uses press, neutralize him with roll-back;
When he closes with you, use split.
Pull-down and push alternate with each other,
And offense and defense all have their principles.
The whole body is as one unbroken *ch'i*,
As unified as a t'ai-chi sphere.
I can draw the opponent in from every point;
My entire body is hands.
However, if offense and defense are not clearly distinguished,
Full and empty will have no basis.
It is like the full moon of the seventh month,
Whose light illuminates the whole world.
When your training has reached the level of emptiness,
Then the distinction of offense and defense no longer exists.

Yang Family Forty Chapters

Analysis of the Texts

Of the forty individual texts contained in the Yang family handwritten manuscripts, fifteen appeared in Yang Ch'eng-fu's 1931 *T'ai-chi ch'üan shih-yung fa*, twenty-four in Tung Ying-chieh's 1948 *T'ai-chi ch'üan shih-i*, and fourteen in T'ang Hao and Ku Liu-hsin's 1963 *T'ai-chi ch'üan yen-chiu*. Yang makes no comment on authorship, and Tung calls them the work of "former masters." Ku Liu-hsin credits as his source Shen Chia-chen, who copied the texts from a collection of forty-three in Yang Ch'eng-fu's possession. The title appearing on the manuscript was *Wang Tsung-yüeh t'ai-chi ch'üan p'u* 王宗岳太極拳譜 (Wang Tsung-yüeh's t'ai-chi ch'üan manual), and Yang told Shen that it was handed down by his grand-father Lu-ch'an. The full forty first appeared as an appendix to a 1985 reprint of Wu Kung-tsao's 1935 *T'ai-chi ch'üan chiang-i* 太極拳講義. The text is a photocopy of Wu Chien-ch'üan's (1870–1942) handwritten manuscript under the title *T'ai-chi fa-shuo* 太極法說 (Methods of t'ai-chi explained) with a preface by Wu's son, Wu Kung-tsao, explaining that the contents represent Yang Pan-hou's teachings to Chien-ch'üan's father Ch'üan Yu (1834–1902) and that the writings have been preserved in the Wu family for more than a hundred years. The Wu family manuscript was reproduced *in toto* in Fang Ch'un-yang's 1992 *Chung-kuo yang-sheng ta-ch'eng* 中國養生大成. More recently in 1993 Yang Ch'eng-fu's son, Yang Chen-chi (1921–), in his *Yang Ch'eng-fu shih t'ai-chi ch'üan* 楊澄甫式太極拳, has published a photocopy of an untitled handwritten manuscript of the same forty texts, which Chen-chi says his mother en-trusted to him in 1961. This edition has no title, author, or date, and the title *Yang Family Forty Chapters* has been created for convenience by the present author. Both manuscripts share the idiosyncrasy that the table of contents lists thirty-two texts, whereas the body actually contains forty. Shen Shou's 1991 *T'ai-chi ch'üan p'u* 太極拳譜 also acknowledges and reproduces the 1985 Wu Kung-tsao edition, but without explanation arbi-trarily divides them into four chapters and omits the last three texts, those purporting to be the words of Chang San-feng. Even more mysteriously, Meng Nai-ch'ang's 1993 *T'ai-chi ch'üan p'u yü mi-p'u chiao-chu* 太極拳譜與秘譜校註 randomly distributes thirty-seven of the forty in two different chapters interspersed with other texts. The thirty-seven repro-duced include two of the "Chang San-feng" texts, and there is no discernible common denominator to the three omitted. The source cited for these texts is a generic "T'ai-chi ch'üan mi-p'u" 太極拳秘譜 (Secret t'ai-chi ch'üan manuals). The book lacks any prefatory material or bibliography, and because of its posthumous publication it may have been hastily com-piled from Meng's articles and unpublished manuscripts.

The two virtually identical manuscripts preserved in the Yang and Wu families suggests a common ur-text, but this poses some difficult prob-lems of authorship and dating. The Wu family manuscript of the forty chapters is in Wu Chien-chüan's hand, so it cannot be later than 1942; Shen Chia-chen told Ku Liu-hsin that he copied the texts from Yang Ch'eng-fu, so they cannot be later than 1936.[4] As the forty texts contain quotations from the Wu/Li classics, they must have been written after 1852, when the Wang Tsung-yüeh material was reportedly discovered by the Wu brothers in Wu-yang. Since the forty texts do not resemble Li I-yü's style, this leaves Yang Lu-ch'an's sons Chien-hou and Pan-hou. To date we have no writings attributed to Chien-hou, which leaves Pan-hou, whom Wu Kung-tsao identifies as the source of these teachings in his preface to Chien-ch'üan's manuscript. The only published body of writings traceable to Yang Pan-hou are the *Nine Secret Transmissions* published by Wu Meng-hsia in his 1975 *T'ai-chi ch'üan chiu-chüeh chu-chieh.* Wu received them from Pan-hou's student, Niu Lien-yüan. Comparing the style and content, the *Nine Secret Transmissions* are exclusively in verse form, whereas the *Forty Chapters* include a mixture of verse and prose texts. The contents of the *Nine* are confined to self-defense applications of the form and "thirteen-postures," whereas the *Forty Chapters* include a varied curriculum of t'ai-chi technique, movement and meditation theory, and martial arts philosophy. The *Forty Chapters* also feature the most advanced seizing techniques and combat tactics found anywhere and a conscious effort to contextualize the martial arts in the mainstream of Chinese high culture. Nevertheless, there is nothing so strikingly similar or dissimilar about the two corpuses to allow us to claim that they came from the same or different hands and even less that they did or did not come from Pan-hou. As other late Ch'ing and early Republican texts come to light, it might be possible to make more of clues in the forty Yang family texts such as the fact that Chang San-feng is mentioned only in those chapters that fall outside the Contents and that five of these last eight are titled "Treatise" 論, whereas none of the first thirty-two are so titled, and a reference to obscure T'ang dynasty Taoist poet Hsü Hsüan-p'ing, whose name appears in published documents linking him to t'ai-chi ch'üan no earlier than Hsü Yü-sheng's 1921 *T'ai-chi ch'üan shih t'u-chieh.*

Let us take our speculation on the authorship of the *Yang Family Forty Chapters* one step further. Do these teachings originate in Ch'en village, Yung-nien, or Beijing? And are these oral or written transmissions? Yang Lu-chan, his sons and grandsons all spent their entire lives, or at least childhood and early manhood, under the Manchu dynasty when the imperial examination system was still in place, yet there is no record in the *Yung-nien Gazetteer* of any of the Yangs passing even the lowest-level examination and no extant specimens of their calligraphy until the generation of Ch'eng-fu's sons. This together with other evidence developed by T'ang Hao and

Hsü Chen points to the illiteracy of the Yangs. Whoever wrote these texts was not only literate, which in traditional China meant thoroughly steeped in the classics, but conversant with the very arcane language of the inner alchemy tradition as well. The nearly total absence of explicit patriotic sentiment and the promotion of martial arts for national salvation that marks post–May Fourth Movement (1919) martial arts literature points to a pre-Republican genesis for these texts. The *Yang Family Forty Chapters* have many elements that set them apart both from the classics and from the modern manuals that followed the publication of Hsü Yü-sheng's 1921 *T'ai-chi ch'üan shih t'u-chieh* 太極拳勢圖解. The only published work on t'ai-chi ch'üan from the late Ch'ing/early Republican period is Ch'en Hsin's (1849–1929) *Ch'en-shih t'ai-chi ch'üan t'u-shuo* 陳氏太極拳圖說 which was begun in 1908 and completed in 1919.[5] It is the only work comparable in the scope and detail of its medical, metaphysical, and meditational content, and Ch'en is Pan-hou's generation. The two works share many parallel passages and themes and breathe the same atmosphere. For example, Ch'en Hsin's "Although the martial arts are a minor path (*tao*), we can by means of the lesser glimpse the greater"[6] might be a summary of the *Yang Family Forty Chapters* "Treatise on Chang San-feng Realizing the *Tao* through Martial Arts." This may enable us to say with some confidence that the *Forty Chapters* seem to belong to this period, but it is very unlikely that Pan-hou possessed this degree of learning, and if he did, why did he not write in his own name? The depth of familiarity with the inner alchemy tradition far surpasses what the typical martial artist or examination candidate scholar would possess. How then did this learning find its way into the Yang family? Was it through the Wu family of Yung-nien or later after coming to Beijing? Of the forty texts in the collection, the twelve that have never been published before (numbers 25, 29, 30–33, 35–40) are precisely those that present the more esoteric martial arts techniques and meditation theory. Their earlier omission in published works is understandable in light of the strong movement for popularization in the martial arts from the 1920s forward, but should we locate the intellectual nexus that produced the *Forty Chapters* mix of martial arts, medicine, metaphysics, and meditation as far back as Ch'ang Nai-chou in the eighteenth century, Ch'en Village and Yung-nien in the nineteenth, or a coterie of conservative intellectuals in the twentieth century?

Written transmission of martial arts theory and practice in premodern times has depended on the talents of educated men like Ch'i Chi-kuang, Huang Pai-chia, Wang Tsung-yüeh(?), Ch'ang Nai-chou, Wu Yü-hsiang, Li I-yü, and Ch'en Hsin, and research to date has largely focused on questions of lineage and style evolution. Answering questions like who wrote the classics and *Yang Family Forty Chapters* requires: (1) closer and more comparative textual analysis; (2) exploitation of neglected historical resources, such as local gazetteers, family genealogies, examination registers, and official and unofficial histories and biographies; and (3) understanding the martial arts in the broader context of Chinese intellectual and cultural history.

Because of the large number of texts in the *Yang Family Forty Chapters*, they will be grouped below for discussion under the following categories: (1) definitions of terms and cosmology, (2) training keys and stages of progress, (3) esoteric martial arts techniques, (4) medicine and inner alchemy in the martial arts, (5) t'ai-chi as a *tao* of self-cultivation. A few of the texts have been cross-listed where contents overlap.

The first group of texts, those devoted to definitions and cosmology (numbers 1, 17, 18, 21, 25), apply the terminology of Chinese cosmology —*yin* and *yang*, the eight trigrams, the sixty-four hexagrams, the Five Phases, heaven and earth, sun and moon, circle and square, the cardinal and intermediate directions—to the martial arts. The prototype for these texts would be the "Thirteen Postures" 十三勢 in the Wu/Li manuscript, which relates the "eight hand techniques" to the trigrams and compass points and the "five steps" to the Five Phases. Text 17, after presenting a long list of correspondences for *yin* and *yang*, other cosmological categories, and martial movement, goes on to employ the Before Completion 未濟/After Completion 既濟 paradigm from the *I ching* to explain the meditational benefits of t'ai-chi ch'üan. This theory—taking the mind as fire (trigram *Li* 離) and body as water (trigram *K'an* 坎)—seeks to remedy body-mind disharmony by concentrating the mind in the *tan-t'ien* point in the lower abdomen (placing fire under water) and thereby restoring integration and producing *ch'i*. Text number 18 provides a comprehensive outline of the cosmological correspondences in the human microcosm. Beginning with the Five Phases' correspondences with the organs, flavors, and vocal qualities, the text goes on to reveal the physiological loci of the *ching* (sexual energy), *ch'i*, and spirit, the inner and outer "six unities," the "seven orifices," "seven emotions," the seats of the emotions in the organs, relation of the Terrestrial Branches and trigrams with the meridians, numerology of the body map, and the relation of the Celestial Stems and organs. Text 21 explains the round and square aspects of t'ai-chi movement.

I ching cosmology became the official language of meditation theory as early as Wei Po-yang's (25–220 C.E.) *Ts'an-t'ung ch'i*. In this form the meditation tradition merged with the sexual alchemy literature during the Ming (1368–1644). The fusion of *I ching* cosmology with the martial arts is not apparent from the historical record until the Ch'ing. Thus we see none of this influence in Ch'i Chi-kuang's *Classic of Pugilism* 拳經 or writings on the "Internal School" 內家 of Huang Tsung-hsi and Huang Pai-chia during the Ming. Wholesale transfer of metaphysics to the martial arts is not found until Ch'ang Nai-chou of the middle Ch'ing, more, in fact, than the Wu/Li classics of the late Ch'ing. In this sense, the use of cosmo-logical analysis in the martial arts in the *Yang Family Forty Chapters* reso-nates more closely with Ch'ang than with the Wu/Li material.

As might be expected, the largest category of texts in the *Forty Chapters* is training keys and stages of progress. The first block of texts, numbers 2 through 12, begin with the notion of "conscious movement" (*chih-chüeh yün-tung* 知覺運動) as a prerequisite for "interpreting energy" (*tung-chin* 懂勁), which in turn leads to the development of "spiritual illumina-tion" (*shen-ming* 神明). However, these stages of progress are really a rever-sion to the state of "innate wisdom and ability" (*liang-chih liang-neng* 良知良能) that are our birthright. "Wisdom" and "ability" imply a dichot-omy that recalls the "dual cultivation" (*shuang-hsiu* 雙修) debates among the various schools of Chinese meditation. Here, however, rather than the terms intrinsic nature (*hsing* 性) and life (*ming* 命), the emphasis is on the need for the tandem development of the "spiritual" 文 and the "martial" 武. Having established this general framework for the discussion, the author begins to draw on the central training concepts in the classics, including "sticking, adhering, connecting, and following"; "butting, insufficiency, separation, and resistance"; "the eight hand techniques"; and "five steps." All of these principles are embodied in the postures and form, but must be prevented from degenerating into "facile gesturing" (*hua-ch'üan* 滑拳) or "hard style" (*ying-ch'üan* 硬拳) (number 16). Alignment images such as "plumb line and balance" (number 24) are derived from the Wu/Li classics, but the *Forty Chapters* goes outside the classics in presenting new descriptive models of movement qualities such as "light, heavy, floating, and sinking"(number 22). Stages of mastery are measured as progressions from "expansive to compact" and from "feet to inches to fractions." In interacting with opponents, one must first overcome errors of "butting, insufficiency, separation, and resistance," and then correct errors associated with "break-ing contact, connecting, leaning forward, and leaning backward." Accord-ing to number 23, at intermediate stages of practice the "four corners" 四隅 (pull-down, split, elbow-stroke, and shoulder-stroke) are necessary to compensate for errors of "light, heavy, floating, and sinking," but at ad-vanced levels the "four-sides" 四正 techniques alone (ward-off, roll-back, press, and push) are sufficient to respond to any situation. Number 30 provides a concise lexicon of technical terms and stages, outlining twelve hand techniques, twelve conditions of the *ch'i*, eight states of response and sensory awareness, and four of mental energy. Finally, text 20 explains that t'ai-chi's uniqueness among the martial arts lies in the belief that long practice of softness ultimately produces internal hardness. Thus the goal of all techniques and training methods is the crystallization of "essential hardness" from liquid-like softness, or the "iron grip" (*wo-ku* 握固) of Lao tzu's infant. Here in this category, it is the *tao* that explains t'ai-chi's methods in the martial arts; while in other texts it is the martial arts that are justified as a method of attaining the *tao*.

The texts considered to this point provide the basic techniques and movement theory that characterize the art. In the third category of texts we find advanced, even esoteric, techniques and concepts that go well beyond the specificity of the classics and beyond most of what has appeared in print in the twentieth century. These teachings begin with advanced grappling and pressure point concepts (numbers 29, 31, 35), noting especially their physiological effects in terms of traditional medicine. On a more advanced conceptual level, text 32 provides a sophisticated model for analyzing an opponent's energy pattern. Taking the opponent's energy as "empty" or "bound," one employs techniques of "breaking" or "rubbing" in order to destabilize the balance of *ch'i* and strength (number 33). Text 36 is a catalogue of hand and finger techniques so rich in its detail and variety as to rival anything in all of martial arts literature.

It may be a revelation to contemporary practitioners to discover the variety of martial arts techniques that once formed part of the t'ai-chi ch'üan repertoire, but the *Yang Family Forty Chapters* goes well beyond this, drawing on the medical, meditational, and inner alchemy traditions as well. Numbers 26 and 27 use traditional medical concepts to explain the distinction between blood and *ch'i*, and how these relate to strength and *ch'i*, external and internal development. Number 18 applies the body microcosm paradigm of Chinese yoga and meditation to set the stage for a theory of physical and spiritual transformation. This transformation, as described in texts 15 and 39, borrows the concept of "the battle of essences" (*ts'ai-chan* 探戰) from sexual practices and inner alchemy to explain a process of mating *yin* and *yang* and mutual exchange and supplementation of essences. The author here proposes a novel third path—not the theft of essence from the opposite sex in sexual practices or etheric parthenogenesis in solo meditation—but a form of asexual dual cultivation based on "the opposition of *yin* and *yang* between two males." This demonstrates once again that within Chinese culture wherever there is an interplay of *yin* and *yang* (and where isn't there?) one may find an opportunity to work with the two forces and, by bringing them into balance, harmonize one's own nature. In the context of t'ai-chi ch'üan practice this experience of dynamic harmony is effected through the complementary coupling of *yin* and *yang* in the "eight hand techniques" and "five steps."

That martial arts are a system of self-defense is self-evident, and the medical benefits of martial exercise is not a great leap. However, Chinese culture has taken the martial arts several steps further, merging them with meditation and inner alchemy, and finally presenting them as a path of ultimate self-realization through the *tao*. Text number 13 links martial arts with the Confucian concept of "sincerity" (*ch'eng* 誠) the neo-Confucian concept of "heaven and humanity as one body" (*t'ien-jen t'ung-t'i* 天人同體), and the Taoist concept of "the root of the tao" (*tao chih pen* 道之本). The martial path of realization of the *tao* stresses the dual cultivation of the spiritual and the martial so that we may fully develop our heavenly and earthly natures and take our place as "human beings" (*jen* 人) in the "cosmic triad" (*san-ts'ai* 三才). In this way we learn that "the *tao* is not far from us" (*tao pu yüan jen* 道不遠人) and that by realizing the "human microcosm" (*i hsiao t'ien ti* 一小天地) we can recover what the philosopher Mencius called "our great primal *ch'i*" (*hao-jan cheng-ch'i* 浩然正氣), or what Wang Yang-ming called "innate wisdom and ability" (*liang-chih liang-neng* 良知良能). In advocating the path of body-based self-realization, the author makes a distinction between "physical culture" (*t'i-yü* 體育) and "martial arts" (*wu-shih* 武事). Several passages, very Confucian in their tone, note that the grace, skill, and softness developed through physical culture must be matched with the hardness and application of martial arts to qualify for the highest attainment. Simultaneous cultivation of the spiritual and martial leads to the highest level; cultivating one through the other is middle; and exclusive one-sided cultivation of either is the lowest (numbers 14, 19, 38).

If there is any doubt left regarding the legitimacy of the martial arts as a vehicle for realizing the *tao*, the highest spiritual aspiration of Chinese high culture, the last three texts in the *Forty Chapters*, attributed to Chang San-feng, are intended to dispel them. Records of the Immortal Chang's association with the martial arts go back as early as Huang Tsung-hsi's description of the origins of the Internal School 內家 in his "Epitaph for Wang Cheng-nan" (1669) and Li I-yü's description of the origins of t'ai-chi ch'üan in his preface to the Ma T'ung-wen classics (1867). Giving Chang a first-person voice, the author here has Chang place himself in direct line of descent from prehistoric culture hero Fu Hsi, through legendary emperors Yao and Shun to Confucius and Hsü Hsüan-p'ing (number 38). Claiming that his transmission represents a new dispensation, Chang explains that former sages taught only physical culture and not this new method of dual-cultivation inner alchemy through the martial arts. The very last text, number 40, is a grand summation of the Chinese conception of spiritual realization, a kind of nontheistic rational mysticism, recognizing and reconciling all opposites, and transcending dualism by equally perfecting our physical and spiritual natures. These last three texts, using Chang San-feng as a mouthpiece, create the impression that it is not just the martial arts that are reaching out to embrace the meditative arts, but that a Taoist adept is reaching out to embrace the martial arts. The body is a crucible containing the reagents of self-realization. *Yin* and *yang* can be aroused, mated, and induced to bear fruit by many methods, but the author here calls martial arts "the fastest and surest." It is interesting that Chinese culture created unique systems of self-defense, but from the point of view of intellectual history, it is even more revealing that these could be reconciled and synthesized with the culture's highest spiritual teachings. The West could at various historical times and places offer salvation through the sword (martyrdom in defending or extending the faith), but the art of war itself owes no debt to the teachings of the prophets, Jesus, or Mohammed in the way that t'ai-chi ch'üan is informed by Taoism.

Translation of the Texts

1. The Eight Gates and Five Steps

Ward-off (south)/ *K'an*, Roll-back (west)/ *Li*, Press (east)/ *Tui*, Push (north)/ *Chen*, Pull-down (northwest)/ *Hsün*, Split (southeast)/ *Ch'ien*, Elbow-stroke (northeast)/ *K'un*, Shoulder-stroke (southwest)/ *Ken*. These are the compass points and "eight gates."

The compass points and "eight gates" demonstrate the principle of the cyclical exchange of *yin* and *yang* that operates unendingly in its course. Thus it is indispensable to understand the "four sides" and "four corners." The "four sides" techniques are ward-off, roll-back, press, and push; the "four corners" techniques are pull-down, split, elbow-stroke, and shoulder-stroke. Combining the corners and sides techniques, we derive the trigrams of the gate positions. The division of the steps contains the concept of the Five Phases and allows us to control the eight directions. The Five Phases correspond to advance (fire), retreat (water), gaze-left (wood), look-right (metal), and central equilibrium, or earth. Advance and retreat are the steps that correspond to water and fire; gaze-left and look-right correspond to metal and wood; and earth at the center is the axis around which everything turns. Our body contains the eight trigrams, and our feet step out the five phases. Hand techniques and steps; eight plus five; together they make up the sum of thirteen. Thus the thirteen postures derive from nature, and we call them the eight gates and five steps.

2. The Practice of the Eight Gates and Five Steps

The eight trigrams and five phases are part of man's natural endowment. We must first understand the meaning of the words *conscious movement*. After grasping conscious movement, we can begin to interpret energy, and finally, from interpreting energy, proceed to spiritual illumination. However, at the beginning of practice, we must gain an understanding of conscious movement, which, although it is part of our natural endowment, is very difficult to grasp.

3. Our Natural Powers of Discrimination

When we are born into the world, we have eyes to see, ears to hear, a nose to smell, and a mouth to eat. Color, sound, odors, and flavors all appeal to our natural sensory endowment; gestures and steps and the various functions of our limbs are all derived from our natural endowment for movement. Considering this carefully, is it without reason that, while similar in nature but different in habits, we have lost our original endowment?[7] Thus, wishing to regain our original endowment, it is impossible to discover our movement potential without physical exercise or to find the source of consciousness without intellectual activity. This then leads us to movement with consciousness. With mobilization, there is sensation; and with movement, awareness; without mobilization there is no sensation, and without movement there is no awareness. When mobilization reaches its peak there is movement, and when sensation reaches its peak there is awareness. Movement and awareness are easy, but mobilization and sensation are difficult. By first seeking to develop conscious movement in yourself and realizing it in your own body, you will naturally be able to know it in others. If you seek it first in others, it is likely that you will miss it in yourself. It is essential that you understand this principle, and the ability to interpret energy follows from this.

4. Stick, Adhere, Connect, and Follow

Sticking means lifting and raising high; *adhering* means clinging and attachment; *connecting* means giving up yourself and not separating from the opponent; and *following* means that I respond to my opponent's movements. It is impossible to understand conscious movement without being clear about sticking, adhering, connecting, and following, but this skill is very subtle.

5. Butting, Insufficiency, Separation, and Resistance

Butting means leading with the head; *insufficiency* means falling short; *separation* means losing contact; and *resistance* means excessive force. If you want to understand the errors represented by these four words, it is not only a failure of sticking, adhering, connecting, and following, but a total lack of appreciation for conscious movement. When beginning to study sparring, it is essential to understand this, and even more important to eliminate those errors. What is difficult is sticking, adhering, connecting, and following without butting, insufficiency, separation, or resistance. This is truly not easy.

6. Sparring without Errors

Butting, insufficiency, separation, and resistance are shortcomings in sparring. The reason we call them errors is because having failed to stick, adhere, connect, and follow, how can you achieve conscious movement? If you do not understand yourself, how can you understand others? What we mean by sparring is that you do not use butting, insufficiency, separation, and resistance in relation to your opponent, but rather use sticking, adhering, connecting, and following. If you can accomplish this, you will not only be without errors in your sparring, but naturally achieve conscious movement and advance to the level of interpreting energy.

7. Training Methods for Sparring, or Holding the Central Earth
(What Is Popularly Called "Post-Standing")

In central equilibrium the feet develop root,
And then you may study the "four sides" and advance and retreat.
Ward-off, roll-back, press, and push are the four hand techniques,

But it will require much effort to perfect them.
The body, waist, and top of the head must all be considered,
And in sticking, adhering, connecting, and following, the mind and *ch'i*
    must be balanced.
Movement and consciousness must complement each other,
For spirit is the ruler and flesh and bones his subjects.
Clearly distinguish the seventy-two stages of progress
And you will naturally develop the martial and mental aspects of the art.

8. The Body, Waist, and Crown of the Head

How can we forget the body, waist, and crown of the head,
For by ignoring any of these, we are simply wasting our time.
The waist and crown can be studied for a lifetime,
And the body can be trained to stretch and relax.
If you abandon this truth, what can you expect?
After ten years you will still be in the dark.

9. The T'ai-chi Circle

The circle of retreat is easy, but the circle of advance most difficult.
Never forget the waist or crown of the head, the front or back.
What is difficult is holding to the central earth.
Retreat is easy but advance most difficult, so study them carefully.
This is movement training and not standing equilibrium.
When closing with an opponent, advance and retreat shoulder to
    shoulder.
Imitate the windmill, grinding fast and slow,
While the cloud dragon and wind tiger go round and round.
By using the heavenly circle to seek your goal,
After much time, all will come naturally.

10. T'ai-chi Never-Ending Advance and Retreat

Ward-off, roll-back, press, and push follow natural principles;
Yin and *yang*, water and fire, complement each other.
First perfect the "four sides" hand techniques,
And then learn pull-down, split, elbow-stroke, and shoulder-stroke.
When you can execute the "four corners" techniques,

Then the thirteen postures go on forever without end,
And this is why we call it Long Boxing.
Now you may expand and contract as you desire,
But never violate the principle of t'ai-chi.

11. *T'ai-chi Above and Below Are Called Heaven and Earth*

The "four sides" hand techniques, above and below, are divided into
  heaven and earth;
Pull-down, split, elbow-stroke, and shoulder-stroke have their origins
  and applications.
If you seek to balance pull-down from heaven and shoulder-stroke from
  earth,
Why fear that above and below will be out of harmony?
If, however, you attempt to execute split and elbow-stroke at long range,
You will have lost the relationship of *Ch'ien* (The Creative) and *K'un*
  (The Receptive) and know nothing but regret.
This theory explains the circles of heaven and earth;
When advancing use elbow-stroke and split and return to the position of
  humanity.

12. *Song of the Eight Words T'ai-chi Human Circle*

The eight trigrams—sides and corners—constitute the "Song of the
  Eight Words."
The number thirteen, after all, is not so large.
However, if these few are not in balance,
And the waist and head are not aligned, we will find ourselves panting
  and out of breath.
The secret of maintaining perfect continuity may be summed up in just
  two words;
Carefully cultivate ruler and subject, flesh and bones.
When your internal and external skill have been perfected,
How could errors still appear in your sparring?
In sparring with opponents be completely natural,
Moving back and forth between heaven and earth.
If your ability to give up yourself is without serious error,
Then high and low, advancing and retreating, will always flow with
  continuity.

13. An Explanation of the Essence and Applications of T'ai-chi

Principle (*li* 理) is the essence of *ching, ch'i,* and spirit; *ching, ch'i,* and spirit are the essence of the body. The body is the application of the mind, and power is the application of the body. The mind and body have an absolute ruler, and that is principle (*li*); *ching, ch'i,* and spirit have an absolute ruler, and that is sincerity. Sincerity is the way of heaven, and he who is sincere follows the way of humanity. Both of these are inextricably bound up with consciousness. If you understand the principle of the unity of heaven and humanity, you will naturally absorb the circulating *ch'i* of sun and moon. This *ch'i* is the circulation of consciousness, for spirit is naturally concealed within principle. Finally, we can speak of the martial and the spiritual, sagehood and immortality. If one speaks of the body and mind from the point of view of the martial arts and applies these principles to the cultivation of power, it must be in the context of the essence of the *tao*. It is a mistake to focus exclusively on physical skills.

Power (*chin* 勁) comes from the tendons, and strength (*li* 力) from the bones. Speaking strictly from a material point of view, a man with great strength can lift several hundred pounds, but this is a superficial matter of bones and joints that produces brute strength. By contrast, the unified power of the whole body, though it appears unable to lift even a few pounds, represents the internal strength of the *ching* and *ch'i*. In this way, after you have perfected your skill, you will manifest marvels far surpassing those of mere hard strength, for this is the way of true self-development through physical culture.

14. An Explanation of the Spiritual and the Martial in T'ai-chi

The spiritual is the essence, the martial is the application. Spiritual development in the realm of the martial arts is applied through the *ching, ch'i,* and spirit—the practice of physical culture. When the martial is matched with the spiritual and it is experienced in the body and mind, this then is the practice of martial arts. With the spiritual and the martial we must speak of the "firing time," for their development unfolds according to the proper sequence. This is the root of physical culture. As the spiritual and the martial are applied to sparring, we must consider the appropriate use of storing and issuing. This is the root of the martial arts. Therefore, the practice of the martial arts in an spiritual way is soft-style exercise, the sinew power of *ching, ch'i,* and spirit. When the martial arts are practical in an exclusively martial way, this is hard style, or simply brute force. The spiritual without martial training is essence without application; the martial without spiritual accompaniment is application without essence. A lone pole cannot stand; a single palm cannot clap. This is not only true of physical culture and martial arts, but all things are subject to this principle. The spiritual is internal principle; the martial is external skill. External skill without internal principle is simply physical ferocity. This is a far cry from the original nature of the art, and by bullying an opponent one eventually invites disaster. To understand the internal principles without the external skill is simply an armchair art. Without knowing the applications, one will be lost in an actual confrontation. When it comes to applying this art, one cannot afford to ignore the significance of the two words: spiritual and martial.

15. An Explanation of Interpreting Energy in T'ai-chi

Interpreting energy approaches the level of spiritual illumination. *Yin* within the body numbers seventy-two, and this is without exception. When *yang* is matched by *yin*, water and fire cooperate, *Ch'ien* (heaven) and *K'un* (earth) are in harmony, and intrinsic nature (*hsing*) and life (*ming*) retain their original purity. The human ability to interpret energy relies on the senses to respond to changing conditions and naturally produces marvelous results. Our body achieves perfect clarity without effort, and our movement becomes supremely sensitive. When your skill reaches this level, whatever you do will come easily and you can move without thinking.

16. An Explanation of the Eight Gates-Five Steps-Thirteen Postures Long Boxing

As you practice posture by posture, and after mastering each one, you will begin to connect them in a long series that flows on and on, round and round without end. This is why we call it Long Boxing. It is necessary to have standard postures, lest after a long period the art degenerate into sloppiness or hardness. We must at all cost avoid losing our continuity and softness. As the body moves back and forth, the spirit and consciousness over time will naturally become all-pervading and invincible. When sparring, the "four hand techniques," derived from the "eight gates" and "five steps," should be your first resort. From a fixed standing posture the "four hand techniques" revolve in circles about the body. The advance-retreat "four hand technique," including the "middle four hand techniques," the "high and low four hand techniques," and the "heaven, earth, and human four hand techniques," all derive from the lower-level Long Boxing "four

71

hand techniques," which are very open and expansive. When your form becomes very compact and your movements free, then you have attained the middle and advanced levels.

17. An Explanation of the Reversal of Yin and Yang in T'ai-chi

Yang is the trigram *Ch'ien* (The Creative), heaven, the sun, fire, the trigram *Li* (The Clinging), projecting, emitting, issuing, confronting, opening, subject, application, *ch'i*, the body, the martial (supporting life), square, exhalation, high, advancing, and corners. *Yin* is the trigram *K'un* (The Receptive), earth, the moon, water, the trigram *K'an* (The Abysmal), rolling up, penetrating, storing, relating, uniting, the ruler, bones, essence, principle, mind, the spiritual (fulfilling intrinsic nature), circular, inhaling, low, retreating, and sides. The principle of the reversal of *yin* and *yang* can be summarized by the two words *water* and *fire*. Fire flames upward and water flows downward. If we place fire under water, then we have brought about their reversal. However, without the proper method, this is impossible. To illustrate this principle, if water is poured into a cauldron and placed over fire, the water will be heated by the fire, and not only will the water not flow downward, but it will become hot. At the same time, the fire, which tends to flame upward, can only rise as high as the bottom of the cauldron and thus is controlled and limited, while the water, which tends to flow downward is prevented from escaping. This is what we mean by the principle of water and fire in mutual harmony, as represented by the hexagram *Chi-chi* (After Completion), or the principle of reversal. If fire is permitted to flame upward and water flow downward, the two will inevitably separate as in the hexagram *Wei-chi* (Before Completion). Therefore we may refer to this as the principle of division into two and two into one, or from one to two and from two to one. Summarizing this principle, we derive the three universal aspects: heaven, earth, and humanity. Understanding this principle of the interchange of *yin* and *yang*, one can begin to speak of the *tao*. Knowing that we can never separate ourselves from the *tao*, we can begin to speak of humanity. If you can magnify the *tao* by means of humanity and realize that the *tao* never separates itself from humanity, then we can begin to discuss the unity of heaven and earth. Heaven is above and earth below, and humanity is in the middle. If you can model yourself on heaven and earth, combine the brilliance of sun and moon, endure with the Five Sacred Mountains and Four Great Rivers, flow with the four seasons, flourish and decay with the grasses and trees, comprehend the favorable and unfavorable influences of the gods and ghosts, and understand the rise and fall of human events, then we can speak of *Ch'ien* (The Creative) and *K'un* (The Receptive) as macrocosm and humanity as microcosm. In terms of the human body and mind, by studying the wisdom and ability of heaven and earth, we can begin to speak of humanity's innate wisdom and ability. If we do not lose our original capabilities, then by cultivating and not harming our great *ch'i*, we can endure forever. What we mean by a person's body comprising a microcosmic heaven and earth is that heaven is our intrinsic nature and earth is our life. Humanity's invisible essence is spirit. Without understanding these things, how can you form a triad with heaven and earth? If we fail to fulfill our intrinsic natures and support our lives, how can we expect to complete the process of spiritual transformation?

18. An Explanation of T'ai-chi in the Human Body

In the human body, the heart is the ruler. The ruler is t'ai-chi. The two eyes are sun and moon, or *yin* and *yang*. The head is heaven and the feet earth. These together with humanity, symbolized by the *jen-chung* point in the middle of the upper lip and the *chung-wan* point on the solar plexus form the universal triad (*san-ts'ai*). The four limbs are the four duograms. Kidney-water, heart-fire, liver-wood, lung-metal, and spleen-earth all belong to *yin*; bladder-water, small intestine-fire, gall bladder-wood, large intestine-metal, and stomach-earth all belong to *yang*. This is our internal aspect. The head-fire, the lower jaw-water, the left ear-metal, the right ear-wood, and the two *ming-men* are our external aspect. The spirit arises in the heart, and the eyes are the sprouts of the spirit; *ching* arises in the kidneys, and the brain and kidneys are the root of the *ching*; *ch'i* issues from the lungs, and the gall bladder *ch'i* is the source of the lungs. When the power of vision functions clearly, then as the heart is moved the spirit runs; when the power of hearing functions clearly, then as the brain is moved the kidneys flow. The flavors detected by the nose and the movement of the breath in and out of the mouth consist of water-salty, wood-sour, earth-sweet, fire-bitter, and metal-hot, together with our voice qualities, which are wood-bright, fire-harsh, metal-smooth, earth-dusty, and water-floating. The flavors distinguished by the nose and mouth are all based on the movement of *ch'i*, the gate of the lungs, and the wind and thunder of the liver and gall bladder, represented by the trigrams *Hsün* (The Gentle) and *Chen* (The Arousing). It issues forth as sound and enters and exits as the five flavors. This describes the mouth, eyes, nose, tongue, spirit, and mind, which are the six senses that must be unified in order to conquer the six desires. This is our internal aspect. The hands, feet, shoulders, knees, elbows, and hips all must be unified in order to rectify the six *tao*. This is the external aspect. The eyes, ears, nose, mouth, anus, urethra, and navel are the seven external orifices. Happiness, anger, anxiety, concern, sorrow, fear, and surprise are the internal seven emotions. The heart is the ruler of the seven emotions. Happiness belongs to the heart, anger to the liver, anxiety to the spleen, sorrow to the lungs, fear to the kidneys, surprise to the gall bladder, concern to the small intestines, apprehension to the urinary bladder, melancholy to the stomach, and sadness to the large intestines. This is the internal aspect. The trigram *Li* (The Clinging) corresponds to the south, the Terrestrial Branch *wu*, fire, and the heart meridian; the trigram *K'an* (The Abysmal) corresponds to the north, the Terrestrial Branch *tzu*, water, and the kidney meridian; the trigram *chen* (the Arousing) corresponds to the east, the Terrestrial Branch *mao*, wood, and the liver meridian; the trigram *Tui* (The Joyful) corresponds to the west, the Terrestrial Branch *yu*, metal, and the lung meridian; *Ch'ien* (The Creative) corresponds to the northwest, metal, the large intestines, and it transforms water; *K'un* (The Receptive) corresponds to the southwest, earth, the spleen, and it transforms earth; *Hsün* (The Gentle) corresponds to the southeast, the gall bladder, wood, and it transforms earth; *Ken* (Keeping Still) corresponds to the northeast, the stomach, earth, and it transforms fire. These are the internal eight trigrams. As for the external eight trigrams, the numbers two and four correspond to the shoulders; six and eight to the feet; above to nine and below to one; left to three and right to seven. The trigram *K'an* is one, *K'un* is two, *Chen* is three, *Hsün* is four, the center is five. *Ch'ien* is six, *Tui* is seven, *Ken* is eight, and *Li* is nine. These are the "nine palaces," and this describes the internal nine palaces. In terms of the external and internal aspects of human physiology, the Celestial Stem *i* corresponds to the liver and left side of the ribs, transforms metal, and connects to the lungs; the Celestial Stem *chia* corresponds to the gall bladder, transforms earth, and connects with the spleen; Celestial Stem *ting* corresponds to the heart, transforms wood, and connects to the liver; the Celestial Stem *ping* corresponds to the small intestines, transforms water, and connects with the kidneys; Celestial Stem *chi* corresponds to the spleen, transforms earth, and connects with the stomach; Celestial Stem *wu* corresponds to the stomach, transforms fire, and connects with the heart; the back and chest, like mountain and marsh, exchange their *ch'i*; Celestial Stem *hsin* corresponds to the lungs and right side of the ribs, transforms water, and connects with the kidneys; Celestial Stem *keng* corresponds to the large intestines, transforms metal, and connects with the lungs; Celestial Stem *kuei* corresponds to the kidneys and lower part of the body, transforms fire, and connects with the heart; Celestial Stem *jen* corresponds to the urinary bladder, transforms wood, and connects with the liver. This describes the internal and external correspondences of the Ten Celestial Stems. The Twelve Terrestrial Branches also have their internal and external correspondences. Understanding these principles, one can begin to discuss the *tao* of self-cultivation.

19. An Explanation of the Three Levels of the Spiritual and Martial in T'ai-chi

Without self-cultivation, there would be no means of realizing the *tao*. Nevertheless, the methods of practice can be divided into three levels. The term *level* means attainment. The highest level is the great attainment; the lowest level is the lesser attainment; the middle level is the attainment of sincerity. Although the methods are divided into three levels of practice, the attainment is one. The spiritual is cultivated internally and the martial externally; physical culture is internal and martial arts external. Those whose practice is successful both internally and externally reach the highest level of attainment. Those who master the martial arts through the spiritual aspect of physical culture, and those who master the spiritual aspect of physical culture through the martial arts attain the middle level. However, those who know only physical culture but not the martial arts, or those who know only the martial arts without physical culture represent the lowest level of attainment.

20. An Explanation of the Martial Aspect of T'ai-chi

As a martial art, t'ai-chi is externally a soft exercise, but internally hard, even as it seeks softness. If we are externally soft, after a long time we will naturally develop internal hardness. It is not that we consciously culti-vate hardness, for in reality our mind is on softness. What is difficult is to remain internally reserved, to possess hardness without expressing it, always externally meeting the opponent with softness. Meeting hardness with soft-ness causes the opponent's hardness to be transformed and disappear into nothingness. How can we acquire this skill? When we have mastered stick-ing, adhering, connecting, and following, we will naturally progress from conscious movement to interpreting energy and finally spiritual illumina-tion and the realm of absolute transcendence. If our skill has not reached absolute transcendence, how could we manifest the marvel of four ounces deflecting a thousand pounds? It is simply a matter of what is called "under-standing sticky movement" to the point of perfecting the subtlety of seeing and hearing.

21. An Explanation of the Orthodox Practice of T'ai-chi

T'ai-chi is round. Regardless of whether inner or outer, up or down, left or right, it never leaves this roundness. T'ai-chi is square. Regardless of whether inner or outer, up or down, it never leaves this squareness. In and out with roundness; advancing and retreating with squareness. From squareness to roundness, and back and forth. Squareness is for opening and expanding; roundness is for tightening and contracting. The square and the round are the highest normative standard. Can anything fall outside this standard? In this way one achieves complete freedom of movement. Higher and deeper, subtler and ever more subtle, visible and invisible, brighter and brighter, it goes on forever without end.

22. An Explanation of Lightness and Heaviness, Floating and Sinking, in T'ai-chi

Double-weightedness is an error because it is overly full, which is not the same as sinking. Double-sinking is not an error because it is naturally nimble, which is not the same as heaviness. Double-floating is an error because it is simply insubstantial, which has nothing to do with lightness. Double-lightness is not an error because it is natural agility, which cannot be compared with floating. Half-light or half-heavy are not errors; too-light and too-heavy are errors. *Half* means that one is half grounded, and therefore it is not an error; *too* means that it is too ungrounded, and is therefore an error. When one is too ungrounded, one will deviate from the proper squareness and roundness; when one is half grounded, why should one deviate from squareness and roundness? Half-floating and half-sinking are errors, erring on the side of insufficiency; too-floating and too-sinking err on the side of excess. Half-heaviness or too-heaviness are stiff and disordered; half-light or too-light are agile but not round. Half-sinking or too-sinking are empty and disordered; half-floating or too-floating are vague and not round. Double-lightness that does not become floating is then nimbleness; double-sinking that does not become heaviness is then liveliness. Therefore we say that the highest technique is light and heavy; half-groundedness is average technique. Apart from these three, all techniques are erroneous. When one's internal lightness is not clouded, then it will express itself as clarity in the external *chi* as it flows into the limbs. If you do not get to the bottom of the techniques of lightness, heaviness, floating, and sinking, you will be wasting your time digging a well and never reaching water. When one has mastered the techniques of squareness, roundness, and the "four sides," together with inner and outer, gross and fine, then this is a great accomplishment. How can one say that the "four corners" depart from the concept of squareness and roundness? This is what is meant when we say that from square to round and round to square, one ultimately transcends the form and attains the realm of the highest technique.

23. An Explanation of the Four Corners in T'ai-Chi

The "four cardinal directions" refer to the four sides, or ward-off, roll-back, press, and push. If in the beginning one does not understand the principle that from squareness we can apply roundness, and that squareness and roundness exchange infinitely, then how can one demonstrate the corners techniques? When our external limbs or internal spirit are unable to sensitively execute the square and round four-sides techniques, we begin to see errors of lightness, heaviness, floating and sinking, and thus the need for the four corners arises. For example, half-heavy and too-heavy cause one to be stiff and disordered, naturally giving rise to the corner techniques—pull-down, split, elbow-stroke, and shoulder-stroke. Or double-weightedness and the resulting excessive fullness will also produce the corner techniques. Practitioners with faulty technique have no choice but to compensate by using the corner techniques in an attempt to return to proper roundness and squareness. Although practitioners of the lowest order must resort to elbow- and shoulder-stroke to compensate for their deficiencies, even the most advanced practitioners must acquire skill in pull-down and split to return to proper form. Thus the function of the four corners is to compensate for a loss of the principle of the art.

24. An Explanation of the Waist and Crown of the Head As Plumb and Balance in T'ai-chi

The crown of the head is like a plumb line, and therefore we speak of "suspension from the crown of the head." The two arms are like a balance that circle to the left and right. The waist is like the stem of the balance. If one stands like a plumb line and balance, then the slightest deviation in lightness, heaviness, floating, or sinking will be obvious. The plumb line suspending the head and the base of the balance located in the waist connect the *wei-lü* point in the coccyx and the *hsin-men* point at the crown of the head.

The top and bottom of the body are united by a single thread;
All depends on the turning of the two arms of the balance.

Through movement measure the inches and fractions;
You yourself can distinguish the precise degree.
With one wave of the signal flag,
The wheels of the two *ming-men* begin to turn.
When orders are issued by the mind, the *ch'i* goes into action like army
  banners,
And one naturally experiences complete freedom of movement.
Now the whole body is agile,
And you have become an *arhat* of steel.
During sparring, back and forth,
Sooner or later you will be successful.
When you make contact, repel the opponent,
Though you need not fling them to the heavens.
By maintaining your composure,
You can repel the opponent for a great distance with a single breath.
This oral teaching must be secretly transmitted;
Open the gate and behold heaven.

25. *Explanation of the T'ai-chi Symbol, the Four Seasons, and the Five* Ch'i

Summer
Fire
The sound *he*
SOUTH

Spring
Wood   EAST
The sound *hsü*

Autumn
WEST   Metal
The sound *hsi*

NORTH
The sound *ch'ui*
Water
Winter

Inhalation-Exhalation
Earth
The Center

26. *An Explanation of the Fundamentals of the Blood and Ch'i in T'ai-chi*

In human physiology, blood has a nutritive function and *ch'i* a defensive function. The blood circulates in the flesh, membranes, and arms; the *ch'i* circulates in the bones, sinews, and blood vessels. The sinews and nails are the superfluity of the bones; the cranial and body hair are the superfluity of the *ch'i*. When the blood is abundant, the cranial and body hair flourish; when the *ch'i* is sufficient, the sinews and nails are strong. Therefore, the courage and strength of the blood and *ch'i* express themselves in the external strength of the bones, skin, and body hair; the essence and function of the *ch'i* and blood express themselves in the internal strength of the flesh, sinews, and nails. The *ch'i* depends upon the fullness or deficiency of the blood; the blood depends upon the rise and fall of the *ch'i*. Round and round without end, the body can never exhaust these processes.

27. *An Explanation of Strength and Ch'i in T'ai-chi*

Ch'i travels in the membranes, bones, sinews, and blood vessels; strength issues from the blood, flesh, skin, and bones. Therefore, those with great brute force have external strength in their skin and bones, or physical form. Those with great *ch'i* have internal strength in their sinews and blood vessels, or physical image. The *ch'i*-blood expresses itself in internal strength; the blood-*ch'i* expresses itself in external strength. If you understand the function of the *ch'i* and blood, you will naturally understand the source of strength and *ch'i*. If you understand the nature of *ch'i* and strength, you will naturally grasp the distinction between using strength and circulating *ch'i*. Circulating the *ch'i* in the sinews and blood vessels and using strength in the skin and bones are very different.

28. *An Explanation of Feet, Inches, Hundredth Parts, and Thousandth Parts in T'ai-chi*

In your training, you should first practice opening and expanding and later practice tightness and compactness. After you have mastered opening and expanding, then pay attention to tightness and compactness; when tightness and compactness are mastered, then pay attention to the feet, inches, hundredth parts, and thousandth parts. This then is an explanation of the principle of feet, inches, hundredth parts and thousandth parts. Now, there are ten inches to the foot, ten hundredth parts to the inch, and ten thousandth parts to the hundredth part. This is the measure. Therefore, we say that sparring is a matter of measure. If you understand the measure, you will be able to grasp the feet, inches, hundredth parts, and thousandth parts. If you want to understand the measure, is this possible without the secret teachings?

29. An Explanation of the Membranes, Blood Vessels, Sinews, and Acupoints in T'ai-chi

Controlling the membranes, grabbing the blood vessels, seizing the sinews, and sealing the acupoints are examples of skills that can be pursued only after one has mastered feet, inches, hundredth parts, and thousandth parts. If you can control your opponent's membranes, his blood cannot circulate freely; if you can grab your opponent's blood vessels, his *ch'i* will have difficulty in circulating; if you seize your opponent's sinews, he will not be able to control himself; if you can seal the opponent's acupoints, he will faint. Seizing the membranes and controlling them will produce near death. If you can expose the blood vessels and grab them, the opponent will be as if dead. If you can isolate the sinews and seize them, this breaks the opponent's power. Sealing the death points terminates the opponent's life. To summarize, how can the opponent control himself if you have deprived him of *ch'i*, blood, or spirit. However, mastery of the techniques of controlling, grabbing, seizing, and sealing is impossible without the true teaching.

30. An Explanation of T'ai-chi Terminology

Break, bend, beat, and *pound* (relating to ourselves and to the opponent). *Press down, rub, push,* and *grab* (relating to ourselves and to the opponent). *Open, close, rise,* and *fall* (relating to ourselves and to the opponent). These twelve terms describe hand techniques. *Flex, extend, move,* and *rest* (relating to ourselves and to the opponent). *Rise, drop, speed up,* and *slow down* (relating to ourselves and to the opponent). *Evade, return, provoke,* and *cease* (relating to ourselves and to the opponent). These twelve terms describe one's own *ch'i* and the opponent's hand techniques. *Turn, exchange, advance,* and *retreat* (relating to one's own body and to the opponent's steps). *Gaze left, look right, forward,* and *backward* (relating to one's own eyes and to the opponent's hand techniques), or gaze forward, gaze to the left and look to the right. These eight terms describe one's spirit. *Break, connect, bend forward,* and *bend backward.* These four terms describe awareness and power. *Connect* describes the spirit and the *ch'i.* *Bend forward* and *bend backward* describe the hands and the feet. The power breaks, but the awareness does not break; the awareness breaks, but the spirit does not break. When power, awareness, and spirit all break, then one resorts to bending forward or backward because the hands and feet have lost their contact and footing. *Bending forward* means to bow; *bending backward* means to arch the back. To avoid bowing and arching, it is imperative to break and reconnect. In terms of sparring, *bending forward* and *bending backward* represent a serious situation. At all times avoid a break in the mind, body, hands, and feet. If you have lost your connection, do not attempt bending forward or backward. If you want to gain the ability to break and reconnect, you must be able to observe the hidden and disclose the subtle. The hidden and the subtle means that there appears to be a break, but there is no break; observing and disclosing means that there appears to be a connection but there is no connection. Connecting and breaking; breaking and connecting. When the consciousness, mind, body, substance, spirit, and *ch'i* become superior in concealing and disclosing, what fear need one have of not being able to stick, adhere, connect, and follow?

31. An Explanation of the Feet, Inches, Hundredth Parts, and Thousandth Parts in T'ai-chi Controlling, Grabbing, Seizing, and Sealing

When you have mastered the skills of sparring, then you can measure the feet, inches, hundredth parts, and thousandth parts in hand techniques. However, although controlling, grabbing, seizing, and sealing may be easy, controlling the membranes, grabbing the blood vessels, seizing the sinews, and sealing the acupoints is assuredly difficult. If you do not begin by measuring feet, inches, hundredth parts, and thousandth parts, it is impossible. If you have not yet perfected the precise measure in your *control* technique, you can locate the *membranes* by press-down. If you have not yet perfected the precise meaure in your *grab* technique, you can use *rub* to find the *blood vessels.* If you have not yet perfected the precise measure in your *seize* technique, you can use *push* to find the *sinews.* If your *seal* technique is not precise, you will not be able to locate the acupoints. From feet one must refine one's technique to the level of inches, hundredth parts, and thousandth parts. Although these four techniques require advanced teachings, without long training they cannot be mastered.

32. An Explanation of Increasing or Draining the Ch'i and Strength in T'ai-chi[8]

To increase or drain your own *ch'i* and strength is very difficult; to increase or drain the opponent's *ch'i* or strength is also difficult. Increasing is called for when there is a deficiency in your consciousness; draining is called for when there is an excess in your movement. Therefore we say that this is not easy to achieve in relation to ourselves. Increasing the opponent is called for when his *ch'i* is excessive; when his strength is excessive, then drain it. This is why we are victorious, whereas the opponent fails. Draining excessive *ch'i* and increasing excessive strength is based on the same principle, but requires a detailed explanation. Increasing excess means that one is adding excess to excess. When dealing with an opponent in a diminished condition, by further retarding what is insufficient, he will react by overcompensating and becoming excessive. Increasing the opponent's *ch'i* and draining his strength both cause the opponent to become excessive. Increasing the *ch'i* is called the "*ch'i* binding method," and draining the strength is called the "strength emptying method."

33. The Theory of Empty and Bound, Breaking and Rubbing, in T'ai-chi

There is a distinction between emptiness caused by a breaking force and binding caused by a breaking force; between emptiness caused by a rubbing force and binding caused by a rubbing force. When emptiness is caused by a breaking force, the strength is isolated; when binding is caused by a breaking force, the *ch'i* is suspended; when emptiness is caused by rubbing, the strength is divided; when binding is caused by rubbing, the *ch'i* is isolated. If binding is caused by rubbing or breaking, then the *ch'i* and strength reverse; if emptiness is caused by rubbing or breaking, then the strength and *ch'i* are spoiled. When binding is caused by rubbing or breaking, then the strength exceeds the *ch'i*, that is, the strength is superior to the *ch'i*; when emptiness is caused by breaking or rubbing, then the *ch'i* exceeds the strength, that is, the *ch'i* is excessive and the strength deficient. In the case of break-binding rubbing and rub-binding breaking, the *ch'i* is sealed off by the strength; in the case of break-emptying rubbing and rub-emptying breaking the strength is drilled by the *ch'i*. To summarize, the technique of binding caused by breaking and emptying caused by rubbing is also a matter of measuring feet, inches, hundredth parts, and thousandth parts. Otherwise, how could one achieve breaking and rubbing or subtle binding without accurate measurement?

34. The Theory of Before and After Gaining the Ability to Interpret Energy

Before gaining the ability to interpret energy one often commits the errors of butting, insufficiency, separation, and resistance; after learning to interpret energy one may also commit the errors of suspending, connecting, bending foreword, and bending backward. It is natural that before learning to interpret energy we might commit errors, but how could there still be errors after mastering it? These errors result from being unclear about our interpretation and inaccurate in suspending and connecting. When spiritual illumination is not yet perfectly achieved and bending forward and backward are unstable, one can also commit errors. If you do not manifest errors in suspending, connecting, bending forward, and bending backward it can only be the result of truly interpreting energy. What is true interpreting energy? If your vision and hearing have no basis, it is difficult to achieve accuracy. When your vision takes in far and near, left and right; when your hearing takes in rising, falling, slow and fast; when your understanding of movement encompasses evading, returning, provoking, and completing; and when your sense of action embraces turning, exchanging, advancing, and retreating, then this is true interpreting. It approaches spiritual illumination and is a clear basis for one's movement. Having a basis, meaning based on interpreting energy, one naturally achieves the marvel of bending, extending, movement, and stillness. If you have achieved the marvel of bending, extending, movement, and stillness, then opening, closing, rising, and descending will also have a basis. Based on your bending, extending, movement, and stillness, when you meet penetration you open, when the opponent issues you unite, when he approaches you descend, and when he withdraws you rise. This then is true spiritual illumination. After reaching this level, how could one not be cautious in regard to daily activities, diet, and elimination. This would then bring one to middle and great accomplishment.

35. Theory of Feet, Inches, Hundredth-Parts, and Thousandth-Parts after Mastering Interpreting Energy

If before mastering interpreting energy, you attempt to first learn the feet, inches, hundredth parts, and thousandth parts, even though you make some small progress, this will merely be a superficial martial art. The ability to measure the opponent is impossible without being able to interpret energy. After learning to interpret energy, and reaching the level of spiritual illumination, one can naturally measure feet and inches. After mastering feet and inches you can then execute controlling, grabbing, seizing, and sealing. In order to understand the principle of the membranes, blood vessels, sinews, and acupoints, you must understand the life and death hand techniques; in order to understand the life and death hand techniques, you must understand the life and death acupoints. How can one fail to be familiar with the acupoint techniques? Knowing the life and death acupoint techniques, how can one fail to understand sealing them so as to terminate life? How can one fail to understand sealing them so that life is no more? Thus the two words *life* and *death* both turn on the one word *sealing*.

36. An Explanation of Fingers, Palm, Fist, and Whole Hand in T'ai-chi

The area from the base of the fingers to the wrist is the palm. All of the fingers together are the hand. Each of the five fingers is a finger. The outside of the hand is called the fist. In terms of their application, push down and push forward use the palm; grab, rub, seize, and seal use the fingers; break and chafe use the whole hand; and punch uses the fist. Among punches, there are "deflect downward and parry," "aim for crotch," "below the elbow," and "turn the body." Apart from these four fist techniques, there is also "upside down punch." Among the palm techniques there are "brush knee," "rotate body," "single whip," and "penetrate the back." Apart from these four palm techniques there is also "linked palms." Among hand techniques, there are "cloud hands," "raise hands," "grab," and "cross hands." Apart from these four hand techniques, there is also "reverse hand." Among finger techniques, there are "bent finger," "extended finger," "pinch fingers," and "sealing finger." Apart from these four finger techniques, there are also "measure finger," also called "feet and inches finger," or "seeking acupoint finger." Now, there are five fingers, and each has its applications. The five fingers together constitute one hand, but they still retain their function as fingers, and therefore they are also called "hand fingers." The first application is "rotating fingers" or "rotating hand." The second application is "root fingers" or "root hand." The third application is "bow fingers" or "bow hand." The fourth application is "central unity" or "hand fingers." Apart from these four "hand finger" techniques, there is also "single finger" or "single hand." The index finger is the "fighting finger," "sword finger," "helping finger," or "sticky finger." The middle finger is the "heart finger," "uniting finger," "hook finger," or "rubbing finger." The third finger is the "complete finger," "ring finger," "substitute finger," or "plucking finger." The little finger is the "serving finger," "mending finger," "seductive finger," or "hanging finger." These names are easy to learn, but the techniques are difficult to apply. Even after receiving the secret oral transmissions, it is still not easy. Secondary techniques include, "facing palm," "push mountain palm," "shoot goose palm," "spread wings palm," "apparent seal up finger," "twist step finger," "bend bow finger," "work shuttles finger," "pat horse hand," "bend bow hand," "embrace tiger hand," "jade lady hand," "straddle tiger hand," "open mountain punch," "under leaf punch," "reverse punch," "power portion punch," and "rolling break punch." Beyond this, you must remember that if the footwork follows the body and never deviates from the Five Phases, then one will commit no errors. If you follow the principles of adhere, stick, and follow, give up yourself and follow the opponent, allow the body to follow the footwork, then if you do not violate the Five Phases, and your postures are natural, what is there to worry about in a few minor mistakes?

37. Oral Transmission of the Theory of Life and Death Acupoints

There are life and death acupoints, but to learn them requires oral transmissions. Why is this? One, because of the difficulty; two, because it relates to life and death; and three, because it depends on the character of the individual. First, one must not teach those who are not loyal and filial; second, one must not teach those who do not have a good background; third, one must not teach those with evil intentions; fourth; one must not teach those who are careless and crude; fifth, one must not teach those who have no consideration for others; sixth, one must not teach those who are outwardly polite but not compassionate; seventh, one must not teach those who are not reliable; eighth, one must not teach those who are quick to learn and quick to forget. It is important to know the eight disqualifications; as for outright criminals, they need not even be mentioned. Those who do qualify may be given the secret transmissions orally. You may teach those who are loyal and filial, emotionally stable, faithful to the teaching, respectful to the teaching, and always consistent. Given these five qualities, if the student is truly consistent from beginning to end and never wavers, then you may transmit every aspect of the art. From generation to generation, this is the way of the transmission. Alas, is it not a pity that there are still criminals in the martial arts!

38. The Legacy of Chang San-feng

Heaven and earth are *Ch'ien* and *K'un*;
Fu Hsi is the father of humankind.
The drawing of the trigrams and naming of the *tao*
Came with Yao, Shun, and the sixteen mothers.
The highest truths
Were passed to Confucius and Mencius.
The spiritual practices for cultivating body and mind
Were exemplified in the seventy-two disciples, Emperors Wen and Wu.
This was handed down to me
Through Hsü Hsüan-p'ing.
The elixir of long life is within the body
That we may restore our primal purity.
Spiritual cultivation brings great virtue;
Regulate it well and the *ch'i* and body will be whole.
For ten thousand years chant the praises of eternal spring;
Truly the mind is the genuine article.
The Three Teachings are not separate schools,
But all speak of the one Great Ultimate,
Whose greatness fills the universe,
One standard fixed for all eternity.
The teachings of the ancient sages are a lasting heritage,
Opening the way for truth seekers down through the ages.
Water and fire form the hexagram *Chi-chi* (After Completion),
Which represents the culmination of our life's quest.

39. Oral Transmission of the Words of Master Chang San-feng

I know that the common thread of the Three Teachings is the dual cultivation of body and mind, taking the mind as ruler of the body, and preserving the body and mind so that *ching, ch'i,* and spirit endure forever. Possessing *ching, ch'i,* and spirit, we are capable of mental composure and martial activity. By developing composure and activity, we can approach sagehood and immortality. The first enlightened attained spiritual transcendence; the later enlightened emulated the abilities of the former. Although these are innate abilities, they cannot be acquired without emulation. Human abilities naturally include both the spiritual and martial. Our vision and hearing naturally belong to the spiritual; gesturing with the hands and stepping with the feet naturally belong to the martial. Thus it is obvious that these are innate abilities. Our ancestors who were masters of the spiritual and the martial taught the arts of self-cultivation through physical culture, but not through the martial arts. As the transmission was handed down to me, I learned the gesturing and stepping "battle of essences," wherein *yin* essence within the body is borrowed to strengthen the *yang* essence. *Yang* within the body is male, and *yin* is female, yet both are within one body. The male body contains only one *yang* and the rest is *yin*. The female, by stealing this one *yang* is able to repair her *yin*, and thus it is said that for the female the *yang* returns to its original state. When it comes to the *yin* within this body, it is not only the female who possesses postpubescent essence. Matching the "fair maiden" and "baby boy" through infinite transformations is the basis for the "fair maiden battle of essences." How is it that there are also those who attempt to carry out these practices using the physical bodies of men and women? Using the microcosmic heaven and earth within our own body to assist this process is the true "*yin-yang* battle of essences." In this way it can be seen that male bodies all belong to *yin*, and to gather the *yin* within our own bodies, to seize the female within our own bodies, is not as good as the interaction of *yin* and *yang* between two males, for this is a more rapid method of self-cultivation. I have applied this to the martial arts, but it must not be viewed as a superficial technique. It must remain on the level of physical culture, self-cultivation, the dual development of body and mind, and the realm of sagehood and immortality. Now the "battle of essences" involving the interaction of two males is based on the same principle as the "battle of essences" within one's own body. When our own body encounters an opponent, this is the "battle of essences," or "mercury and lead." When doing battle with an opponent, the *yin* and *yang* of trigrams *K'an* (The Abysmal) and *Li* (The Clinging) and *Tui* (The Joyous) and *Chen* (The Arousing) demonstrate the principle of *yang* seizing *yin*, or the four sides of the square; the *yin* and *yang* of *Ch'ien* (The Creative) and *K'un* (The Receptive) and *Ken* (Keeping Still) and *Hsün* (The Gentle), demonstrate the principle of *yin* gathering *yang*, or the four corners. Thus the eight trigrams in action are the "eight gates." The feet begin in the central earth position. When we advance we use *yang* to seize the opponent; when we retreat we use *yin* to gather the opponent; when we gaze-left we use *yang* to gather him; and when we look-right we use *yin* to seize him. Thus the Five Phases in action are the "five steps." Together these are the "eight gates and five steps." What I have just taught you can be used for a lifetime without exhausting it. My teachings should be transmitted as a martial art for self-cultivation. The practice of self-cultivation is the same whether based on the martial or spiritual. The source of the "three teachings" and "three levels" is none other than t'ai-chi. I hope that students in the future will use the principles of the *I Ching* to test them in the body and pass them on to future generations.

40. *Treatise on Chang San-feng Realizing the Tao through Martial Arts*

Before the creation of heaven and earth, natural law (*li*) already existed. Natural law controls the *yin* and *yang* of *ch'i*. Through the control of natural law, heaven and earth came into existence with the *tao* in its midst. *Yin* and *yang* govern the movement of the *tao* of *ch'i*, and thus there is the interaction of opposites. The interaction of opposites is *yin* and *yang*, or number. One *yin* and one *yang* constitute the *tao*. Nameless, the *tao* is the beginning of heaven and earth; nameable, the *tao* is the mother of all things. Before the creation of heaven and earth was the infinite, the unnameable; after the creation of heaven and earth was the finite, the nameable. What preceded the creation of heaven and earth was called natural law; what succeeded the creation of heaven and earth was called motherhood. This is the transformation of natural law. Precreation *yin-yang*, *ch'i*, and number are born of mother; postcreation eggs develop in the watery environment of the womb. Located between heaven and earth and sustaining all life, the *tao* works harmoniously. Therefore, *Ch'ien* and *K'un* are the greater father and mother, belonging to the prenatal realm; our biological father and mother are the lesser father and mother, belonging to the postnatal realm. Receiving *yin* and *yang* and prenatal and postnatal *ch'i* as we come into the world, this is the beginning of human life. In coming into this world, the human being receives life, intrinsic nature, and reason from its greater father and mother and *ching*, blood, and body from its lesser father and mother. Combining body and life from our pre- and postnatal sources, we then become a human being. Wishing to form a triad with heaven and earth, can we afford to lose the root of our intrinsic nature? If we are able to act in accordance with our intrinsic nature, then we will not lose the root. Since we have not lost our original nature, then how could we lose the direction of our physical bodies? Wishing to find our direction, we must first know where we came from. Knowing our origin, we will find the path, for the means are surely at hand. But what are the means? It is simply our own innate knowledge and ability. No matter whether brilliant or foolish, virtuous or otherwise, all can use their innate knowledge and abilities to approach the *tao*. Being able to cultivate the *tao* and understanding our origins, we will understand the direction we must go. Knowing our origins and direction, we must understand self-cultivation. Therefore, it is said that from the emperor down to the common people, all take self-cultivation as their foundation. But how should we go about self-cultivation? It is on the basis of innate wisdom and abilities. From the vision of our eyes and the hearing of our ears we have acuity and clarity. The hands naturally gesture and the feet stamp; we are endowed with both martial and spiritual capacities. Thus we must extend our knowledge and investigate the world, so that our thoughts will be sincere and our hearts straight. The mind is the ruler of the body, and thus we must rectify the mind and make our hearts sincere. The feet step out the Five Phases and the hands gesture the eight trigrams. As the hands and feet enact the "four images" and their various applications, our innate abilities revert to their origin. As our eyes perceive the "three unities" and our ears hear the "six ways," the eyes and ears enact the "four forms," and combining their essence in one, our own innate wisdom reverts to its root. The ears and eyes, hands and feet, being divided into pairs are like *yin* and *yang,* and their uniting into one is like *t'ai-chi.* Thus the external becomes concentrated in the internal, and the internal expresses itself externally. In this way we develop within and without, the fine and the gross, and with penetrating understanding, we realize the work of the wise men and sages. Wisdom and knowledge, sagehood and immortality, these are what we mean by fulfilling our intrinsic nature and establishing life. Herein lies the perfection of spirit and divine transformation. The way of heaven and the way of humanity is simply sincerity.

SIGNIFICANCE
OF THE NEW TEXTS

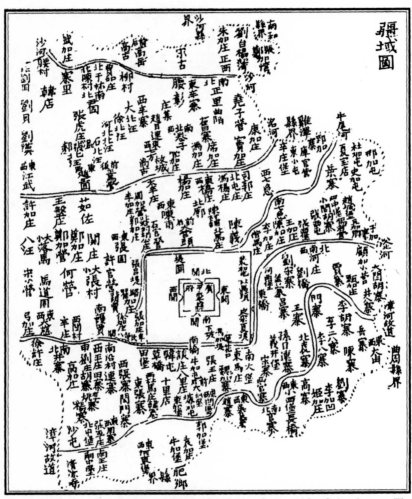

Detail of area surrounding Kuang-p'ing City showing farms, villages, and fortified settlements. The "Wu chia-chuang" (Wu family farm) in the upper left-hand corner of the map may or may not have belonged to the Wu family of t'ai-chi fame.

Significance of the New Texts

In view of the many gaps and controversies concerning the origins and development of t'ai-chi ch'üan, one would hope that the revelation of new premodern documents could shed light directly or indirectly on t'ai-chi's formative period. Wu Yü-hsiang's role was absolutely pivotal, as putative discoverer of the salt shop manuscripts, patron of Yang Lu-ch'an, student of Ch'en Ch'ing-p'ing, redactor of the classics, and creator of the Wu (Hao) style. Works by his brothers, Ch'eng-ch'ing and Ju-ch'ing, coming out of the same historical, intellectual, and familial milieu, can thus be expected to illuminate the background of the classics and to amplify them. Li I-yü is the next generation, and it is in Li's hand that we have our earliest extant authentic autographs of the classics, together with examples of his own writings. Hence new texts by Li I-yü must also be considered significant additions to the primary literature. Writings tracing their origins to Yang Pan-hou are our closest link to Yang Lu-ch'an and to the richness of the art before it moved into the mainstream of Chinese culture in the twentieth century.

In assessing the significance of this new material, we must ask if it provides (1) new teachings, (2) light on controversial questions, or (3) general historical background. The question of new teachings has been discussed in detail in the analytical introductions to each set of texts, and it has been demonstrated that these materials represent a significant infusion of new theoretical and practical concepts. In terms of the third criterion, general historical background, the sum of all four sources multiplies by many times the sheer volume of pre-twentieth-century literature on t'ai-chi ch'üan and gives the scholar a much broader base or "feel" for the territory and the intellectual tone of the time. It is inevitably significant in providing a richer linguistic environment in which to carry out hermeneutic studies. In the absence of the kinds of detailed discussions of schools and lineages we find in Ch'i Chi-kuang, Huang Tsung-hsi, Huang Pai-chia, or Ch'ang Nai-chou, we are forced to conclude that the primary documents of t'ai-chi ch'üan are virtually sterile and devoid of internal historical evidence or clues. Li I-yü's "Short Preface" and "Postscript," Wu Ch'eng-ch'ing's "Postscript," Wu Lai-hsü's "Biography of Wu Yü-hsiang," Wu Yen-hsü's "Biographies of the Li Family," and the anonymous "Preface to the Yin-fu Spear Manual" are all secondary sources and of dubious credibility. With the exception of Li I-yü's very sketchy "Short Preface" and "Post-script," the absence of historical references in the primary writings on t'ai-chi ch'üan, previously received or recent, contrasts sharply with the relative richness of lineages and historical references in the "Classic of Pugilism," "Epitaph for Wang Cheng-nan," or Ch'ang Nai-chou's writings. This may point to either forgery of the classics, ignorance as to the origin of the texts, or political constraints on truthfulness. Historical referents in the previously received literature are conspicuous by their absence, and a similar blackout in the new material reinforces the impression of something to hide.

As for the ability of these new texts to shed light on controversial questions in t'ai-chi scholarship, there is a good deal more room for speculation. Let us examine ten of the most controversial questions in t'ai-chi ch'üan scholarship in light of these new documents under the following four headings: authorship, editions, figures, and anomalies. Organizing the discussion in this way produces the following outline:

I. Authorship
  1. Who wrote the previously received "classics?"
  2. Are the new texts authentic? And when were they written?
II. Editions
  1. Why is there a difference between the Wu/Li classics and the Yang editions?
  2. Are the bookstall classics authentically Wang Tsung-yüeh's, partly authentic, or complete forgeries?
III. Figures
  1. Was Chang San-feng an historical figure? And who introduced the notion of his connection with t'ai-chi ch'üan?
  2. Is Wang Tsung-yüeh an historical figure? And did he transmit the art to the Ch'en family or learn it from them?
  3. What was the period and role of Chiang Fa?
IV. Anomalies
  1. How can we explain why where we find the art (Ch'en Village) we find no pre- twentieth-century theory, and

where we find the theory (Wu-yang salt shop) we find no t'ai-chi?

2. How do we explain verbatim and close parallels between Ch'ang Nai-chou's writings and the Wu/Li classics?

3. Is it possible we have original texts of Ch'eng-ch'ing and Ju-ch'ing, but not of Yü-hsiang? And why were the Wu brothers' manuscripts preserved in the Li and Hao families but not in the Wu family?

Let us take these topics up in turn, beginning with authorship.

Authorship of the Previously Received Classics

With the exception of the "Song of Sparring," there is no record in Ch'en Village of any of the classics as we know them.[1] The Wu/Li transmission, from the Ma T'ung-wen to Lien Jang Hall editions, include attributions to Wang Tsung-yüeh, Wu Yü-hsiang, Li I-yü, and Li Ch'i-hsüan. Yang editions are mutually contradictory, variously attributing the texts to Chang San-feng, Wang Tsung-yüeh, or Yang Lu-ch'an. Appendix 2, p. 158, indicates some of the pre-Ch'ing sources of the language and concepts in the "Treatise"; and Appendix 2, pp. 186–88 shows parallels between the classics and Ch'ang Nai-chou's writings. The three characters 是爲論 ("This is the treatise") that appear at the end of the "Wang Tsung-yüeh of Shanxi's Treatise on T'ai-chi Ch'üan" tend to mark it off from the rest of the manuscript as being an older stratum. Li I-yü's "Postscript" appended to his own personal copy and to the "handwritten copy" shown by Hao Yüeh-ju to Hsü Chen states: "This manual was obtained in a salt shop in Wu-yang County. I have gathered together the theories of various masters and added my own views." Does this mean that the boundaries are clear-cut, that "manual" equals "treatise," "various masters" includes Wu Yü-hsiang, and "my own views" refers to the three texts that follow the "Short Preface" in the original manuscript? Or does Li's ambiguity allow us to consider that portions of the Wang Tsung-yüeh material are distributed throughout the classics, or even that Wang is a fiction? The "Postscript," citing the "Wu-yang salt shop" as the site of the found "manuals," does not mention Wang Tsung-yüeh, and the "Short Preface," citing Wang as "pre-eminent theoretician," does not mention the source of these writings. Likewise Wu Lai-hsü's "Biography" of his grandfather, Yü-hsiang, credits Wang's "writings" (*lun-shuo* 論說) as authoritative, but does not recount the salt shop story. Nevertheless, the title "Wang Tsung-yüeh of Shanxi's Treatise on T'ai-chi Ch'üan" indicates that Li wanted us to believe that at least this text belonged purely to Wang. Whatever other language or passages belong to Wang is open to interpretation.

Any attempt to fabricate Wang as a cover for forgery would involve one of two scenarios: (1) The Wu brothers forged the Wang Tsung-yüeh "manual" and foisted it on the credulous Li brothers, or (2) the Wu and Li brothers conspired together to foist the Wang plot on the public. This is not the place to examine the conspiracy theories of Chao Hsi-min, T.Y. Pang, and others, but to ask what light the new material might shed on this critical issue. If the Ch'eng-ch'ing texts are authentic, the "Postscript" mentioning Wang by name and the reference to "the original treatise" and "the original manual" in the "Notes" and "Postscript" reinforce either Ch'eng-ch'ing's role in the actual find in Wu-yang, where he was posted as magistrate in 1852, or, conversely, his active participation in a conspiracy. Although I believe conspiracy theories have considerable merit in this environment, on balance, and if these texts are authentic, Ch'eng-ch'ing's writings tend to support the veracity of the salt shop find. From the point of view of motivation, since it took more than a century for these texts to surface, we must ask whom they would have been intended to deceive? Even the "three old manuscripts" were not known outside of Yung-nien until the 1930s.

If the Ch'eng-ch'ing pieces tend to support the salt shop find and Wang Tsung-yüeh's authorship, there is still a question of which portions of the Wu/Li manuscript may be attributed to him. The "Treatise" must be considered an irreducible minimum, but the number of phrases associated with "original treatise" or "original manual" in Ch'eng-ch'ing's writings that fall outside the "Treatise" means that Wang material cannot be confined to the "Treatise" alone (see Appendix 2, pp. 164–66). This may suggest that the "Treatise" was found as a complete piece and that other fragments were incorporated into texts by the Wu brothers. Still, how do we explain the fact that the preponderance of parallels between Ch'ang and the Wu/Li manuscript fall not in the "Treatise" but in the "Essentials?" Also, the large number of quotations from general literary sources (see Appendix 2, pp. 158–59) means that the "Treatise" could as easily have been written in Wu's time (the nineteenth century) as in Wang's (presumably the eighteenth, if we can believe the "Preface to the Yin-fu Spear Manual"). The expression "this art" in the "Treatise" phrase "This art has many rivals" suggests a high level of distinctiveness and makes us wonder why Wang's name appears in no gazetteers or histories. The preponderance of quotations in Ch'eng-ch'ing's "Notes" appear in the Wu/Li

"Treatise," but the "Postscript" shows a majority in the "Essentials," leaving the situation less than clear. Thus, although the new material cannot definitively establish the authenticity of the "Wang Tsung-yüeh of Shanxi's Treatise on T'ai-chi Ch'üan," to deny it in the face of the new material means bringing into the conspiracy the older Wu brothers or even those who have recently published these works.

Continuing with the Wu/Li manuscript, and considering each text in order of appearance, we come next to the "Thirteen Postures Form" 十三勢架. Neither it nor the "Broadsword Techniques" 刀法 nor the "Spear Techniques" 槍法 is illuminated by the new material, as there is no reference to specific form postures or to weapons. The "Body Techniques" 身法, however, presents some possibilities. Ku Liu-hsin[2] attributes the text to Wu Yü-hsiang, as does Hsü Chen;[3] however, the juxtaposition of phrases paralleling the Wu/Li "Treatise" and "Body Techniques" in Ch'eng-ch'ing's "Notes" and Ju-ch'ing's "Treatise" introduced with the generic phrase "body techniques" suggests that these may be standard two-character expressions compiled by, but not original with, Yü-hsiang. Whether they derive from a body of material found in the Wu-yang salt shop or from oral transmissions cannot be said at this point. At any rate, the phrases "relax the chest and raise the back" and "enclose the crotch and protect the ribs" are so intermingled with other phrases in the "Notes" and Ju-ch'ing's "Treatise" that it is hard to imagine that the authors were not looking at material that predates the Wu/Li "Body Techniques." Therefore, while it might be justifiable to credit Yü-hsiang with compiling the "Body Techniques" as it appears in the Wu/Li manuscript, it cannot be based exclusively on his personal "insight."

The "Thirteen Postures (Also Called Long Boxing)" 十三勢一名長拳一名十三勢 is attributed by Ku Liu-hsin to Wang Tsung-yüeh,[4] but Hsü Chen allows only that portion naming the postures, attributing to Wu the poetic passage "Long Boxing is like long rivers . . ." that precedes it and the trigram and Five Phases analysis that follows it.[5] The term "Long Boxing" 長拳 is absent from the new Wu brothers and Li I-yü material, as is trigram and Five Phases analysis. However, the phrase "The *ch'i* is like the water of the Yangtze River, flowing unceasingly to the east" in Li's "Song of Circulating the *Ch'i*" is obviously inspired by the language of the "Thirteen Postures" or its antecedents. Nevertheless, the basic question remains: Was the text of the "Thirteen Postures," or parts of it, found by Yü-hsiang or composed by him? The Ch'eng-ch'ing and Ju-ch'ing material contains no quotations from the "Thirteen Postures" and does not develop trigram or Five Phase analysis, which does not reappear until the *Yang Family Forty Chapters.* Ch'ang Nai-chou uses Five Phases medical theory in relation to the organs and meridians, but the "Thirteen Postures" is the first received example of either Five Phase or trigram analysis in the martial arts. The frequency of quotations from other Wu/Li texts in Ch'eng-ch'ing and Ju-ch'ing and the total absence of any hint of the "Thirteen Postures" in the new material do not strengthen the case for Wang authorship, but neither do they make it look any more like exclusively Wu Yü-hsiang's.

Hsü Chen lists the "Song of the Practice of the Thirteen Postures" 十 三 勢 行 工 歌 訣 as Wang Tsung-yüeh's,[6] but Ku Liu-hsin notes it as "author unknown."[7] The language and spatial arrangement of the handwritten Wu/Li manuscript (confirmed by Appendix 2, pp. 160–61) make it very clear that the first "The commentary says" 解曰 section of the "Essentials of Sparring" is fundamentally a commentary to the "Song." Since the "Essentials" is most unequivocally the work of Wu Yü-hsiang, it is unlikely he would write a commentary to his own composition. Unfortunately, Ku does not explain why he dissents from his mentor, T'ang Hao,[8] in not assigning the text to Wang or siding with Chang Shih-i 張士一, who considered it earlier than the "Treatise."[9] The verse form of this text resonates more with the new Li I-yü material than anything else in the Wu/Li manuscript, but it is unlikely that Li interpolated one of his own compositions at this point and then proceeded to forge the "Essentials" commentary over Wu's name. It is equally unlikely that Wu wrote a commentary to his student I-yü's verse. The only other verse piece in the Wu/Li collection is the "Song of Sparring," which, because of its existence in Ch'en Village and quotation in the "Treatise," appears to represent the oldest stratum of the classics. Unfortunately, there is nothing comparable in Ch'ang Nai-chou's eighteenth-century writings. The two most striking features of the "Song of the Practice of the Thirteen Postures" in relation to the new material—its nonquotation in the Ch'eng-ch'ing texts and formal similarity with Li I-yü's writings—sheds no light on its authorship. Ku Liu-hsin should be applauded for breaking ranks and withholding judgment.

The byline "All written by Wu Yü-hsiang" 禹襄武氏並識 following the "Essentials of Sparring" 打手要言 has been used by many scholars to argue that the classics are not the work of Chang San-feng and, more recently, by a few to argue that they are not the work of Wang Tsung-yüeh. Whether the "All" refers to all of the "Essentials," all of the preceding texts, or the whole manuscript is a question, although one must ask why the title of the "Treatise" would include the name of Wang Tsung-yüeh if written by Wu.[10] The insertion of the attribution "All written by Wu Yü-hsiang" implies that at least the "Essentials" belongs to Wu. However, only parts of the text of the Wu/Li "Essentials," distributed under the two titles "Explanation of T'ai-chi Ch'üan" 太極拳解 and "Summary of the Thirteen Postures" 十三勢說略, are attributed to Wu in Li Huai-yin's 1935 Lien-jang Hall edition. The first and second "It is also said" 又曰 sections are appended to the "Treatise" as if to credit them to Wang Tsung-yüeh, and the first "The commentary says" 解曰 is also given a separate rubric and credited to I-yü. Huai-yin's editing and attribution appear to be guesswork, and reinforce the impression given by the Wu/Li "Essentials" itself that this was never a single organic composition, but assembled by Li from Wu's fragments. The first "Commentary" section is clearly an explanation of the "Song of the Practice of the Thirteen Postures" and most closely resembles Ch'eng-ch'ing's "Notes," but what of the second "Commentary" section? Is it a commentary to a lost text, a collection of epigrammatic phrases, or an original composition? There is a marked tendency to cluster Ch'ang Nai-chou parallels in this second "Commentary" section, but the Ch'ang-Wu connection has yet to be traced. Can the new Ch'eng-ch'ing and Ju-ch'ing material help us sort this out? Although we do not know what Yü-hsiang was looking at when he wrote his manuscripts, we can assume that his brothers were privy to the same material. The large number of parallels between the new Wu brothers' texts and the "Essentials" leaves us with two alternatives: Either Ch'eng-ch'ing and Ju-ch'ing were quoting from Yü-hsiang's compositions, or they were quoting from an earlier corpus of writings. I believe it is a highly unlikely they were quoting from their younger brothers' original compositions and far more probable that they based their writings on a corpus that preceded and was the textual antecedent of the Wu/Li "Essentials." Whether this was all part of the salt shop find is yet unclear. At the very least, the appearance of numerous phrases from the "Essentials" in Ch'eng-ch'ing's "Notes" and "Postscript" in contexts associated with the words *original treatise* and *original manuals* suggests an older strata in the "Essentials" and comports with the eclectic appearance of the "Essentials."

The "Four-Character Secret Transmission" 四字秘訣 was originally believed by Ku Liu-hsin to be the work of Li I-yü or Li Ch'i-hsüan.[11] After receiving a photograph of Li I-yü's personal copy of the "three old manuscripts" with the title "Uncle Yü-hsiang's Four-Character Secret Transmission" 禹襄母舅太極拳四字不傳秘訣, he realized his error. In its language and intent it most closely resembles Ch'eng-ch'ing and Ju-ch'ing's theory of "stalled, incoming, and retreating" energies. Both go beyond technique to the level of mobilizing energy, although the "three energies" equally emphasizes reading and response, whereas the "Four-Character Secret" emphasizes deployment exclusively. Many of the new Wu brothers and Li I-yü theoretical principles are shared with the previously received classics, but the new material opens the door much wider and allows us a fuller glimpse of the period and state of development of the art.

The "Song of Sparring" is unusual in that it was found in both the Ch'en Village manuscripts and the Wu/Li classics, as well as quoted in the "Treatise." The Ch'eng-ch'ing eight-line version joins the previously received Ch'en Village four- and six-line "Songs"[12] and the Wu/Li six-line version. With the exception of four characters, the Ch'en six-line and Wu/Li versions are identical. Whether the Ch'en six is a development of the Ch'en four or whether the four is a contraction of the six is difficult to determine, since the first four lines of the Tzu-ming six-line version are close to the four-line version. Nevertheless, the Ch'eng-ch'ing "Song" contains three lines not seen in previously received versions. It is also unknowable whether the three new lines—describing the "four-corners technique," "five steps," and role of the waist—are Ch'eng-ch'ing's original contribution or an older variant. Whatever the case, it would be difficult to argue that it was the true ur-text from which all the others derive and easy to argue that it was a newer variation on a theme. The more vital question, perhaps, is whether Yü-hsiang found his version among the salt shop manuscripts or received it from the Ch'en family. The Wu/Li and Ch'en Tzu-ming six are identical save for seven characters, four of which are merely synonymous variations found in the Ch'en four-line version. In terms of thematic development, Ch'eng-ch'ing's eight-line treatment harkens back to the Ch'en four-line version in ending with the most climactic lines, "Let him attack with all his might,/While with but four ounces I deflect a thousand pounds." Though denouement is not unknown in Chinese poetry, it is more typical for the most telling line to come at the end in short works. It is this that makes me feel that Ch'eng-ch'ing was not just idly reworking an old form but consciously attempting to improve the prosody, especially in light of the very weak rhyme scheme of the earlier versions.

T'ang Hao,[13] Hsü Chen,[14] and Ku Liu-hsin[15] all attribute the "Repelling in Fighting" 撒放秘訣 to Wu Yü-hsiang. In the Wu/Li manuscript it falls in the crack between the "All this is written by Wu Yü-hsiang" at the end of the "Essentials" and Li I-yü's "Short Preface to T'ai-chi Ch'üan." The Lien-jang Hall edition lists it under "Songs," thereby avoiding the issue of authorship. It is difficult to know whether the four works in this section are here because of their shared form or as a catchall for unattributed texts. From the point of view of content, the "Repelling in Fighting" is a list of eight characters—five with tones indicated and three characters without—representing eight sounds, or *kiyas*, presumably used to accompany and augment the power of repelling or issuing energy. There is no explanation for and no indication of correspondence between the various sounds and specific techniques. The new material illuminates this very cryptic piece chiefly by its absence. If we assume that the Wu brothers confined their quotations to the older strata of material and were not likely to quote from original compositions of their younger brother, then the absence of any reference to the "Repelling in Fighting" probably indicates it was not part of the found manuscripts but either a collection of oral transmissions or original composition on Yü-hsiang's part.

The "Short Preface to T'ai-chi Ch'üan" 太極拳小序 is our earliest document concerning the history and development of t'ai-chi ch'üan. Its position near the end of the Wu/Li manuscript rather than at the beginning is apparently an attempt to demarcate the works of earlier masters, including Wang Tsung-yüeh, Wu Yü-hsiang, and perhaps others, from Li's own compositions that follow the "Short Preface." The "Preface" itself names only the "Five-Character Secret Transmission" 五字訣, although it is followed by two additional texts—"Secrets of Repelling" 撒放密訣 and "Essentials of the Practice of Form and Sparring" 走架打手行工要言 —that we can only assume are also Li's.

The contents of the "Short Preface," tantalizingly terse, refer to Wang Tsung-yüeh, Ch'en Village, Chao-pao Village, Yang Lu-ch'an, Wu Yü-hsiang, Ch'en Ch'ing-ping, and Li I-yü himself. Its demurring on the question of t'ai-chi's creator, ambiguity in reference to the relationship of Wang Tsung-yüeh and Ch'en Village, introducing the identity of Lu-ch'an with the words *a certain Yang*, the suggestion that Lu-ch'an traveled to Ch'en village as an adult, and Wu's seeking out Ch'en Ch'ing-p'ing have all been the subject of intense debate among martial arts historians. One would hope this new material could break some of the deadlocks. Ch'eng-ch'ing's "Postscript" begins promisingly with "Wang Tsung-yüeh's discussion of t'ai-chi ch'üan is most excellent," but gives no further details. The Ma T'ung-wen manuscript (1867), Wu Lai-hsü "Biography of Wu Yü-hsiang" (1935) and Wu Yen-hsü "Li Family Biographies" (c.1930s) all credit "Chang San-feng of the Sung dynasty" as creator of the art. Li's "three old manuscripts," however, state "I do not know who is the creator of t'ai-chi ch'üan." The Ch'eng-ch'ing "Postscript," in going no further than Wang Tsung-yüeh and omitting any reference to Chang San-feng, may be said to be aligned with Li's later (1880) "Short Preface." If the Chang story was invented by Wu (it does not exist in Ch'en Village) and repeated by Li in his Ma T'ung-wen phase, but later discounted in his "three old manuscripts" phase, what is the significance of its omission from Ch'eng-ch'ing's "Postscript"? This is intriguing because the "Postscript's" theme—parallels between the *Lao tzu* and t'ai-chi theory—presents the obvious opportunity to associate the Immortal Chang with t'ai-chi ch'üan. Unfortunately, the new material cannot resolve contradictions between the various late-nine-teenth-century documents or twentieth-century theories. At the very least, we can say that in the Ch'eng-ch'ing "Postscript," the truncation of the t'ai-chi transmission tends to promote Wang as the ultimate authority.

The "Five-Character Transmission" 五字訣, "Secrets of Repelling" 撒放秘訣, and "Essentials of Form and Sparring Practice" 走架打手行工要言 are the last three texts in the Wu/Li manuscript and by all indications ("Short Preface" and Lien-jang Hall edition) are the work of Li I-yü. The "Secrets of Repelling" and "Essentials of Form and Sparring" are prose pieces, derivative in their content, perfect in their form, and addressed to Li's generation of practitioners. How do these two prose pieces relate to the six poems in the new Li material, and can we at least tell which were written first? In his "Short Preface," Li tells us he began to study with Uncle Yü-hsiang in 1853; Ma T'ung-wen, dated 1867, does not include the Li-authored texts, so they must have been written after 1867. Given Li's death date of 1892, should we assume the poems were written after 1880, or before and simply not included in the "three old manuscripts" redaction? In view of the poem's wider technical purview, should we assume that the greater detail was present in the Ch'en-Yang-Wu collaboration or developed in the decade after Wu's passing? The three Li-authored pieces in the Wu/Li manuscript deal with the general theory of t'ai-chi energetics and mechanics. The six poems in the new material provide much greater detail on the energy pathways and the specifics of self-defense applications. Taken together, then, the three old and six new texts of Li I-yü represent the earliest significant sample of unequivocally authored literature on the art of t'ai-chi ch'üan.

Authenticity of the New Texts

Given the history of martial arts forgeries and fabrications, any new release of pre-Republican texts must be considered guilty until proven innocent. Generally, clues suggesting possible forgery include (1) anach-ronisms of historical events, figures, or language; (2) inconsistencies in theo-retical content; and (3) motivation for forgery. Using these criteria, I have not been able to discover any self-incriminating slips in the four new sources. Motivation for forgery is also hard to come by, as publication royalties cannot have been a factor, and it is difficult to understand how revelation at this time significantly advances the fortunes of any one style, school, or teacher.

Ku Liu-hsin tells us that Li I-yü's personal copy of the "three old manuscripts," last in Yao Chi-tsu's possession, "disappeared" during the Cultural Revolution;[16] hence the publication of this material at this time might be explained as seizing the current climate of liberalism as insurance against future book burnings. Although I know little about the men who came forward with the new Wu brothers and Li I-yü documents, much less having had an opportunity to examine the manuscripts, I am inclined to accept them as authentic.

In seeking to authenticate the new Ch'eng-ch'ing texts, a most intriguing piece of evidence may be found in two prefaces to Sun Lu-t'ang's (1861–1932) *T'ai-chi ch'üan hsüeh* 太極拳學. Sun's work was published in 1924, but the "Author's Preface" is dated 1919, making its composition even earlier than Hsü Yü-sheng's seminal *T'ai-chi ch'üan shih t'u-chieh* 太極拳勢圖解. Although I cannot identify the authors, Wu Hsin-ku 吳心穀 and Ch'en Ts'eng-tse 陳曾則, their prefaces to Sun's *T'ai-chi ch'üan hsüeh* contain, respectively, the exact language of the first third and second two-thirds of Ch'eng-ch'ing's "Postscript." This coincidence forces us to decide whether the Wu and Ch'en "Prefaces" lifted the language of the Ch'eng-ch'ing "Postscript," made known to them sometime during or before 1919, or whether Wu Wen-han concocted the "Postscript" by conflating portions of the *T'ai-chi ch'üan hsüeh* prefaces. Plagiarism by Wu and Ch'en would tend to authenticate the "Postscript," whereas originality on their part would unequivocally expose at least the "Postscript" as a hoax by Wu Wen-han or his sources.

In considering the case for Wu/Ch'en plagiarism and its concomitant tendency to confirm the authenticity of the Ch'eng-ch'ing "Postscript," it is useful first to remember that Sun was in direct disciplic descent from Wu Yü-hsiang, through Wu's nephew, Li I-yü, to Hao Wei-chen, who was Sun's teacher. Additionally, we know that the Hao family was in possession of Wu family manuscripts, as it was Wei-chen's grandson, Shao-ju, who showed the Wu/Li classics to Hsü Chen in the 1930s. It is also interesting that Sun's work contains none of the Wang/Wu classics but only the three Li I-yü's pieces. It was not really until Ch'en Wei-ming's 1925 *T'ai-chi ch'üan shu* that the contents of the classics as we know them today came to be widely circulated. A possible scenario might have Hao Wei-chen showing the Wu manuscripts to Sun and Sun showing portions to Wu and Ch'en for "inspiration" when he called upon them to write prefaces to his book. The fact that the Wu and Ch'en prefaces appear side by side in the same work and precisely split the "Postscript" material between them makes it appear that they sat down together and agreed to divide the spoils in a calculated way. Sun may or may not have known that Ch'eng-ch'ing was the author and may or may not have made that representation to Wu and

Ch'en. It is unlikely, however, that they viewed this as a dishonest act or experienced any pangs of conscience.

If this explains how the Ch'eng-ch'ing material found its way into Wu and Ch'en's hands and why they felt comfortable quoting it verbatim and unacknowledged in their prefaces, we must contrast this with Wu Wen-han's risk/benefit ratio in passing off portions of Wu and Ch'en's prefaces as a lost composition of Wu Ch'eng-ch'ing. Although martial arts scholarship in China is highly politicized, there is little political (or financial) capital to be made from a misrepresentation of this kind by Wu Wen-han. My reading, then, of the circumstantial evidence surrounding the 1919 prefaces and the present publication of the Ch'eng-ch'ing material makes it very unlikely that Wu and Ch'en would hesitate to borrow passages from some old manuscripts in their teacher's possession and even more unlikely that Wu Wen-han would risk his reputation by stealing from a well-known work of a major style founder.

An internal textual analysis may provide more conclusive evidence. We must begin by asking why the Wu and Ch'en prefaces both emphasize theoretical parallels between t'ai-chi ch'üan and the *Lao tzu.* If the prefaces were written with consultation between the authors, we have an inappropriate redundancy; if they were written without consultation, we have a startling coincidence. The next question is whether any splices can be detected between the lifted material and the author's own words. The second "Preface," that of Ch'en Ts'eng-tse, is simply the whole first two paragraphs of the Ch'eng-ch'ing "Postscript," followed by a line and a half of formulistic apologies for the author's lack of depth and so forth. There is nothing here, either structurally or semantically, that precludes a wholesale transfer of text from a preexisting source. The Wu Hsin-ku "Preface," consisting of the last paragraph of the Ch'eng-ch'ing "Postscript," is framed by three lines before and three lines after, thus providing more-ample opportunity to examine segues and possible splices. The three lines preceding the interpolated text (if that indeed is what it is) set up the theme of t'ai-chi ch'üan and Taoist philosophy in fairly seamless fashion. It is the last third of the "Preface," the portion directly following the suspected Ch'eng-ch'ing "Postscript" final paragraph, that shows subtle discontinuities with what precedes it. The Ch'eng-ch'ing text matches precise quotations from the *Lao tzu* with precise quotations from the t'ai-chi classics, whereas the three lines following the suspected interpolation mix language from the *Lao tzu* with unpedigreed Taoist clichés, and without any quotations from the t'ai-chi classics. The rhythm of the Ch'eng-ch'ing paragraph involves three quotations from the Wu/Li classics, each followed by a parallel line from the *Lao tzu*, and ending with a fourth pair in reverse order, leaving the taste of t'ai-chi in the reader's mouth. I believe that Wu Hsin-ku attempted to conceal the splice by continuing with the other half (actually the final half in the original) of the *Lao tzu* line and then coupling it with the Taoist formula "Refine the *ch'i* and transform it into spirit" rather than with a line from the classics. It may well be that Wu and Ch'en never saw the classics. Sun does not reproduce them in his book, and he mentions only Li I-yü's writings in his "Author's Preface," saying nothing of Wu Yü-hsiang's writings. This may explain why the copious quotations from the Wu/Li classics that characterize Ch'eng-ch'ing's writings suddenly run dry two-thirds of the way into the Wu Hsin-ku "Preface." It is also interesting that the Ch'eng-ch'ing "Postscript" begins with the words "The art of t'ai-chi ch'üan has been described most brilliantly by Wang Tsung-yüeh," whereas Wu's "Preface" begins, "According to tradition, t'ai-chi ch'üan was created by Chang San-feng." If my conclusion that Wu Hsin-ku and Ch'en Ts'eng-tse copied the Wu Ch'eng-ch'ing "Postscript" into their "Prefaces" for Sun Lu-t'ang's *T'ai-chi ch'üan hsüeh* is correct, this confirms the first half of Wu Wen-han's statement, "Ch'eng-ch'ing's writings were circulated and copied by a small number of Wu style practitioners and were not widely disseminated," but it leaves us wondering whether Wu Wen-han was aware that at least the "Postscript" reached a wider audience under other names.

Differences between the Wu/Li and Yang Editions of the Classics

The differences between the Wu/Li and Yang editions of the classics is one of the questions that divided Hsü Chen and T'ang Hao in the 1930s that has not been pursued by later martial arts historians. Hsü considered the differences testimony to Yang editions' being based on an earlier Wu version, whereas T'ang believed it was simply a question of Yang revisions.[17] Our efforts are hampered in the first instance by lack of reliable dates for Lu-ch'an's return from Ch'en Village and for his departure for Beijing. Nevertheless, no theory has ever been advanced claiming that Yang transmitted the classics to Wu, or, with the exception of Ch'eng-fu's *T'ai-chi ch'üan shih-yung fa*, that he authored any of the texts himself.[18]

Hsü uses Wu Chien-ch'üan and Li Hsien-wu to get at Ch'üan Yu's edition and Ch'en Wei-ming and Li Hsien-wu's to glimpse Yang Chien-hou's version, all of which he considers closer to the original than Ch'eng-fu's. According to Hsü's reconstruction, the ten passages in the first paragraph (*chieh yüeh* 解曰) of the "Essentials" represent Yü-hsiang's first addition to the Wang Tsung-yüeh texts, the two paragraphs of the Yang "Mental Elucidation" represents the second addition, and the Wu/Li redaction represents the third stage, possibly containing Li's revisions. If it could be shown that all of the Ch'eng-ch'ing and Ju-ch'ing quotations are within the boundaries of the Yang editions, it might support Hsü's claim that Yang Lu-ch'an took an early version of Wu's manuscript with him to Beijing. Although it is true, in fact, that none of the Ch'eng-ch'ing and Ju-ch'ing quotations fall outside of the parameters of the Yang editions, that language that appears only in Yang editions is not quoted in any of the new material; this tends to support T'ang's view that Yang texts represent not an earlier redaction but simply a corruption.

The most significant difference between the Wu/Li and Yang editions of the classics can be seen in their handling of the "Essentials of Sparring." Hsü recognizes only the phrases "Concentrate your spirit within and be externally relaxed" and "When the opponent does not move, you do not move; when the opponent makes the slightest move, you move first" as original Wang Tsung-yüeh language and considers the rest Wu's commentary. Hsü concludes that the words "The commentary says" 解曰, introducing the first two paragraphs of the "Essentials" and corresponding to the Yang "Shih-san shih hsing-kung hsin-chieh" 十三勢行工心解 (Mental elucidation of the practice of the thirteen postures) and Lien-jang Hall "Shih-san shih hsing-kung ke-chieh" 十三勢行工歌解 (Song of the practice of the thirteen postures), indicates that Wu's original title was "Mental Elucidation" and that Li I-yü changed it back to Wang's original "Ta-shou yao-yen" 打手要言 (Essentials of sparring), conflating Wang's core passages with Wu's commentary. Unfortunately, the two nuclear passages Hsü considers original Wang language are not quoted in the new Ch'eng-ch'ing or Ju-ch'ing material, which is not friendly to Hsü's case, but neither is it sufficient to demolish it.

Authorship of the Bookstall Classics

T'ang Hao's 1935 *Wang Tsung-yüeh t'ai-chi ch'üan ching* takes the bookstall classics as ur-text, while Hsü Chen's 1936 *T'ai-chi ch'üan k'ao-hsin lu* takes the Wu/Li classics as ur-text.[19] Hsü's evaluation of the bookstall find may be summarized in two points: (1) It was not compiled by Wang Tsung-yüeh or a disciple of Wang, and (2) the "Master Wang of

Shanxi" mentioned in the bookstall manuscript's "Preface to the Yin-fu Spear Manual" and Wang Tsung-yüeh are one and the same.[20] Thus Hsü attempts to preserve the historicity of Wang Tsung-yüeh and the authenticity of portions of the text, while denying that the three-text bookstall manuscript, as a compilation, represents Wang's work. Although at the time of the writing of the *Wang Tsung-yüeh t'ai-chi ch'üan ching*, T'ang was willing to concede only that the form manual portion of the manuscript did not belong to Wang, later in his *T'ai-chi ch'üan yen-chiu* he writes: "In 1930 I found Wang Tsung-yüeh's 'Yin-fu Spear Manual' and Yang family 'T'ai-chi Ch'üan Manual' bound together in one manuscript in the Beijing bookstalls."[21] T'ang thus came to agree with Hsü on this issue, though both men apparently died in disagreement over whether Wang brought t'ai-chi to Ch'en Village or learned it there and whether the Wu/Li or Yang recension is the oldest. Nevertheless, more than sixty years after T'ang's discovery, the fundamental question remains: How did the compiler of the bookstall manuscript come into possession of an authentic specimen of Wang Tsung-yüeh's writing in the "Spear Manual" and combine it with a Yang version of the form manual and classics, plus a preface dated 1795 written by an anonymous contemporary of Wang? This makes a highly suspicious package, especially from a source as notorious for its forgeries as the Beijing bookstalls. The bookseller from whom T'ang obtained the manuscript must have purchased it from someone. T'ang was a lawyer by profession, and it is inconceivable he did not question the bookseller as to the manuscript's history, though this is never reported.

The value of the bookstall manuscript is certainly not in its reproducing the five core classics or form manual, as these are identical with the Yang version, nor is it the "Spear Manual," which contains little beyond vague clichés easily derived from general t'ai-chi principles; rather its value lies in the "Preface" with its biographical details on the life of Wang Tsung-yüeh, or, more accurately, "Master Wang of Shanxi." In 1930 T'ang Hao was virtually the only critical mind in China working on the origins of the martial arts, yet this manuscript fell precisely into his hands and he fell for it! For the salt shop classics to be a hoax would require the complicity of the Wu and Li families; for the bookstall classics to be a hoax would require only one anonymous pen. Li's "Postscript" does not specifically say whether the salt shop manuscript was purchased or copied, but it is certain that the profit motive was involved in the bookstall transaction. The highly unusual anonymity of the author of the "Preface to the Yin-fu Spear Manual" prevents us from checking his background, and the even more unusual absence of a given name for "Master Wang" seems a calculated insinuation.

Historicity of Chang San-feng

Based on the first sentence in Li I-yü's "Short Preface to T'ai-chi Ch'üan," which states, "The Creator of t'ai-chi ch'üan is unknown," Hsü Chen concluded that the source of Chang San-feng's association with t'ai-chi must have been Yang family partisans no earlier than the Kuang-hsü reign (1875–1904) of the Ch'ing dynasty.[22] T'ang Hao initially concurred,[23] but later he shifted the blame to Wu Yü-hsiang himself, based on agreement between the Ma T'ung-wen manuscript and the writings of Wu's grandsons, Lai-hsü and Yen-hsü, all of which credit Chang San-feng as the originator of the art.[24] Wu's grandsons could have been influenced by Yang propaganda, as Hsü suggests (though it is unlikely this would have been more persuasive than their grandfather's version, had there been a contradiction), but the Ma T'ung-wen manuscript, dated 1867, is too early to reflect anything but Wu Yü-hsiang's point of view. In this way, Yang Lu-ch'an must have heard the story from Wu Yü-hsiang himself, though by all accounts Lu-ch'an spent many years in Ch'en Village, where no tradition of Chang San-feng has been recorded, and one wonders how Wu might have presented the link between Chang and the Ch'en family to Yang. This picture is further complicated by the presence of the Chang San-feng creation story in Sun Lu-t'ang's 1919 *T'ai-chi ch'üan hsüeh*, which indicates either Yang influence (not otherwise very apparent in the work) or the persistence of the Ma T'ung-wen tradition, in spite of Li I-yü's later "The creator of t'ai-chi ch'üan is unknown."

Two central questions emerge from the foregoing: (1) Why did Li change his story between the Ma T'ung-wen (1867) and Hao Wei-chen (1881) copies of the "three old manuscripts"? And (2) Why did Wu put out the story to begin with? If Wu told Li the story of Chang San-feng, then one explanation for Li's change is that he believed it in 1867, or was too respectful to contradict his teacher, and later in 1881 after Wu Yü-hsiang's death, he had become skeptical, or felt free to express the skepticism he harbored from the beginning. Li's "Postscript," also dated 1881, likewise passes up the opportunity to reinforce the Chang San-feng story, as does Ch'eng-ch'ing's recently published "Postscript." If Ch'eng-ch'ing's writings are authentic, then considering that he was the discoverer of the salt shop manuscript, his failure to mention Chang in his "Postscript" must be considered a blow to the Chang San-feng theory and to cast further doubt on the authenticity of the "T'ai-chi Ch'üan Manual" in the bookstall classics, the title of whose first text is "Treatise on the Thirteen Postures Handed Down by Masters Chang San-feng and Wang Tsung-yüeh."

The second question, why Wu advanced the story of Chang San-feng, implies a more fundamental question, namely, where did he get the notion of Chang San-feng as martial arts master? Neither T'ang Hao nor Hsü Chen discovered any evidence of its being part of the written or oral tradition in Ch'en Village during their researches of the 1930s, and it is not mentioned in the text of the Wu/Li "classics."[25] He could have borrowed and modified the story of Chang San-feng as founder of the Internal School recounted by Huang Tsung-hsi in his "Epitaph for Wang Cheng-nan" 王征南墓志銘 and later taken up by the "Ningpo Gazetteer" 寧波府志 and Wang Yü-yang's note appended to P'u Sung-ling's *Strange Stories from a Chinese Studio* 聊齋志異, "Wu-chi p'ien." Fully developed grafting of the Internal School lineage onto the Ch'en family lineage can already be seen in Yang transmission works as early as Hsü Yü-sheng's 1921 *T'ai-chi ch'üan shih t'u-chieh*, Ch'en Wei-ming's 1925 *T'ai-chi ch'üan shu*, and Yang Ch'eng-fu's 1931 *T'ai-chi ch'üan shih-yung fa*. Whether this reflects Wu Yü-hsiang's original belief or Yang embroidery cannot be traced through written documents at this time. Recent claims by Chao-pao partisans, based on Tu Yüan-hua's 1935 *T'ai-chi ch'üan cheng-tsung*, that trace the transmission from Chang San-feng through Wang Tsung-yüeh, and Chiang Fa, to Ch'en Ch'ing-p'ing even go so far as to assert that Ch'ing-p'ing not only taught Yü-hsiang the art of t'ai-chi ch'üan but revealed to him the texts we now revere as the classics.[26] This, of course, is in direct contradiction to the salt shop story. The possibility of Huang "Epitaph" influence seems somewhat strengthened by the coincidence that both the Ma T'ung-wen manuscript and the "Epitaph" cite a Chang San-feng of the "Sung dynasty," by contrast with most records that place him in the Ming and mention no association with the martial arts. It is weakened, however, by discrepancy of name (王宗 and 王宗岳) and native place (陝西 and 山西) and by Wu's failure to explicitly connect the Internal School with t'ai-chi ch'üan. We are thus left with Huang's "Epitaph" as our earliest record associating Chang San-feng with the martial arts, the Ma T'ung-wen manuscript as our earliest record associating Chang and t'ai-chi ch'üan, and no way to link the two. Had there been indications internal to the salt shop manuscript, Li I-yü would probably have been forced to respect these and would not have felt at liberty to change his tune in the 1881 "Short Preface." This leaves Wu Yü-hsiang himself as borrower from an oral or written tradition or as inventor. Since the possibility of invention involves the question of why, or motivation, let us first attempt to turn over some new stones in the borrowing, or where, field. T'ai-chi's origins have been intensively studied using modern historical methods for at least sixty years, as has the hagiography of Chang San-feng. Li I-yü told us over a century ago that the Wang Tsung-yüeh manuals were discovered in Wu-yang County,

Henan, yet apparently no one has examined the *Wu-yang County Gazetteer*, where we find the following entry:

> The "Cave of the Immortal Chang" at West Pass is tradi-
> tionally regarded as the site where San-feng realized immor-
> tality. The *Fu-kou Gazetteer* says that the people of Fu-kou
> believe Chang San-feng left his body in the T'ai-chi Temple
> on the Wu-tang Mountains. An image of him may still be
> seen there. He wore a copper cymbal as a straw hat, which he
> allowed the people of Fu-kou to strike without becoming an-
> gry, for he was very good-natured. The people of Wu-yang
> also believe that San-feng was a native of Wu-yang and that
> they have the exclusive privilege of striking his hat.[27]

Thus it is possible that Wu Yü-hsiang found the Wang manual and the Chang myth in the same place—Wu-yang—and combined them as the rudiments of a lineage. This may be no more than coincidence, but it deserves to be considered at least as much as theories that have produced no documentation at all.

Intellectual historian Huang Tsung-hsi 黃宗羲 (1610–95), was a major figure in anti-Manchu resistance during the mid seventeenth century, and his "Epitaph for Wang Cheng-nan," along with "Methods of the In-ternal School" 內家拳法 by his son, Huang Pai-chia 黃百家, were vehicles for expressing their patriotic sentiments. They include a lineage linking the god of war, Hsüan Wu 玄武, to the Immortal Chang San-feng, to the martial artist Wang Cheng-nan 王征南. I believe that, by combining sacred elements from Chinese culture—divine, semidivine, and mortal—and focusing them on righteous martial activity, the Huangs at-tempted in an environment of strict censorship to issue a spiritual rallying cry against alien aggression. In the nineteenth century, revival of the cult of Chang San-feng was heralded by Li Hsi-yüeh's 李西月 *Complete Works of Chang San-feng* 三丰全集, published in 1844 just between the disas-trous Opium War and the outbreak of the Taiping Rebellion.[28] Li was the leading light of a circle of Sichuan Taoists, calling themselves the "Hidden Immortal Sect" 隱仙派 or "Dragon-like Sect" 猶龍派, who claimed to communicate with Chang San-feng through face-to-face encounters and planchette. Li was Ju-ch'ing's generation, and if Ju-ch'ing shared his older brother's interest in "Taoism and occultism," it may be that Ju-ch'ing made contact with members of this group or their ideas while he was posted in Sichuan in 1850. Triangulating from references to Chang San-feng in Huang Tsung-hsi, Li Hsi-yüeh, and the Wu-yang Gazetteer, it might be possible that, against a background of national crisis, Wu sought to raise the banner of Chang San-feng as a coded gesture of patriotism. Taking this semiotic interpretation one step further, if Wang Tsung-yüeh was a fabricated cover for Wu Yü-hsiang's own writings or anonymous transmissions, the name *Tsung-yüeh* ("Revering Yüeh") might refer to the twelfth-century Sung general Yüeh Fei 岳飛 (1103–41), who battled the Nü-chen (ancestors of the Manchus) invaders. The T'ung-chih Restoration (1862–74) made the period of the 1870s and 1880s one of relative calm between storms. The major rebellions were behind the dynasty, the Tsung-li Yamen had a working relationship with the Western powers, and Japan had not yet threatened China's heartland. In a more optimistic atmosphere, where it appeared that the dynasty and the Confucian elite might survive, Li I-yü and Wu Ch'eng-ch'ing may not have felt the need to invoke the spirit of Chang San-feng, explaining why Li's "Short Preface and "Postscript" and Ch'eng-ch'ing's "Postscript" are without it.

Historicity and Role of Wang Tsung-yüeh

No issue divided T'ang Hao and Hsü Chen more sharply than that of the role of Wang Tsung-yüeh. Both fully accepted Wang as a historical figure, but T'ang believed he was a student and recorder of the teachings of Ch'en masters, whereas Hsü believed he brought the art to Ch'en Village, which previously had no knowledge of it.[29] Both advanced elaborate arguments to bolster their positions that will be discussed in future studies and do not concern us here. T'ang's interpretation gained more or less official status in mainland China during the Mao era and is still clung to by champions of the Ch'en style revival today, even as Chao-pao and Wu-tang partisans construct alternative lineages leading to their doors. Wu T'u-nan is probably the most famous figure in recent years to associate himself with Hsü's view that the original Ch'en family art was p'ao-ch'ui 炮捶 and that t'ai-chi came from the outside.[30]

Li I-yü's "Short Preface" is a masterpiece of ambiguity: "The original creator of t'ai-chi ch'üan is unknown. Its subtlety and skill were thoroughly described by Wang Tsung-yüeh. Later it was transmitted to the Ch'en family of Ch'en-chia-kou in Henan." If we interpret this narrative as a linear chronology, then it would appear that Wang received the art first and the Ch'en family received it second. However, because Wang's role as theoretician is stressed, and because he is not the stated subject of the sentence beginning "Later it was transmitted to the Ch'en family," the possibility is left open that there is no chronology, but simply three discontinuous statements implied. Hsü exploits this syntactical slack to deny Wang's disciplic relationship to the Ch'en family, while T'ang struggles bravely to bring the loose ends in line with his theory of Ch'en Wang-t'ing's foundership.

Wang's biography is also an area of great uncertainty. The "Wang Tsung-yüeh of Shanxi's Treatise on T'ai-chi Ch'üan" gives Wang's native place but not his dates; Li's "Short Preface" gives neither. The "Master Wang of Shanxi" described in the "Preface to the Yin-fu Spear Form," dated 1795, has been accepted by T'ang, Hsü, and most other martial arts historians as none other than Wang Tsung-yüeh, in spite of the unusual anonymity of the "Preface" and failure to state Wang's full name and native county. The author records that in 1791 Wang was in Loyang and later in Kaifeng, where he served as a teacher. His status as a teacher suggests that he held at least the *kung-sheng* 貢生 degree (see Appendix 2, p. 192) and thus should have been recorded in the gazetteer of his native place. A search of the Shanxi gazetteers has not been undertaken by the present author because of the sheer volume of gazetteers, the popularity of the surname Wang 王, and the likelihood that Tsung-yüeh 宗岳 is not a given but an assumed name, or style. Ch'ang Nai-chou is accorded space in the Ssu-shui 汜水 gazetteer, why not Wang in his? The two must have known of each other, if only secondhand, or they could not share so many verbatim quotations and parallel passages, yet there is no acknowledgment on either side.

Whatever truth may exist in any account of Wang Tsung-yüeh is purely accidental, as we do not have a single bona fide historical document. Nevertheless, this inconvenience has not prevented generations of authors from assigning specific dates and native places to Wang. Appendix 2, p. 183, shows that native place ranges from "Shensi" to "Shanxi" to "Sian" (provincial capital of Shaanxi) and dates run from the Sung to the Ch'ing, a span of approximately six hundred years. None of these authors felt obliged to cite their sources, but it is clear that Kuan Pai-i launched the first published attempt to splice the Internal School lineage onto the t'ai-chi transmission by equating Wang Tsung 王宗 and Wang Tsung-yüeh 王宗岳, and that subsequent authors have struggled to reconcile contradictions in dates, native place, and form, while preserving the links from Chang Sanfeng through Wang to Ch'en Village. Ch'en Kung's 1943 *T'ai-chi ch'üan tao chien kan san-shou ho-pien* even takes the novel approach of placing both "Wang Tsung of Shaanxi" and "Wang Tsung-yüeh of Shanxi" in his account of t'ai-chi's development, and Wu T'u-nan, not to be outdone, considers "Wang Tsung" the given name and "Wang Tsung-yüeh" the style of one man.[31] T'ang Hao's publication of the "Yin-fu Spear Manual Preface" and Hsü Ch'en's revelation of the Hao family manuscripts by Li

I-yü seemed to clinch Wang's historicity, but they could not prevent authors even as late as Cheng Man-ch'ing's 1946 *Thirteen Chapters* from assigning Wang to the Ming Dynasty. In fact, using this singular dating as a tracer adds confirmation to the widely held suspicion that Cheng ghostwrote Yang's 1934 *T'ai-chi ch'üan t'i-yung ch'üan-shu,* which is the only other work to assign the Ming date to Wang.

Regardless of when or where one thinks Wang Tsung-yüeh was born, most authors accept all or parts of the classics in their various redactions as Wang's, thus ultimately the first act of faith hinges on the salt shop story and Wu's record through Li and Yang. Assuming for the moment the veracity of the Li "Postscript" account, the manuscript either did or did not bear the name of Wang Tsung-yüeh. If the manuscript reached the salt shop with Wang's name, this suggests that it is either genuine or affixed by someone further up the line. If without signature, the name could have been supplied verbally to Wu by the salt shop staff or invented by Wu. Li, a nephew of Wu Yü-hsiang, tells us he commenced study with Wu in 1853, and given Wu's death in 1880, they had close contact for nearly thirty years, yet Li gives us only two sparse phrases: "T'ai-chi ch'üan's subtlety and skill were most thoroughly described by Wang Tsung-yüeh" ("Short Preface") and "This manual was found in a salt shop in Wu-yang" ("Postscript"). Li's writings show the utmost reverence for Wang's legacy, yet in spite of his intimacy with the Wu brothers, he shares suspiciously little concerning the circumstances of its discovery. This suggests three possibilities: (1) The salt shop story was a hoax, and the paucity of detail in Li's writings was intended to make tracing it more difficult; (2) the Li manuscripts were intended not for publication but only for the eyes of those already familiar with the details of the Wu-yang story; or (3) Li recorded everything he knew. Examining just the last of these for the moment, it is not impossible that Ch'eng-ch'ing showed Yü-hsiang a manuscript identified only as authored by "Wang Tsung-yüeh of Shanxi" and containing a refined theoretical explanation for what he had observed in Yang Lu-ch'an and Ch'en Ch'ing-p'ing, although he did not know the specific links between Wang and Ch'en Village. In this case, Wu might have told Li only as much as he himself knew. However, Li's caginess in introducing and then withdrawing the Chang San-feng creation story and concealing the identity of Yang Lu-ch'an somewhat undercuts the consistency and forthrightness necessary to sustain this interpretation.

The insertion of the Ch'eng-ch'ing "Postscript" in the Wu Hsin-ku and Ch'en Ts'eng-tse prefaces to Sun Lu-t'ang's *T'ai-chi ch'üan hsüeh* establishes that this text cannot be later than 1919 and antedates the earliest Yang influenced publications of Hsü Yü-sheng (1921) and Ch'en Wei-ming (1925). The absence of Yang influence, including scarcity of quotations from the classics, points to the purity of Sun's t'ai-chi lineage and reinforces the authenticity of the Ch'eng-ch'ing "Postscript." The fact that all the Wu brothers' and Li I-yü's writings read like commentaries to the classics suggests that there really was a manuscript find in Wu-yang. Shared language between the classics and Chang Nai-chou suggests that the "core Wang material" was composed not much before or after the Ch'ien-lung period; differences between Ch'ang and "Wang" suggests that Wu Yü-hsiang probably did not just lift portions of Ch'ang, mix them with Ch'en and Yang teachings and market them under the brand name "Wang Tsung-yüeh." Whether or not the name Wang Tsung-yüeh appeared on the salt shop manuscript cannot be determined based on received evidence, although the title "Wang Tsung-yüeh of Shanxi's Treatise on T'ai-chi Ch'üan" as it stands is unlikely to have been that of the author. Li I-yü's 1881 confession, "The creator of t'ai-chi ch'üan is unknown," may be seen as heightening his credibility when he says, "Its subtlety and skill were most thoroughly described by Wang Tsung-yüeh," and seems to indicate he had some convincing basis for the latter. Ch'eng-ch'ing's silence on Chang San-feng and acknowledgment of Wang Tsung-yüeh weighs more heavily on the scales of scholarship than a century of apocrypha.

Period and Role of Chiang Fa

Chiang Fa 蔣發 is another quasi-historical figure, like Chang San-feng and Wang Tsung-yüeh, caught in the crossfire of contending styles and scholars. Ch'en family stalwarts Ch'en Hsin, Ch'en Tzu-ming, and Ch'en Chi-fu in their 1930s publications portray Chiang as a servant or disciple under Ch'en Wang-t'ing (c. sevententh century).[32] Wu T'u-nan, however, claims that in a personal interview with Ch'en Hsin conducted in Ch'en Village, Ch'en told him that Chiang Fa was Ch'en Ch'ang-hsing's (1771–1853) teacher.[33] This is at odds with Ch'en Hsin's published account, but agrees with Yang family versions, which since Hsü Yü-sheng's 1921 *T'ai-chi ch'üan shih t'u-chieh* have held that Wang Tsung-yüeh transmitted the art to Chiang Fa, who transmitted it to Ch'en Ch'ang-hsing.[34] The idea that the Ch'en family art came from Chiang was apparently popular in Ch'en Village, as T'ang Hao reports from research there in the early 1930s[35] and as is attested to by a 1928 note appended to the Wen-hsiu Hall manuscript (*Wen-hsiu t'ang pen* 文修堂本) by Ch'en Hsin specifically forbidding his clansmen to repeat a story contradictory to his own claims of Ch'en family originality.[36] Thus Ch'en Hsin has left us with a theory of "two Chiangs": one a renegade refugee and servant (Chiang P'u 蔣僕) in Ch'en Wang-t'ing's household, and one a martial arts master (Chiang Pa-shih 蔣把式, 蔣把拾, 蔣八式) of the Ch'ien-lung period (1756–95). Hsü Chen seized on this to reinforce his theory of external transmission to Ch'en Village,[37] but T'ang Hao dismisses any need for external transmission, citing the "Ch'en Family Genealogy" (*Ch'en-shih chia-p'u* 陳氏家譜), which states that Ch'ang-hsing's father was a martial artist.[38] Thus for Ch'en family standard-bearers and their scholar supporters, Chiang Fa is probably historical, possibly double, but certainly not the transmitter of t'ai-chi to Ch'en Village; for the Yangs and their supporters on this issue, Chiang Fa represents the fact or likelihood of external transmission to Ch'en Village.

While the Yang's have sought to elevate Chiang Fa to the status of vital link from Wang Tsung-yüeh to the Ch'en family, and the Ch'ens themselves have sought to marginalize his role, another movement has arisen built on Chiang leading not to Ch'en-chia-kou but neighboring Chao-pao-chen. Tracing their inspiration to Tu Yüan-hua's 1935 *T'ai-chi chüan cheng-tsung* 太極拳正宗, Chao-pao 趙堡, Ho 和, Li 李, and Wu-tang 武當 stylists have hailed Chang San-feng as progenitor and adopted Chiang Fa as native son, thus shifting the cradle of t'ai-chi ch'üan from Ch'en-chia-kou to Chao-pao-chen. In scores of articles published during the past decade Chao-pao advocates have traced a lineage including Chang, Wang, and Chiang but also interspersing a host of lesser-known figures all leading to Chao-pao Village. Without advancing any significant new historical documents, their accounts have variously placed Chiang in the sixteenth, seventeenth, and eighteenth centuries and made him the teacher of Ch'en Wang-t'ing, Ch'en Ch'ang-hsing, or Ch'en Ch'ing-p'ing.

Can the new Wu brothers' and Li I-yü material finally solve the mystery of the identity of the figure holding a sword and standing behind the portrait of Ch'en Wang-t'ing discovered by T'ang Hao on the ancestral alter in Ch'en Village[39] and reproduced in Ch'en Tzu-ming's *Ch'en-shih shih-ch'uan t'ai-chi ch'üan shu?*[40] If we interpret Li I-yü's 1881 "Short Preface" and Wu Ch'eng-ch'ing's "Postscript" as expunging the mythological figures from the t'ai-chi creation story, then the absence of Chang San-feng and Chiang Fa from their narrative indicates a stand for historical accuracy. Although we can only speculate on the reason why Chang San-feng appears in the 1867 Ma T'ung-wen version of the "Short Preface" and disappears in the 1881 "three old manuscripts" versions, the fact that Chiang Fa appears in neither is a question Chiang proponents must address. Thinking in this vein also makes us wonder why Chiang Fa is featured in Yang accounts of t'ai-chi's history but absent from Wu/Li sources, and why, if Chiang Fa figures in Ch'en Village folklore, Wang Tsung-yüeh does not?

Paucity of Theoretical Texts in Ch'en Village

T'ang Hao and his Ch'en-centered camp credit Ch'en Wang-t'ing with creating t'ai-chi ch'üan based on a note in the "Ch'en Family Genealogy": "Ch'en Wang-t'ing . . . , the creator of the Ch'en family hand, broadsword, and spear forms."[41] Hsü Chen and the Wang-centered camp rejoice in this passage in Li I-yü's "Short Preface": "T'ai-chi ch'üan's subtlety and skill was most thoroughly explained by Wang Tsung-yüeh. Later it was transmitted to the Ch'en family of Ch'en Village in Henan."[42] The Chang San-feng-centered camp, including possibly Wu Yü-hsiang himself, the Yangs, Wus, Suns, Sung Shu-ming, Tu Yüan-hua, and more recently Wu-tang and Chao-pao advocates take comfort in Huang Tsung-hsi's "The Internal School began with Chang San-feng of the Sung" and Ma T'ung-wen's "T'ai-chi ch'üan was created by Chang San-feng of the Sung dynasty."

From the point of view of intellectual history, the divisions outlined above may be seen as a typical example of the idealist versus materialist, or fundamentalist versus evolutionist, modes of thought. That is, when tracing origins on the level of theory, one is free to go all the way back to the *Lao tzu* and *I ching*, add any number of legendary Taoists and martial arts heroes, and pick up the Internal School on the way to Ch'en Village or Chao-pao. However, if one is tracing the evolution of a specific movement form, then, starting with Yang and Wu, one works backward to the Ch'en family, Ch'i Chi-kuang and his antecedents. It is this radical bifurcation of perspectives that causes idealists to dismiss Ch'en Village as a hick town and Wang-t'ing as a lowly militia battalion commander, and materialists to minimize the perennial influence of Taoist ideas and the possibility of multiple advents of old wine in new bottles. T'ang Hao in his later writings painstakingly attempts to trace the development of t'ai-chi theory in Ch'en Village based on its very fragmentary "Song of the Classic of Pugilism" (*Ch'üan-ching tsung-ko* 拳經總歌) and four- and six-line versions of the "Song of Sparring,"[43] but it does not appear that they were self-consciously creating a radically new system based on a diametrical set of principles in the sense of Huang Pai-chia's "Chang San-feng was a master of Shao-lin, but reversing its principles developed the Internal School" or Wang Tsung-yüeh's "This art has many rivals, but although their forms vary, in reality they are nothing more than the strong bullying the weak." In the case of Huang and his teacher, Wang Cheng-nan, we know that Huang must have either recorded the principles recited to him by Wang Cheng-nan or given theoretical expression to what he observed as unique in Wang. In the case of "Wang Tsung-yüeh," we do not know if he recorded or gave theoretical expression to what he saw or heard in Ch'en Village, brought the art and theory to Ch'en Village personally or through an intermediary, or is an invention of Wu Yü-hsiang. Thus for the Ch'en family, either their art was not so theoretically unique as to require special theoretical expression, or it was unique but they were not disposed to commit their discoveries to writing. Alternative interpretations have recently been advanced by Wu T'u-nan and others positing a two-track scenario in Ch'en Village, where the traditional family art, p'ao-ch'ui, was in competition with Chiang Fa's t'ai-chi ch'üan, which Ch'en Ch'ang-hsing was ostracized for embracing.[44] In the absence of adequate documentation in Ch'en Village or, indeed, Yung-nien, we can expect further proliferation of theories presented as fact explaining the transmission of t'ai-chi ch'üan. Unless Chao-pao claims are correct, the absence of received theoretical texts in Ch'en Village is even more inexplicable in view of the proximity of Ch'ang Nai-chou's hometown, Ssu-shui, just across the Yellow River and the extreme sophistication of Ch'ang's writings.

The only source for the Wu-yang Wang Tsung-yüeh manuscript find is Li I-yü's "Postscript." The "Short Preface" mentions no trip to Wu-yang, but only "My uncle [Yü-hsiang] went to Henan on business and on the way visited [Ch'en Ch'ing-p'ing] . . . . I [I-yü] began studying with my uncle when I was a little over twenty in 1853." "Business" (*kung* 公) has always been interpreted to mean visiting his brother Ch'eng-ch'ing at his new post in Wu-yang, which he took up in 1852.[45] Whatever "business" meant in Li's "Preface" could not have been "business as usual," since 1852 was the midst of the Nien Rebellion and the eve of the Taiping Northern Expedition. The only reason for Yü-hsiang to enter the hornets nest of central Henan at this time would be to assist his brother in organizing militia defense. Whether Mrs. Wu would have allowed another son to risk his life at this time is a question, and certainly a rich gentleman traveling alone on the roads would be in danger even before arriving. The *Yung-nien Gazetteer* tells us that in 1852 Wu-yang was surrounded by a hundred thousand "bandits" but was spared because of Ch'eng-ch'ing's bold tactics. Against this background we must wonder why there is no mention in any source of Yü-hsiang's taking part in these heroics and how anyone had time for manuscript collecting under siege or, at best, extremely tense conditions.

As a setting for the Wang Tsung-yüeh manual discovery, the "Wu-yang salt shop" strikes one as singularly mundane and unromantic. Most important manuscript finds seem to turn up in caves or tombs, crumbling walls, or at least under floorboards. It is perhaps useful to recall that salt in late imperial China was a government monopoly, a means of generating revenues for the imperial treasury. As county magistrate, Ch'eng-ch'ing would have been responsible for transferring funds from the salt shop to the next collection point, and thus it is virtually certain he had dealings with the man in charge. Since tax revenue destined for Beijing traveled under armed guard, and such guards were a class, or brotherhood, of professional martial artists (*piao-k'o* 鏢客), it is reasonable that the subject of martial arts came up in conversation between Wu and the salt shop official, and that the official might have shown him an interesting old manuscript. The question then becomes one of whether the salt shop is a more plausible site on account of its humbleness than, say the "Cave of the Immortal Chang," or just a more subtle cover for a deception. Assuming there was only one such manuscript in existence, what were the chances that the one family in China best able to appreciate its contents happened to be in Wu-yang? Why was fate able to bring together Wang Tsung-yüeh's writings and Wu Yü-hsiang in an obscure salt shop yet powerless to leave any authentic record of the relationship between Wang Tsung-yüeh, Ch'ang Nai-chou, and the Ch'en family, even though they all lived less than a hundred miles apart in northern Henan?

Ch'ang Nai-chou and the Wu/Li Classics

Ch'ang Nai-chou 萇乃周 was a scholar and martial artist who flourished during the Ch'ien-lung reign (1736–95) of the Ch'ing dynasty. A native of Ssu-shui County, Henan, his name and biography appear in the local gazetteer, and although precise birth and death dates are not recorded, his older brother, Shih-chou 仕周, passed his metropolitan degree (*chin-shih*) in 1742. Since Ch'ang and his life and writings are the subject of a separate study in progress, it is sufficient for our purposes here simply to point out that both Ch'ang and Wu Yü-hsiang are attested historical figures and that both left bodies of writings. Appendix 2, p. 186, begins to illustrate the necessity of some direct or indirect relationship between Ch'ang and the Wu/Li classics; however, notwithstanding Hsü Chen's theory of Ch'ang's discipleship in the Wang Tsung-yüeh lineage or Ch'en Hsin's account of Ch'ang's indiscretion and humiliation in Ch'en Village, we have no reliable evidence of contact between Ch'ang, Wang, and Ch'en Village.[46] Furthermore, in spite of an even larger dose of Ming/Ch'ing meditation terminology and theory in Ch'ang than "Wang," there is no mention of Chang San-feng or anything but a mortal-to-mortal transmission.

The points of similarity between Ch'ang and the t'ai-chi classics are so striking, on the one hand, and evidence for the historicity of Wang Tsung-yüeh so weak, on the other hand, that one might be tempted to speculate that Wu came into contact with Ch'ang's writings (Wu-yang and Ssu-shui are both in Henan) and concocted the "classics" out of elements from Ch'ang, Yang Lu-ch'an, and Ch'eng Ch'ing-p'ing using Wang Tsung-yüeh as a cover for political reasons. This scenario seems plausible except for certain fundamental divergences between Ch'ang and the Wu/Li classics. T'ai-chi's concept of "interpreting energy" has no real equivalent in Ch'ang's writings, although there is nothing that contradicts it and much that could be said to imply it, yet it does not emerge as a full-blown free-standing concept in Ch'ang. Moreover, the concept of "placing most of the weight on one foot and avoiding double-weightedness" (偏沈 . . . 雙重) is flatly contradicted in Ch'ang's "The weight of the body should rest between the two legs."[47] Should we look, then, to Ch'en Village as the source of "avoiding double-weightedness"? Ch'en documents from the late Ch'ing are sparse and inconclusive, but judging from photographs of Ch'en Fa-k'e 陳發科 (1887–1957) from the 1930s and 1940s[48] and contemporary practitioners of Ch'en style, we may say it is unlikely this teaching had its origin in Ch'en Village. Moreover, Ch'ang's form, with its emphasis on bending forward and backward, bears no resemblance to any known style of t'ai-chi ch'üan.

Curiously, in spite of an abundance of compelling verbatim and close parallel passages between Ch'ang and the Wu/Li classics, in reading Ch'en Hsin's *T'u-shuo* one feels more in the world of Ch'ang than of the classics. Ch'en Hsin's use of the terms "central energy" (*chung-ch'i* 中氣) and "balancing hard and soft" (*gang-jou hsiang-chi* 剛柔相濟), as well as massive transplants from traditional medicine and the *I ching,* all give the impression of a strong resonance between Ch'ang and Ch'en Hsin. Ch'en actually records a visit by Ch'ang to Ch'en Village in his "Biographies of Ch'en Family Masters" (Ch'en-shih chia-sheng 陳氏家乘) under the biography of Ch'en Chi-hsia 陳繼夏, who lived at the end of the Ch'ien-lung reign (1736–95).[49] Ch'en's account depicts Ch'ang as committing an impropriety and being put in his place by Chi-hsia. On the surface this might seem no more than a crude advertisement for his own ancestor, but we cannot help but wonder whether there is a kernel of historical truth in Ch'ang's visit and whether Ch'en Hsin might have glimpsed Ch'ang's writings. For Ch'en apologists, then, both Wang Tsung-yüeh and Ch'ang Nai-chou owe their art to Ch'en Village.

Passages like the following from Ch'ang's writings leave us with a host of tantalizing questions:

> At the beginning of study do not be concerned with cultivating the *ch'i*, but strive rather for precision in your body, leg, and eye techniques. It is also important not to use strength, but following the natural movement of each posture perform them slowly and deliberately. Be sure that the body moves as one unit . . . . All the joints and bones should be relaxed and open.[50]

The author of these words, so compellingly in sympathy with t'ai-chi principles, was a native of northern Henan and contemporary of Wang Tsung-yüeh (if the "Spear Manual Preface" can be believed), and yet neither mentions the other in their writings. Why is there such a rich written record with Ch'ang and so relatively poor with Ch'en Village or Wu Yü-hsiang? Why does Ch'ang give us a form and Wang does not? Why did Wu find a few fragmentary writings of a shadowy undocumented figure, Wang Tsung-yüeh, while missing a substantial historical figure, Ch'ang Nai-chou, with an extensive and highly developed body of literature? Can the new Wu and Li material help us answer any of these questions regarding the relationship between Ch'ang Nai-chou and the t'ai-chi classics? The quantity of verbatim parallels, together with the attested dates of Ch'ang Nai-chou, indicates that the core of the classics is no later than the Ch'ien-lung period and cannot simply be a pseudograph of Wu Yü-hsiang. If, on the other hand, Yü-hsiang was stealing directly from Ch'ang, one might expect to see stray passages from Ch'ang surface in the new works of Yü-hsiang's brothers and nephew that did not become enshrined in the t'ai-chi "classics." However, no such exceptions exist, and thus, just as the quantity of quotations from the "core Wang material" in the writings of Ch'eng-ch'ing and Ju-ch'ing reinforces the impression of a genuine manuscript find in Wu-yang, so the absence of Ch'ang influence in the Wu brothers and Li I-yü also points to an alternative transmission associated with the name Wang Tsung-yüeh.

Survival of Manuscripts in the Wu and Li Families

Given Wu Yü-hsiang's pivotal role in the theory and transmission of t'ai-chi ch'üan in the nineteenth century, it has long greatly chagrined and puzzled scholars that we do not have authentic holographs in Wu's own hand. This must be considered ironic in view of the number of documents at our disposal from periods as remote as the Shang more than three thousand years ago. If the reason for this lack of written materials is peculiar to Wu family custom (indifference to preserving family documents), then we must point to the bibliographies of Ch'eng-ch'ing and Ju-ch'ing's writings in their various biographies; if the reason is peculiar to the subject matter (martial arts in a scholar family), we must ask why the Li family did a better job? Given the educational background of the Wu brothers, the bloody period in which they lived, and their own participation in military defense, it is inconceivable that they were not aware of Ch'i Chi-kuang's *Chi-hsiao hsin-shu* 紀效新書 and its "Classic of Pugilism" 拳經 or could have failed to notice the influence of this work on the Ch'en family art. However, strangely, Wu and his editor, Li, were able neither to acknowledge Ch'i's influence, nor to accept Ch'en family originality, nor to tell us the relationship between Wang and Ch'en. By any standard, Wu was most uncommunicative.

The transmission of the art and the preservation of texts are two different things but equally worthy of examination. The two most influential documents in t'ai-chi historical research—the salt shop and bookstall manuscripts—were both accidental finds and not preserved in family or even martial arts lineages. The third important manuscript, that of the Wu/Li classics, was preserved by the Hao family, two steps removed from Wu. To explain these anomalies, we can begin by looking at Wu Lai-hsü's biography of his grandfather, Wu Yü-hsiang, which tells us that, of Wu's five sons and fifteen grandsons, all failed to apply themselves to the art, and that only nephews Li Ching-lun (I-yü) and Ch'eng-lun (Ch'i-hsüan) mastered it.[51] We might also note that there is no record of Ch'eng-ch'ing or Ju-ch'ing's descendants pursuing the art either. Thus in spite of Yü-hsiang's intense involvement in shaping the theory and practice of the art, he did not teach his sons or grandsons and apparently made no attempt to see that his writings were preserved, or perhaps even recorded beyond the level of fragmentary and random notes. By contrast, both the Ch'ang family art and Nai-chou's writings were preserved for five generations, when they were collected and published by Hsü Chen.

The publishers of the new Ju-ch'ing and Li I-yü material have not favored us with explanations of the backgrounds of these texts, but Wu Wen-han's article makes it clear that the Ch'eng-ch'ing pieces were preserved in Hsing-t'ai 邢台, where Hao Wei-chen taught during the late Ch'ing. Thus the background of the Ch'eng-ch'ing texts seems to confirm our reliance on the Li and Hao families for the survival of Wu family t'ai-chi documents. This comports with the insertion of the Ch'eng-ch'ing "Postscript" in the prefaces by Hao Wei-chen's student, Sun Lu-t'ang. The Ch'eng-ch'ing and Sun Lu-t'ang cases confirm the transmission of texts through Li, not Wu, but confound the impression that we are dependent on Li's editorship, since we now seem to have texts of direct Ch'eng-ch'ing and Ju-ch'ing composition. The question then becomes one of whether the Ch'eng-ch'ing and Ju-ch'ing texts were also edited by Li I-yü. Taken together, the Wu/Li classics and new Wu brothers' and Li I-yü material confirm the impression of three layers of input—core Wang texts (or early Ch'ing language), Wu editorship and original contributions, and Li I-yü reediting and further original contributions—and the tendency for texts to be passed down in transmission rather than family lineage.

Conclusion

This book accidentally coalesced from materials discovered in the course of research on a larger, more comprehensive study of the origins and development of t'ai-chi ch'üan. The four new sets of Wu Ch'eng-ch'ing, Wu Ju-ch'ing, Li I-yü, and Yang family texts published for the first time between 1985 and 1993 have not been analyzed in aggregate in China and have not hitherto been noted in the West. What has held objective t'ai-chi research back during the past fifty years, apart from politics, has been the lack of premodern primary materials and failure to exploit existing historical sources. It seemed logical in analyzing the new texts and their significance to explore the backgrounds of their authors, all of whom shared the same hometown—Kuang-p'ing Prefectural City, Yung-nien County, Henan. In this connection, too, there has been little advance since the pioneering work of T'ang Hao and Hsü Chen in the 1930s. The use of local gazetteers, which has revolutionized the study of Ch'ing history in general, can do the same for Chinese martial arts history. The Wu brothers played not only a leading role in their community and on the national scene but in the editorial shaping of the *Yung-nien Gazetteer*—it presents their family portrait and contains their ideological testament. Grandfather Ta-yung was soldier-turned-scholar and a paragon of selfless generosity. Father Lieh was filial son and promising scholar cut down in the prime of life. Mother Wu was a record holding faithful widow (sixty-five years) and lifelong champion of education. Ch'eng-ch'ing and Ju-ch'ing were the only sibling holders of the *chin-shih* degree in Yung-nien County records, incorruptible officials, and defenders of hearth and home. Their control of the ideological slant of the gazetteer allowed them to project their personal heroes and political orientation. They praise heroes of anti-Manchu resistance and "bandit" suppression and advocate the revival of traditional Confucian virtues of honesty and public service, combined with skill in practical studies. The premise of this book is that for the Yung-nien circle of literati t'ai-chi ch'üan enthusiasts, the art was not merely a hobby but of a piece with the whole of their lives. In the late nineteenth century, being good Confucian scholar-officials meant that every aspect of their lives related to national survival. Because of the blackout of information on t'ai-chi ch'üan in their public writings and silence on the why of t'ai-chi practice in their private manuscripts, there is plenty of room for speculation. Looking at parallels in China's history and other national independence struggles, we find that the Wu and Li brothers' participation in t'ai-chi ch'üan practice and the formulation of theory might very well have been associated with the construction of a national identity. In this sense, t'ai-chi ch'üan for these men functioned as a metaphor in body movement, a metaphor capturing the culture's spiritual essence and providing a plan for its survival.

If it is true that the classics give us a glimpse of the state of t'ai-chi ch'üan in the eighteenth century, the new writings of the Wu brothers, Li I-yü, and the Yang family give us a glimpse of the art in the nineteenth. From these new sources it is apparent that t'ai-chi ch'üan drew more deeply on the meditation tradition and more widely on martial arts techniques than is commonly found in popularized versions of the art taught in the twentieth century. The contents of the new texts range from the mechanics of grappling to the manipulation of an opponent's energy, from the cosmology and physiology of t'ai-chi theory to the philosophy of martial arts as a *tao*.

The historiography of t'ai-chi ch'üan has been a battleground in Chinese culture since T'ang Hao and Hsü Chen's debunking of the Chang San-feng origination myth aroused the ire of traditionalists in the Yang camp. For nearly two decades during the 1930s and 1940s, T'ang and Hsü fought the traditionalists on historical versus mythological grounds and each other on the details of history. After the founding of the People's Republic of China in 1949, T'ang's view that t'ai-chi ch'üan was created by Ch'en Wang-t'ing in the seventeenth century and transmitted by Ch'en's descendants to Wang Tsung-yüeh became official in mainland China. Debate has heated up again since the 1980s, driven by the reemergence of family lineages and the shift from popularization in a socialist context to commercialization in an entrepreneurial environment. In the current period Chang San-feng has been dusted off again to bolster Chao-pao and Wu-tang claims of unique authenticity and as part of a more general "roots seeking" movement to reclaim the colorful and unique artifacts of Chinese culture. From the point of view of the creation of the art and authorship of its classics, the new material provides no bombshells or smoking guns. The Li I-yü material is rich in technical content, but unfortunately does not supplement the "Short Preface" and "Postscript" that remain our earliest sources on history. The *Yang Family Forty Chapters* reinforce the association of the Yang family with belief in Chang San-feng, but in the absence of definitive authorship and date simply raises more questions. Ch'eng-ch'ing, however, seems to give confirmation to the veracity of the salt shop manuscript, the historicity of Wang, and a Wang core to the classics. Taken in aggregate, these four new sets of texts will offer strength both to those who lean to the historical and to those who lean to the mythological interpretations of t'ai-chi history; it will offer sustenance both to those who emphasize the self-defense, and to those who emphasize the health and meditational aspects of the art.

Finally, it is hoped that this book will offer scholars of late imperial China a new window through which to glimpse a neglected aspect of the period. For Western practitioners of t'ai-chi ch'üan, a better understanding of the art in its native cultural and historical context will stimulate fresh perspectives on the role of t'ai-chi ch'üan in Western culture and in our personal lives.

ORIGINAL CHINESE TEXTS FOR
THE LOST CLASSICS

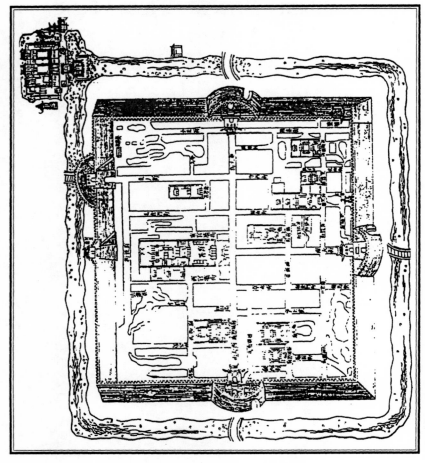

Map of Kuang-p'ing City. From the *Kuang-p'ing Prefectural Gazetteer*.

武澄清

一 釋原論

《動》：“動之則分，靜之則合。”分爲陰陽之分，合爲陰陽之合，太極之形如此：分合皆謂己而言。“人不知我，我獨知人”，懂勁之謂也，揣摩日久自悉矣。

《引》：“引勁落空合即出”，“四兩撥千斤”，合即撥也，此字能悟，眞凤慧者也。

夫練太極拳者須知陰陽，辨識虛實明，然後知進退，固是進中有退，退仍是進，退中隱有進機，此中須有轉合，身法要有虛領頂勁，拔背含胸、氣沉丹田，裹襠護肫。精神總要提起，則周身旋轉自如，兩手支撐八面，活似車輪，所向無敵。人勁方來，未能發出，我即打去，此謂“打悶勁”；人勁已來，我早靜待，著身即便打去，此謂“打來勁”；人已落空，欲將換勁，我隨之打去，此謂“打回勁”。由此體驗，留心揣摩，自然從心所欲階及神明矣。

“左重”、“右重”、“仰之”、“俯之”、“進之”、“退之”，是謂人也。“左虛”、“右杳”、“彌高”、“彌深”、“愈長”、“愈促”，是謂己亦謂人也。虛、杳、高、深是人覺如此，我引彼落空也。“退之則愈

促",,迫無容身之地,如懸崖勒馬,非懂勁不能走也。此
六句上、下、左、右、前、後之謂是矣。

"偏沉則隨,雙重則滯",是比 "活似車輪" 而言,
乃己之謂。一邊沉則轉,兩邊重則滯,不使雙重,即不為
制矣!是言己之病也。硬則如此,軟則隨,隨則舍己從
人,不致膠柱鼓瑟矣!

二 拳 論

初學打手,先學攦、按、肘。此用攦彼用肘,此用按
彼用攦,此用肘彼用按,二人一樣,循環往復,周而復
始,謂之 "老三著"。以後高勢低勢漸漸加多,周身上下
打著何處,何處接應,身隨勁(己之勁)轉,論內功不論
外形。此打手磨練之法,練得到純熟時,能引勁(人之
勁)落空合即出,則藝業成矣。然非懂勁(此勁字兼言
人、己之勁)不能知人勁怎樣來,己之勁當怎樣引進。此
中巧妙必須心悟,不能口授。心知方能身知,身知勝于心
知:悟于心知身知,勁乃靈動。徒心知尚不適用,到得身
知方為懂勁。懂勁詢不易也。

三 打手歌

綳攦擠按須認真,采挒肘靠就曲伸,
進退顧盼與中定,粘連依隨虛實分;
手足相隨腰腿整,引勁落空妙如神,
任他巨力向前打,牽動四兩撥千斤。

四 跋

　　太極拳學，王宗岳論之精矣！其術以柔曲爲體，以剛直爲用。蓋巨力之至，非柔曲不能化之靈，彼力旣化，非剛直不能放之遠，故曰：「曲中求直，蓄而後發。」

　　練習此術，在氣沉丹田，純以神行，不尚後天之拙力；而御敵制勝，如行所無事，雖甚巧而有至道存焉。老子曰：「若欲取之，必固與之。」原譜所謂「左重則左虛，右重則右杳」，即人取我與之意。莊子曰：「得其環中，以應無窮」。所謂氣如車輪，行氣如九曲珠，即得其環中之意也。故其術「專氣致柔」，蓋合于道家，非數十年純功，不能用之精巧。

　　此拳貴空虛忌雙重，非老子之「虛而不屈，動而愈出」者乎！太極之勁斷意不斷，非老子之「綿綿若存」者乎！太極之隨曲就伸，意在人先，非老子之「迎而不見其首，隨之不見其後」者乎！故吾謂有欲以觀其竅者，即太極之十三勢也。

武汝清

太極拳論

　　夫拳名太極者，陰陽虛實也。陰陽明然後知進退，進固是進，進中有退，步退仍是進，退中隱有進機。此中轉關，在於虛領頂勁，而拔背含胸，則精神提得起；氣沉丹田而裹襠護臀，則周旋便捷。肘宜曲，曲而能伸，則支撐得勢。膝宜蓄，蓄而能發，則發勁有力。至與人交手，手先著力，只聽人勁，務要由人，不要由己；務要知人，不要使人知己。知人則上下前後左右自能引進落空，則人背我順。此中轉關在乎松肩，主宰于腰，立根在腳，但聽命于心。一動無有不動，一靜無有不靜。上下一氣，即所謂立如秤準，活似車輪，支撐八面，所向無敵。人勁將來，未能發出，我即打去，謂之"打悶勁"。人勁已來，我早靜待，著身即便打去，所謂"打來勁"。人勁已落空，將欲換勁，我隨打去，此謂"打回勁"。由此體驗，留心揣摩，自能從心所欲，階及神明焉。

李亦畬

一　太極拳體用歌

妙哉太極拳，運行法自然。綿綿如玉環，著著太極圖。渾身如一氣，上下無斜偏。邁步如貓行，運氣把絲盤。一動無不動，一靜俱寂然。上要頂頭懸，下氣沉丹田。垂肩與墜肘，拔背把胸含。尾閭自中正，體松氣騰然。用意不用力，轉腰把身翻。根在腳上升，腿腰認的端。勁由脊中發，膀臂到指尖。伸筋與拔骨，坐腕展指端。手指覺微漲，氣到體自顯。此全是心意，莫當拙力言。虛實分清楚，剛柔隨變遷。陰陽要相濟，往返須轉變。氣隨勢鼓蕩，神要內中斂。動從靜中升，雖動靜猶然。神領氣隨到，腰動掌腕連。步隨勢變化，手眼照當前。快慢隨人動，單沉勢勿延。不丟與不頂，勢勢要領先。引進落空後，發勁似涌泉。任他金鋼汗，四兩撥千斤。

二 十三式歌

十三總式訣，自古少人學。有緣深造化，破格爲君說。繃臂要圓活，出手問知覺。敵空使我擠，敵實墜肘撥。由外斜掤上，後仰站不著。

攦按繃臂後，沉肩轉腰肋。攦著隨化走，誘敵入空穴。擠多偏模用，下沉敵驚愕。轉動向前打，遠側地平坡。按中要帶合，先下後回折。上轉再前按，丈外把敵挫。采必用實力，過輕無效果。從上先沉下，平采身旁過。挒打平旋轉，快刀斬額脖。迫近來打我，挒手爲先著。肘在近處使，屈臂指胸肋。敵若按我肘，開花無處躲。靠先找三角，插襠眼下斜。腰身一起轉，送他見閻羅。進步搶中宮，逼勢人難容。相近上半步，免被敵人乘。退步先後擦，尋隙無蹤影。顧在三前使，盼在七星用。中土不離位，含胸把腰松。細體十三式，式式妙無窮。

三 八字訣

掤臂斜出月上弦，前膝微拱後掌圓。對方斤兩有多少，掤臂觸之似稱盤。敵勁出頭我封采，對方凹陷我擠然。上下渾身一團氣，猶如長蛇摸地盤。

手好似鹿回頭，掌高手低勢自由。神意全在掌中現，腰腿一致順水舟。沾粘不離中土位，攦中帶引是根由。有攦無擠空自攦，無攦有擠枉出頭。

擠手打出賽拱橋，斜中帶摸竟氣豪。逢按打擠先攦化，引進落空單臂找。拱橋閉著敵膀臂，先沉後前勢無繞。擠又從攦無引進，攦後無擠是空著。

打按好似虎撲羊，腰腿手臂各相當。先沉後帶再按出，定將敵人擲當陽。按掤攦化須注意，肘不過膝略無妨。對方撤步來采我，進步肘靠將敵傷。

采似猿猴摘仙桃，沉後斜帶引敵偷。退步采腕要老辣，不傾不脆枉徒勞。無論掤按與拳掌，采用遇之似冰消。用采切防敵肘靠，守著中宮任意拋。

挒打橫勁出驚彈，避開中門走螺旋。單手平掃敵頸頂，予似快馬摧磨轉。挒手還須挒手破，彼以禮來我禮還。肩隨腰轉龍轉身，切忌遲呆不天然。

肘打好似牛低頭，開花連環任自由。此是近取一采手，遠距用之氣人羞。對方封采隨勢用，肘指肋脅一命休。用肘最怕琵琶式，遇之轉身我咽喉。

進步打靠賽游龍，靠腿直入敵襠中。由下斜上急轉身，肩打敵胸不容情。切忌一腿不鼎主，致使對方有余容。靠打多由采手變，敵閃我采招法成。

四 神氣運行歌

氣如長江水，滔滔向東流。來自涌泉穴，路經脊背過。來到泥丸宮，回到印堂關。心意將氣領，從不稍離別。譬如右拳舉，意氣到臂腋。隨勁意氣到，覺之在肘窩。順勢一反拳，氣到內關穴。右拳前按出，掌心微突越。氣經掌陰面，直到五指尖。單雙皆一樣，手足無二般。只能舉一隅，應以三隅反。照此練下去，周身一綫穿。心意導氣力，肢體動周全。一動無不動，一靜俱寂然。一快無不快，一慢皆遲緩。呼合發放出，吸開歸丹田。行如就曲珠，處處運周全。切忌行太速，田脊跳指尖。未經步步點，未經各各關。定要按步走，內外合天然。心意力調合，久練自過關。一年復一年，金鋼鐵羅漢。

意氣爲君，骨肉爲臣。腰腿爲主帥，手掌爲先鋒，眼神皮膚爲偵探。君令臣使，將令君使。偵察速報與軍將，軍將命令與臣軍。主從相依，上下相隨，渾身一氣。

五　亂環歌

圓里乾坤大，沾沾日月長。陰陽百變化，剛柔任消長。沾沾亦是圈，亂環無丟抗。腳隨手進步，腰腿全主張。上下相隨和，運化在兩掌。前後與左右，隨機任端詳。出掌摸前胸，亂環勢難擋。動搖敵根本，一發氣遠揚。敵若用挑手，采按不離行。敵若手按下，隨下在升堂。我上莫忘采，敵旁封閉忙。左右無參差，出手顯高強。太極眞立妙，亂環術中王。

六　太極散手贊

祖師傳我眞妙法，剛柔虛實隨機變。個中有語細參求，表里精粗問根由。彼欲來時我引進，彼欲出時我逐牛。虛中無實不爲虛，實中無虛枉出頭。

虛中隨機變，妙在圓中求。擠時可擺化，迫近出捌

133

手。采按互變化，功守有來由。周身如一氣，渾如太極
球。處處有引進，滿身都是手。攻守不分明，虛實無憑
證。恍如中元月，光霞照九州。練到虛無處，無攻亦無
守。

楊鈺（班候）傳
楊澄甫、吳鑑泉 收藏

太極法說

一 八門五步

掤（南）	擺（西）	擠（東）	按（北）
坎	離	兌	震

采（西北）	挒（東南）	肘（東北）	靠（西南）	方位
巽	乾	坤	艮	八門

　　方位八門，乃爲陰陽顛倒之理，周而復始，隨其所行也。總之，四正四隅，不可不知矣。夫掤、擺、擠、按，是四正之手；采、挒、肘、靠，是四隅之手。合隅正之手，得門位之卦。以身分步，五行在意，支撐八面。五行者，進步（火），退步（水），左顧（木），右盼（金），定之方中土也。夫進退爲水火之步，顧盼爲金木之步，以中土爲樞機之軸，懷藏八卦，腳跳五行，手步八五，其數十三，出于自然十三勢也。名之曰八門五步。

二 八門五步用功法

　　八卦五行，是人生成固有之良，必先明 " 知覺運動 " 四字之本由。知覺運動得之後，而後方能懂勁，由懂勁後，自能接及神明。然用功之初，要知知覺運動，雖固有之良，亦甚難得之于我也。

三　固有分明法

蓋人降生之初，目能視，耳能聽，鼻能聞，口能食。顏色聲音，香臭五味，皆天然知覺固有之良；其手舞足蹈，與四肢之能，皆天然運動固有之良。思及此，是人孰無因人性近習遠，失迷固有，要想還我固有，非乃武無以尋運動之根由，非乃文無以得知覺之本原，是乃運動而知覺也。夫運而覺，動而知，不運不覺，不動不知。運極則為動，覺盛則為知，動知者易，運覺者難。先求自己知覺運動，得之于身，自能知人，要先求知人，恐失于自己，不可不知此理也。夫而後懂勁然也。

四　粘黏連隨

粘者，提上拔高之謂也；黏者，留戀繾綣之謂也；連者，舍己無離之謂也；隨者，彼走此應之謂也。要知人之知覺運動，非明粘、黏、連、隨不可。斯粘、黏、連、隨之功夫，亦甚細矣。

五　頂匾丟抗

頂者，出頭之謂也；匾者，不及之謂也；丟者，離開之謂也；抗者，太過之謂也。要知于此四字之病，不但粘、黏、連、隨，斷不明知覺運動也。初學對手，不可不知也，更不可不去此病。所難者，粘、黏、連、隨而不許頂、匾、丟、抗，是所不易也。

六　對待無病

頂、匾、丟、抗，失于對待也。所以謂之病者，既失粘、黏、連、隨，何以獲知覺運動？既不知己，焉能知人？所謂對待者，不以頂、匾、丟、抗相對于人也，要以粘、黏、連、隨等待于人也。能如是，不但無對待之病，知覺運動自然得矣，可以進于懂勁之功矣。

七　對待用功法

守中土（俗名站樁）：定之方中有根，先明四正進退身。掤、攦、擠、按自四手，須費功夫得其眞。身形腰頂皆可以，粘、黏、連、隨意氣均。運動知覺來相應，神是君位骨肉臣。分明火候七十二，天然乃武並乃文。

八　身形腰頂

身形腰頂豈可無，缺一何必費工夫。腰頂窮研生不已，身形順我自伸舒。舍此眞理終何極，十年數載亦糊涂。

九　太極圈

退圈容易進圈難，不離腰頂後與前。所難中土不離位，退易進難仔細研。此爲動工非站定，倚身進退並比肩。能如水磨催急緩，雲龍風虎象周旋。要用天盤從此覓，久而久之出天然。

十 太極進退不已功

掤進攦退自然理，陰陽水火旣相濟。先知四手得來
眞，采、挒、肘、擠方可許。四隅從此演出來，十三勢架
永無已。所以因之名長拳，任君開展與收斂，千萬不可離
太極。

十一 太極上下名天地

四手上下分天地，采、挒、肘、擠由有去。采天擠地
相應求，何患上下不旣濟。若使挒、肘習遠離，迷了乾坤
遺嘆息。此說亦明天地盤，進用挒、肘歸入字。

十二 太極人盤八字歌

八卦正隅八字歌，十三之數不幾何。幾何若是無平
準，丟了腰頂氣嘆哦。不斷要言只兩字，君臣骨肉細琢
磨。功夫內外均不斷，對待數兒豈錯他。

對待于人出自然，由茲往復于地天。但求舍己無深
病，上下進退永連綿。

十三 太極體用解

理爲精氣神之體，精氣神爲身之體，身爲心之用，勁
力爲身之用。心身有一定之主宰者，理也；精氣神有一定
之主宰者，意誠也。誠者天道，誠之者人道，俱不外意念

須臾之間。要知天人同體之理，自得日月流行之氣，其氣意之流行，精神自隱微乎理矣。夫而後言乃武乃文，乃聖乃神，則得矣。若特以武事論之于心身，用之于勁力，仍歸于道之本也，故不得獨以末技云爾。

勁由于筋，力由于骨。如以持物論之，有力能執數百斤，是骨節皮毛之外操也，故有硬力。如以全體之有勁，似不能持幾斤，是精氣之內壯也。雖然，若是功成後，猶有妙出于硬力者，修身體育之道有然也。

十四　太極文武解

文者體也，武者用也。文功在武，用于精氣神也，為之體育；武功得文，體于心身也。為之武事。夫文武猶有火候之謂，在放卷得其時中，體育之本也。文武使于對待之際，在蓄發當其可者，武事之根也。故云武事文為，柔軟體操也。精氣神之筋勁，武事武用，剛硬武事也，心身之骨力也。文無武之預備，為之有體無用；武無文之侶伴，為之有用無體。如獨木難支，孤掌不響，不惟體育武事之功，事事皆如此理也。文者內理也，武者外數也，有外數無內理，必為血氣之勇，失于本來面目，欺敵必敗爾；有內理，無外數，徒思安靜之學，未知用的，采戰差微則亡耳。自用于人，文武二字之解豈可不解哉？

十五　太極懂勁解

自己懂勁，接及神明，為之文成而後采戰，身中之陰，七十有二，無時不然，陽得其陰，水火既濟，乾坤交

泰，性命葆眞矣。于人懂勁，視聽之際，遇而變化，自得
曲誠之妙，形著明于不勞，運動覺知也。功至此，可爲攸
往咸宜，無須有心之運用耳。

十六　八五十三勢長拳解

　　自己用功，一勢一式，用成之後，合之爲長，滔滔不
斷，周而復始，所以名長拳也。萬不得有一定架子，恐日
久入于滑拳也，又恐入于硬拳也。決不可失其綿軟，周身
往復，精神意氣之本，用久自然貫通，無往不至，何堅不
摧也。與人對待，四手當先，亦自八門五步而來。站四
手，四手碾磨，進退四手，中四手，上下四手，三才四
手，由下乘長拳四手起，大開大展，煉至緊湊伸屈自由之
功，則升之中上成矣。

十七　太極陰陽顚倒解

　　陽乾、天、日、火、離、放、出、發、對、開、臣、
肉、用、氣、身、武（立命）、方、呼、上、進、隅、陰
坤、地、月、水、坎、卷、入、蓄、待、合、君、骨、
體、理、心、文（盡性）、圓、吸、下、退、正。蓋顚倒
之理，“水火”二字詳之則可明。如火炎上，水潤下者，
若能使火在下而用水在上，則爲顚倒。然非有法治之，則
不得矣。譬如水入鼎內，而置火之上，鼎中之水，得火以
然之，不但水不能下潤，藉火氣水必有溫時，火雖炎上，
得鼎以隔之，是爲有極之地，不使炎上之火無止息，亦不
使潤下之水永滲漏，此所謂水火旣濟之理也，顚倒之理
也。若使任其火炎上，水潤下，必至水火必分爲二，則爲

水火未濟也。故云分而爲二，合之爲一之理也。故云一而二，二而一，總斯理爲三，天、地、人也。明此陰陽顛倒之理，則可與言道；知道不可須臾離，則可與言人；能以人弘道，知道不遠人，則可與言天地同體。上天下地，人在其中矣。苟能參天察地，與日月合其明，與五岳四瀆畢朽，與四時之錯行，與草木並枯榮，明鬼神之吉凶，知人事之興衰，則可言乾坤爲一大天地，人爲一小天地也。夫如人之身心，致知格物于天地之知能，則可言人之良知良能。若思不失固有其功用，浩然正氣，直養無害，悠久無疆矣。所謂人身生成一小天地者，天也性也，地也命也，人也虛靈也，神也，若不明之者，烏能配天、地爲三乎？然非盡性立命、窮神達化之功，胡爲乎來哉？

十八　人身太極解

人之周身，心爲一身之主宰。主宰，太極也。二目爲日月，即兩儀也。頭象天，足象地，人中之人及中腕，合之爲三才也。四肢，四象也。腎水，心火，肝木，肺金，脾土，皆屬陰；膀胱水，小腸火，膽木，大腸金，胃土，皆陽也。茲爲內也。顴丁火，地閣承漿水，左耳金，右耳木，兩命門也。茲爲外也。神出于心，眼目爲心之苗；精出于腎，腦腎爲精之本；氣出于肺，膽氣爲肺之原。視思明，心動神流也；聽思聰，腦動腎滑也。鼻之嗅香臭，口之呼吸出入，水鹹、木酸、土甜、火苦、金辣、及言語聲音，木亮、火焦、金潤、土塕、水漂、鼻息口呼吸之味，皆氣之往來，肺之門戶，肝膽巽震之風雷，發之聲音，出入五味。此言口、目、鼻、舌、神、意，使之六合，以破六欲也，此內也；手、足、肩、膝、肘、胯，亦使六合，以正六道也，此外也。眼、耳、鼻、口、大小便、肚臍，

外七竅也；喜、怒、憂、思、悲、恐、驚，內七情也。七
情皆以心爲主，喜心、怒肝、憂脾、悲肺、恐腎、驚膽、
思小腸、怕膀胱、愁胃、慮大腸，此內也。夫離南正午火
心經，坎北正子水腎經，震東正卯木肝經，兌西正酉金肺
經，乾西北隅金大腸化水，坤西南隅土脾化土，巽東南隅
膽木化土，艮東北隅胃土化火，此內八卦也。外八卦者，
二四爲肩，六八爲足，上九下一，左三右七也。坎一，坤
二，震三，巽四，中五，乾六，兌七，艮八，離九，此九
宮也。內九宮亦如此。表里者，乙肝左肋化金通肺，甲膽
化土通脾，丁心化木通肝，丙小腸化水通腎，己脾化土通
胃，戊胃化火通心，後背前胸，山澤通氣，辛肺右肋化水
通腎，庚大腸化金通肺，癸腎下部化火通心，壬膀胱化木
通肝，此十天干之內外也。十二地支亦如此之內外也。明
斯理，則可與言修身之道矣。

十九　太極分文武三成解

　　蓋言道者，非自修身無由得成也。然又分爲三乘之修
法，乘者成也。上乘即大成也，下乘即小成也，中乘即誠
之者成也。法分三修，成功一也。文修于內，武修于外，
體育內也，武事外也。其修法，內外表里成功，集大成即
上乘也；由體育之文而得武事之武，或由武事之武而得體
育之文，即中乘也；然獨知體育不入武事而成者，或專武
事不爲體育而成者，即下乘也。

廿　太極下乘武事解

　　太極之武事，外操柔軟，內含堅剛而求柔軟。柔軟之

于外，久而久之，自得内之堅剛，非有心之堅剛，實有心之柔軟也。所難者，内要含蓄堅剛而不施，外終柔軟而迎敵，以柔軟而應堅剛，使堅剛盡化無有矣。其功何以得乎？要非粘、黏、連、隨已成，自得運動知覺，方爲懂勁，而後神而明之，化境極矣。夫四兩撥千斤之妙，功不及化境，將何以能是？所謂懂粘運得其視聽輕靈之巧耳。

廿一　太極正功解

太極者，元也，無論内外上下左右，不離此元也；太極者，方也，無論内外上下左右，不離此方也。元之出入，方之進退，隨方就元之往來也。方爲開展，元爲緊湊，方元規矩之至，其孰能出此以外哉？如此得心應手，仰高鑽堅，神乎其神，見隱顯微，明而且明，生生不已，欲罷不能。

廿二　太極輕重浮沉解

雙重爲病，干于填施，與沉不同也；雙沉不爲病，自爾騰虛，與重不易也。雙浮爲病，只如漂渺，與輕不例也；雙輕不爲病，天然清靈，與浮不等也。半輕半重不爲病；偏輕偏重爲病。半者，半有著落也，所以不爲病；偏者，偏無著落也，所以爲病。偏無著落，必失方圓；半有著落，豈出方圓？半浮半沉爲病，失于不及也；偏浮偏沉，失于太過也。半重偏重，滯而不正也；半輕偏輕，靈而不圓也。半沉偏沉，虛而不正也；半浮偏浮，茫而不圓也。夫雙輕不近于浮，則爲輕靈；雙沉不近于重，則爲離虛。故曰：上手輕重，半有著落，則爲平手。除此三者之外，皆爲病手。蓋內之虛靈不昧，能致于外氣之清明，流行乎肢體也。若不窮研輕重浮沉之手，徒勞掘井不及泉之嘆耳。然有方圓四正之手，表里精粗無不到，則已極大成，又何云四隅出方圓矣？所謂方而圓，圓而方，超乎象外，得其寰中之上手也。

廿三　太極四隅解

四正即四方也，所謂掤、攦、擠、按也。初不知方能使圓，方圓復始之理無已，焉能出隅之手矣。緣人外之肢體，內之神氣，弗緝輕靈方圓四正之功，始出輕重浮沉之病，則有隅矣。譬如半重偏重，滯而不正，自然爲采、挒、肘、靠之隅手，或雙重塡實，亦出隅手也。病多之手，不得已以隅手扶之，而歸圓中方正之手。雖然，至低者挒靠，亦及此以補其所以云爾。舂後功夫能致上乘者，亦須獲采、挒而仍歸大中至正矣。是四隅之所用者，因失體而補缺云云。

廿四　太極平準腰頂解

頂如準，故云頂頭懸也。兩手即平左右之盤也，腰即平之根株也。立如平準，所謂輕重浮沉，分厘毫絲則偏顯然矣。有準頂頭懸，腰之根下株，尾閭至囟門也。上下一條綫，全憑兩平轉。變換取分毫，尺寸自己辨。車輪兩命門，一纛搖又轉。心令氣旗使，自然隨我便。滿身輕利者，金剛羅漢煉。對待有往來，是早或是晚。合則放發去，不必凌霄箭。涵養有多少，一氣哈而遠。口授秘傳，開門見中天

廿五　太極四時五氣解圖

夏
火
呵
南

秋金呬西　　　　　　　　　　　　東噓木春

北
吹
水
冬
呼　吸
土
中
央

廿六　太極血氣根本解

　血爲營，氣爲衞，血流行于肉、膜、胳，氣流行于骨、筋、脉。筋甲爲骨之餘，髮毛爲血之餘，血旺則髮毛盛，氣足則筋甲壯。故血氣之勇力，出于骨、皮、毛之外壯，氣血之體用，出于肉、筋、甲之內壯。氣以血之盈虛，血以氣之消長，消長盈虛，周而復始，終身用之，不能盡者矣。

廿七　太極力氣解

氣走于膜、胳、筋、脉，力出于血、肉、皮、骨。故有力者皆外壯于皮骨，形也；有氣者是內壯于筋脉，象也。氣血功于內壯，血氣功于外壯。要之明于 "氣血" 二字之功能，自知力氣之由來矣。知氣力之所以然，自能用力行氣之分別，行氣于筋脉，用力于皮骨，大不相侔也。

廿八　太極尺寸分毫解

功夫先煉開展，後煉緊湊。開展成而得之，才講緊湊，緊湊得成，才講尺寸分毫。由尺住之功成，而後能寸住、分住、毫住，此所謂尺寸分毫之理也明矣。然尺必十寸，寸必十分，分必十毫，其數在焉。故云對待者數也。知其數，則能得尺寸分毫也。要知其數，非秘授而能量之者哉！

廿九　太極膜脉筋穴解

節膜、拿脉、抓筋、閉穴，此四功由尺寸分毫得之，後而求之。膜若節之，血不周流；脉若拿之，氣難行走；筋若抓之，身無主地；穴若閉之，神昏氣暗。抓膜節之半死，申脉拿之似亡，單筋抓之勁斷，死穴閉之無生。總之氣血精神，若無身何有主也？如能節、拿、抓、閉之功，非得點傳不可。

卅 太極字字解

挫、柔、捶、打（于己、于人），按、摩、推、拿（于己、于人），開、合、升、降（于己、于人），此十二字皆用手也。屈、伸、動、靜（于己、于人），起、落、急、緩（于己、于人），閃、還、撩、了（于己、于人），此十二字于己氣也，于人手也。轉、換、進、退（于己身、于人步也），顧、盼、前、後（于己目也、于人手也），即瞻前眇後，左顧右盼也，此八字關乎神矣。斷、接、俯、仰，此四字關乎意勁也。接關乎神氣也，俯仰關乎手足也，勁斷意不斷，意斷神可接，勁意神俱斷，則俯仰矣，手足無著落耳。俯爲一叩，仰爲一反而已矣。不使叩反，非斷而復接不可。對待之字，以俯仰爲重，時刻在心身手足，不使斷之。無接則不能俯仰也，求其斷接之能，非見隱顯微不可，隱微似斷而未斷，見顯似接而未接，接接斷斷，斷斷接接，其意心身體神氣，極于隱顯，又何慮不粘、黏、連、隨哉！

卅一 太極節拿抓閉尺寸分毫辨

對待之功既得，尺寸分毫于手，則可量之矣。然不論節、拿、抓、閉之手易，若節膜、拿脉、抓筋、閉穴則難，非自尺寸分毫量之，不可得也。節不量由按而得膜，拿不量由摩而得脉，抓不量由推而得拿，閉非量而不能得穴，由尺盈而縮之寸分毫也。此四者雖有高授，然非自己功夫久者，無能貫通焉。

卅二　太極補瀉氣力解

補瀉氣力于自己難，補瀉氣力于人亦難。補自己者，知覺功虧則補，運動功過則瀉，所以求諸己不易也。補于人者，氣過則補之，力過則瀉之，此勝彼敗，所由然也。氣過或瀉，力過或補，其理雖一，然其有詳。夫過補爲之過上加過，遇瀉爲之緩，他不及他必更過，仍加過也。補氣瀉力，于人之法，均爲加過于人矣。補氣名曰結氣法，瀉力名曰空力法。

卅三　太極空結挫揉論

有挫空、挫結，有揉空、揉結之辨。挫空者，則力隅矣；挫結者，則氣斷矣；揉空者，則力分矣；揉結者，則氣隅矣。若結揉挫則氣力反，空揉挫則氣力敗。結揉挫則力盛于氣，力在氣上矣；空挫揉則氣盛于力，氣過力不及矣。挫結揉，揉結挫，皆氣閉于力矣；挫空揉，揉空挫，皆力鑿于氣矣。總之，挫結、揉空之法，亦必由尺寸分毫，量能如是也。不然無地之挫揉，平虛之靈結，亦何由而致于哉！

卅四　懂勁先後論

夫未懂勁之先，長出頂、匾、丟、抗之病；旣懂勁之後，恐出斷、接、俯、仰之病。然未懂勁故然病亦出勁，旣懂何以出病乎？緣勁似懂未懂之際，正在兩可，斷接無準矣，故出病。神明及猶不及，俯仰無著矣，亦出病。若不出斷、接、俯、仰之病，非眞懂勁，弗能不出也。胡爲眞懂？因視聽無由，未得其確也。知瞻眇顧盼之視，覺起落緩急之聽，知閃還撩了之運，覺轉換進退之動，則爲眞懂勁，則能接及神明，及神明自攸往有由矣。有由者，由于懂勁，自得屈伸動靜之妙。有屈伸動靜之妙，開合升降，又有由矣。由屈伸動靜，見入則開，遇出則合，看來則降，就去則升，夫而後才爲眞及神明也明也。豈可日後不愼行坐臥走，飮食溺溷之功，是所爲及中成、大成也哉！

卅五　尺寸分毫在懂勁後論

在懂勁先求尺寸分毫，爲之小成，不過末技武事而已。所謂能尺于人者，非先懂勁也。如懂勁後，神而明之，自然能量尺寸。尺寸能量，才能節、拿、抓、閉矣。知膜脉筋穴之理，要必明存亡之手，知存亡之手，要必明生死之穴，其穴之數，安可不知乎？知生死之穴數，烏可不明閉而不生乎？烏可不明閉而無生乎？是所謂二字之存亡，一閉之而已盡矣。

卅六　太極指掌捶手解

自指下之腕上里者爲掌，五指之首爲之手，五指皆爲指，五指權里其背爲捶。如其用者，按、推，掌也；拿、揉、抓、閉，俱用指也；挫、摩，手也；打，捶也。夫捶有搬攔，有指襠，有肘底，有撇身，四捶之外有覆捶；掌有摟膝，有換轉，有單鞭，有通背，四掌之外有串掌；手有雲手，有提手，拿，有十字手，四手之外有反手；指有屈指，有伸指，捏指，閉指，四指之外有量指，又名尺寸

指，又名覓穴指。然指有五指，有五指之用，首指爲手仍
爲指，故又名手指，其一用之爲旋指、旋手，其二用之爲
根指、根手，其三用之爲弓指、弓手，其四用之爲中合、
手指。四手指之外爲獨指，獨手也。食指爲卜指，爲劍
指，爲佐指，爲粘指；中正爲心指，爲合指，爲鉤指，爲
抹指；無名指爲全指，爲環指，爲代指，爲扣指；小指爲
幫指，補指，媚指，掛指。若此之名，知之易而用之難，
得口訣秘法，亦不易爲也。其次有如對掌、推山掌、射雁
掌、晾翅掌、似閉指、拗步指、彎弓指、穿梭指、探馬
手、彎弓手、抱虎手、玉女手、跨虎手、通山捶、葉下
捶、背反捶、勢分捶、卷挫捶，再其次步隨身換，不出五
行，則無失錯矣。因其粘、連、黏、隨之理，舍己從人，
身隨步自換，只要無五行之舛錯，身形腳勢出于自然，又
何慮些須之病也。

卅七 口授穴之存亡論

穴有存亡之穴，要非口授不可。何也？一因難學，二
因其關系存亡，三因其人才能傳。第一不授不忠不孝之
人，第二不傳根底不好之人，第三不授心術不正之人，第
四不傳鹵莽滅裂之人，第五不傳授目中無人之人，第六不
傳知禮無恩之人，第七不授反復無長之人，第八不傳得易
失易之人。此須知八不傳，匪人更不待言矣。如其可以
傳，再口授之秘訣。傳忠孝知恩者，心氣和平者，守道不
失者，眞以爲師者，始終如一者。此五者，果其有始有
終，不變如一，方可將全體大用之功，授之于徒也明矣。
于前于後，代代相繼，皆如是之所傳也。噫！抑亦知武事
中烏有匪人哉！

卅八　張三豐承留

天地即乾坤，伏羲爲人祖。畫卦道有名，堯舜十六母。微危允厥中，精一及孔孟。神化性命功，七二及文武。授之至予來，字著宣平許。延年藥在身，元善從復始。虛靈能德明，理令氣形具。萬載詠長春，心兮誠眞跡。三教無兩家，統言皆太極。浩然塞而沖，方正千年立。繼往聖永綿，開來學常續。水火濟旣焉，願至戌畢字。

卅九　口授張三豐老師之言

予知三教歸一之理，皆性命學也，皆以心爲身之主也，保全心身，永有精氣神也。有精氣神，才能文思安安，武備動動，安安動動，乃文乃武，大而化之者，聖神也。先覺者，德其寰中，超乎象外矣；後學者，以效先覺之所知能，其知能雖人固有之知能，然非效之不可得也。夫人之知能，天然文武，目視耳聽，天然文也，手舞足蹈，天然武也，孰非固有也明矣。前輩大成文武聖神，授人以體育修身，進之不以武事修身，傳之至予，得之手舞足蹈之采戰，借其身之陰，以補助身之陽。身之陽男也，身之陰女也，然皆于身中矣。男之身只一陽，男全體皆陰，女以一陽采戰全體之陰，女故云一陽復始，斯身之陰，女不獨七二，以一姹女配嬰兒之名，變化千萬，姹女采戰之可也，亦安有男女後天之身以補之者，所謂自身之天地以扶助之，是爲陰陽采戰也。如此者，是男子之身皆屬陰，而采自身之陰，戰己身之女，不如兩男之陰陽對待，修身速也。予及此傳于武事，然不可以末技視，依然體育之學，修身之道，性命之功，聖神之境也。今夫兩男

之對待采戰，于己身之采戰，其理不二，己身亦遇對待之
數，則爲采戰也，是爲汞鉛也。于人對戰，坎離之陰陽兌
震，陽戰陰也，爲之四正，乾坤之陰陽艮巽，陰采陽也，
爲之四隅。此八卦也，爲之八門。身足位列中土，進步之
陽以戰之，退步之陰以采之，左顧之陽以采之，右盼之陰
以戰之。此五行也，爲之五步。共爲八門五步也。夫如
是，予授之，爾終身用之不能盡之矣。又至予得武繼武，
必當以武事傳之而修身也。修身入首，無論武事文，爲成
功一也。三教三乘之原，不出一太極。願後學以易理格致
于身中，留于後世也可。

卅　張三豐以武事得道論

蓋未有天地先有理，理爲氣之陰陽主宰。主宰理以有
天地，道在其中。陰陽氣道之流行，則爲對待。對待者，
陰陽也，數也。一陰一陽之爲道。道無名，天地始；道有
名，萬物母。未有天地之前，無極也，無名也；既有天地
之後，有極也，有名也。然前天地者曰理，後天地者曰
母，是乃理化。先天陰陽氣數母生，後天胎卵濕化。位天
地，育萬育，道中和然也。故乾坤爲大父母，先天也，爹
娘爲小父母，後天也。得陰陽先後天之氣，以降生身，則
爲人之初也。夫人身之來者，得大父母之命性賦理，得小
父母之精血形骸，合先後天之身命，我得而成人也。以配
天地爲三才，安可失性之本哉！然能率性，則本不失，既
不失本來面目，又安可失身體之去處哉！夫欲尋去處，先
知來處，來有門，去有路，良有以也。然有何以之？以之
固有之知能，無論知愚賢否，固有知能，皆可以之進道，
既能修道，可知來處之源，必能去處之委。來源去委既
知，能必明身不修，故曰自天子至于庶人，壹是皆以修身

為本。夫修身以何？以之良知良能，視目聽耳，曰聰曰明，手舞足蹈，乃武乃文，致知格物，意誠心正。心為一身之主，正意誠心，以足蹈五行，手舞八卦。手足為之四象，用之殊途，良能還原。目視三合，耳聽六道，目耳亦是四形，體之一表，良知歸本。耳目手足，分而為二，皆為兩儀，合之為一，共為太極，此由外斂入之于內，亦自內發出之外也。能如是表里精粗無不到，豁然貫通，希賢希聖之功自臻。于曰睿曰智，乃聖乃神，所謂盡性立命，窮神達化在茲矣。然天道人道，一誠而已矣。

TEXTUAL AND
BIOGRAPHICAL STUDIES

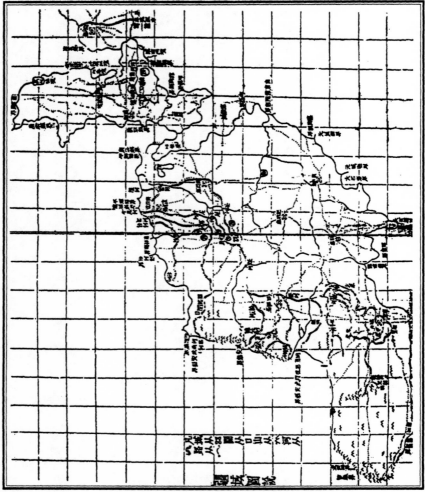

Map of Kuang-p'ing Prefecture with Yung-ning County at the very center. From the *Kuang-p'ing Prefectural Gazetteer*.

Phrases in Wu Ch'eng-ch'ing's "Postscript"
Also Appearing in Wu/Li Classics

"Wang Tsung-yüeh of Shanxi's Treatise on T'ai-chi Ch'üan" 山右王宗岳太極拳論	"Essentials of Sparring" 打手要言
"Sink the *ch'i* to the *tan-t'ien.*" 氣沉丹田	"Seek the straight in the bent; gather and then issue." 曲中求直蓄而後發
"When I feel pressure on the left, I empty the left; when I feel pressure on the right, I empty the right." 左重則左虛右重則右杳	"Move the *ch'i* as if threading a pearl with nine bends." 行氣如九曲珠
"Alternate bending and extending." 隨曲就伸	"The *ch'i* is like a cartwheel." 氣如車輪
"Double-weightedness." 雙重	"The energy stops but the mind does not stop." 勁斷意不斷

LINE	SOURCE OR PARALLEL
"T'ai-chi (The Great Ultimate) is born of the Infinite." 太極者無極而生	Chou Tun-i 周敦頤, *Theory of the T'ai-chi Diagram* 太極圖說: "From the Infinite comes The Great Ultimate." 無極而太極
"T'ai-chi ... is the mother of yin and yang." 太極者…陰陽之母也	*I ching*, "Great Commentary:" "The Changes contain The Great Ultimate and this produces *yin* and *yang*." 易有太極是生兩儀 *Lao tzu*, chap. 1: "Nonexistence names the beginning of heaven and earth; existence names the mother of all things." 無名天地之始有名萬物之母
"In movement it separates; in stillness it unites." 動之則分靜之則合	*I ching*, "Great Commentary," part 1, chap. 6: "*K'un* (The Receptive) unites in stillness; in movement it opens." 夫坤其靜也翕其動也開 *Theory of the T'ai-chi Diagram*: "*Yang* is change and *yin* is unity." 陽變陰合
"Without excess or deficiency." 無過不及 "Do not lean or incline." 不偏不倚	Chu Hsi 朱熹 *Chung-yung chang-chü* 中庸章句: "The 'center' means not leaning or inclining and being without excess or deficiency."; also Chou Tun-i, *Diagram* 中者不偏不倚無過不及
"However, without long effort, one will not attain sudden enlightenment." 然非用力之久不能豁然貫通	"Great Learning" 大學, chap. 5: "After long effort, one day there will be sudden enlightenment." 至於用力之久而一旦豁然貫通
"If pressure is applied to our left side we empty the left; if pressure is applied to our right side we empty the right." 左重則左虛右重則右杳	*Sun tzu* 孫子, chap. 1: "Avoid the enemy's strength." 強而避之
"The opponent cannot fathom me, but I understand the opponent." 人不知我我獨知人	*Sun tzu*, chap. 6: "Cause the enemy to be visible while you remain invisible." 形人而我無形
"Give up yourself and follow the opponent." 舍己從人	*Book of History* 書經, "Ta Yü mo" 大禹謨: "Give up your private interests and serve others." 舍己從人

LINE	SOURCE OR PARALLEL
"Examine the phrase, with four ounces deflect a thousand pounds." 察四兩撥千斤之句	"The Song of Sparring" 打手歌: "Pull aside with four ounces of energy to deflect a thousand pounds." 牽動四兩撥千斤
"*Yang* never leaves *yin* and *yin* never leaves *yang*, when *yin* and *yang* complement each other, this is 'interpreting energy.'" 陽不離陰陰不離陽陰陽相濟方爲懂勁	Chou Tun-i, *Theory of the T'ai-chi Diagram*: "*Yin* and *yang* never separate; this is the marvel of mutual dependence and complementarity." 陰陽不相離又有相須相互之妙
"Sticking is neutralizing; neutralizing is sticking." 粘即是走走即是粘	"The Song of Sparring" 打手歌: "Stick, connect, adhere, and follow without losing your vertical posture." 沾連粘隨不丟頂
"Silently memorize." 默識	*Analects*, "Shu erh" 論語, 述而 默識
"Thoroughly ponder." 揣摩	*Intrigues of the Warring States*, "Intrigues of Ch'in" 戰國策, 秦策 揣摩
"Attaining the level of total freedom." 從心所欲	*Analects*, "Wei cheng" 論語, 爲政 從心所欲
"The slightest error will carry you a thousand miles off course." 差之毫厘謬之千里	Ssu-ma Ch'ien, *Records of the Grand Historian*, "Preface" 史記, 序 差之毫厘謬之千里
Scorning what is near and chasing what is far." 舍近求遠	Proverb 舍近求遠

Internal Repetitions in the "Essentials of Sparring"

PHRASE	1st "The commentary says" 解曰	2nd "The commentary says" 解曰	1st "It also says" 又曰	2nd "It also says" 又曰	3rd "It also says" 又曰
"The mind issues orders and the *ch'i* goes into action like battle flags; the spirit is commander and the body subordinate." 心為令氣為旗神為主帥身為驅使	X				
"First in the mind, then in the body." 先在心後在身		X	X		
"In movement everything moves; in stillness all is still." 一動無有不動 一靜無有不靜		X	X		
"Internally strengthen your spirit and externally appear calm and relaxed." 內固精神 外示安逸		X	X		
"If your opponent does not move, you do not move; if the opponent makes the slightest move, you move first." 彼不動己不動 彼微動己先動		X		X	

PHRASE	1st "The commentary says" 解曰	2nd "The commentary says" 解曰	1st "It also says" 又曰	2nd "It also says" 又曰	3rd "It also says" 又曰
"Move the *chi* as if threading a pearl with nine bends; there is not the slightest recess it does not penetrate." 行氣如九曲珠 無微不到	X	X			
"Seek the straight in the bent; store and then issue." 曲中求直 蓄而後發	X	X			
"See movement as stillness and stillness as movement." 視動猶靜 視靜猶動		X	X		
"If you can raise the spirit, then there will be no worry for slowness or heaviness." 精神能提得起 則無遲重之虞	X				

Phrase Repetitions in the Wu/Li Classics

PHRASE	"Treatise"	"Essentials of Sparring"	"Song of the Practice of the Thirteen Postures"	"Song of Sparring"
"Focus your attention on the waist." 命意源頭在腰隙		X	X	
"Pay attention to changes of full and empty." 變轉虛實須留意		X	X	
"When ch'i fills the body, there is not the slightest awkwardness." 氣遍身軀不稍痴		X	X	
"Maintain movement in stillness and stillness in movement." 靜中待動動猶靜		X	X	
"Mind every posture, paying careful attention." 勢勢存心揆用意		X	X	
"At all times keep your mind on the waist." 刻刻留心在腰間		X	X	

162

PHRASE	"Treatise"	"Essentials of Sparring"	"Song of the Practice of the Thirteen Postures"	"Song of Sparring"
"When the belly is relaxed, the *ch'i* will be lively." 腹內松靜氣騰然		X	X	
"Open the energy at the crown of the head." 虛領頂勁	X	X		
"When the *wei-lü* is properly aligned, the spirit penetrates to the crown. The whole body will be light and agile when the crown is supended from above." 尾閭正中神貫頂 滿身輕利頂頭懸		X	X	
"When the mind and *ch'i* are rulers, the flesh and bones obey." 意氣君來骨肉臣		X	X	
"Give up yourself and follow others." 舍己從人	X	X		
"With four ounces deflect a thousand pounds." 四兩撥千斤	X	X		X

Phrases in Wu Ch'eng-ch'ing's "Notes to the Original Treatise" Also Appearing in the Wu/Li Classics

"Wang Tsung-yüeh of Shanxi's Treatise on T'ai-ch'i Ch'üan" 山右王宗岳太極拳論	"Essentials of Sparring" 打手要言	"Song of Sparring" 打手歌	"Body Techniques" 身法
"In movement it separates; in stillness it unites." 動之則分 靜之則合	"With four ounces deflect a thousand pounds." 四兩撥千斤	"With four ounces deflect a thousand pounds." 四兩撥千斤	"Raise the back and relax the chest." 拔背含胸
"My opponent cannot understand me, but I understand him." 人不知我 我獨知人	"Draw the opponent's energy in, and when it lands on nothing, unite and issue." 引勁落空合即出	"Draw the opponent's energy in, and when it lands on nothing, unite and issue." 引進落空合即出	"Enclose the crotch and protect the buttocks." 裹襠護臀
"When I feel pressure on the left, I empty the left; when I feel pressure on the right, I empty the right. Looking up, it appears higher and higher; looking down, it appears deeper and deeper. Advancing it becomes longer and longer; retreating it becomes more and more pressed." 左重則左虛 右重則右杳 仰之則彌高 俯之則彌深 進之則愈長 退之則愈促	"Always raise the spirit" 精神總要提起 "Control the eight directions." 支撐八面 "Make the energy at the crown of the head empty and light." 虛領頂勁		

"Wang Tsung-yüeh of Shanxi's Treatise on T'ai-ch'i Ch'üan" 山右王宗岳太極拳論	"Essentials of Sparring" 打手要言	"Song of Sparring" 打手歌	"Body Techniques" 身法
"With all the weight on one side one can follow; with double-weightedness one is stuck." 偏沉則隨 雙重則滯			
"As lively as a cartwheel." 活似車輪			
"Make the energy at the crown of the head open and light." 虛領頂勁			
"Sink the *ch'i* to the *tan-t'ien*." 氣沉丹田			
"Approaching spiritual illumination." 階及神明			
"Wherever you go you will have no match." 所向無敵			
"Give up yourself and follow the opponent." 舍己從人			

165

(Phrases in Wu Ch'eng-ch'ing's "Notes to the Original Treatise", continued)

"Wang Tsung-yüeh of Shanxi's Treatise on T'ai-ch'i Ch'üan" 山右王宗岳太極拳論	"Essentials of Sparring" 打手要言	"Song of Sparring" 打手歌	"Body Techniques" 身法
"Follow your desires." 從心所欲			
"With four ounces deflect a thousand pounds." 四兩撥千斤			

Phrases in Li Yi-yü's Six new Texts Also Appearing in Wu/Li Classics

"Wang Tsung-yüeh of Shanxi's Treatise on T'ai-ch'i Ch'üan" 山右王宗岳太極拳論	"Essentials of Sparring" 打手要言	"Song of the Practice of the Thirteen Postures," 十三勢行工歌訣	"Body Techniques" 身法	"Song of Sparring" 打手歌	"The Thirteen Postures, Also Called Long Boxing or the Thirteen Postures" 十三勢一名長拳一名十三勢
"Sink the *ch'i* to the *tan-t'ien*." 氣沉丹田		"Suspension from the crown of the head." 頂頭懸	"Raise the back and relax the chest." 拔背把胸合	"Do not lose contact and do not overextend." 不丟與不頂	"The *ch'i* is like the waters of the Yangtze River, ceaselessly flowing to the east." 氣如長江水滔滔向東流
"Step like a cat." 邁步如貓行		"The *wei-lü* point at the coccyx should be naturally vertical." 尾閭自中正		"Draw the opponent's energy in so that it lands on nothing." 引勁落空後	
"In movement everything moves; in stillness everything is still." 一動無不動一靜俱寂然		"The body is relaxed and the *ch'i* is lively." 體鬆氣騰然		"With four ounces deflect a thousand pounds." 四兩撥千斤	
"Move like a pearl with nine bends." 行如九曲珠		"When the mind and *ch'i* are rulers, the body and bones obey." 意氣為君體肉為臣			

Phrases in Wu Ju-ch'ing's "Treatise on T'ai-chi Ch'üan" Also Appearing in Wu/Li Classics

"Wang Tsung-yüeh of Shanxi's Treatise on T'ai-ch'i Ch'üan" 山右王宗岳太極拳論	"Essentials of Sparring" 打手要言	"Body Techniques" 身法	"Song of Sparring" 打手歌
"I am at ease while the opponent is at a disadvantage." 我順人背	"Make the energy at the crown of the head open and light." 虛領頂勁	"Enclose the crotch and protect the buttocks." 裹襠護臀	"Draw the opponent's energy in so that it lands on nothing." 引進落空
"Stand like a balance and move like a cartwheel." 立如秤準活似車輪	"Raise the spirit." 精神提得起	"Raise the back and relax the chest." 拔背含胸	
"Follow your desires." 從心所欲	"Sink the *ch'i* to the *tan-t'ien*." 氣沉丹田		
"Wherever you go you will have no match." 所向無敵	"In movement everything moves; in stillness all is still." 一動無有不動一靜無有不靜		
"Approaching spiritual illumination." 階及神明	"Draw the opponent's energy in so that it lands on nothing." 引進落空		
"Make the energy at the crown of the head open and light." 虛領頂勁	"Control the eight directions." 八面支撐		

"Wang Tsung-yüeh of Shanxi's Treatise on T'ai-ch'i Ch'üan" 山右王宗岳太極拳論	"Essentials of Sparring" 打手要言	"Body Techniques" 身法	"Song of Sparring" 打手歌
"Sink the *ch'i* to the *tan-t'ien*." 氣沉丹田	"The root is in the feet." 根在腳		
	"Controlled by the waist." 主宰于腰		

169

TITLE	FIRST LINE
"Wang Tsung-yüeh of Shanxi's Treatise on T'ai-chi Ch'üan" 山右王宗岳先生太極拳論	"T'ai-chi is born of the Infinite." 太極者無極而生
"Secret Transmission of the Practice of the Thirteen Postures" 十三勢行工歌訣	"Do not neglect the thirteen postures." 十三總勢莫輕視
"Song of Sparring" 打手歌	"Be conscientious in your practice of ward-off, roll-back, press, and push." 掤攦擠按須認眞
"Essentials of Sparring" 打手要言	"The commentary says: Circulate the *ch'i* with the mind." 解曰以心行氣 "It is also said: If the opponent does not move." 又曰彼不動
"It is also called Long Boxing, or the Thirteen Postures" 一名長拳一名十三勢	"Long Boxing." 長拳者

Texts in Li I-yü Handwritten Manuscripts

TITLE	FIRST LINE
"Wang Tsung-yüeh of Shanxi's Treatise on T'ai-chi Ch'üan" 山右王宗岳太極拳論	"T'ai-chi is born of the Infinite." 太極者無極而生
"Body Techniques" 身法	"Relax the chest, raise the back." 涵胸拔背
"Broadsword Techniques" 刀法	"Inner scissors wrist." 裹剪腕
"Spear Technique" 槍法	"Horizontal thrust at heart." 平刺心窩
"The Thirteen Postures, Also Called Long Boxing, or the Thirteen Postures" 十三勢一名長拳一名十三勢	"Long Boxing." 長拳者
"Verse Transmission on the Practice of the Thirteen Postures" 十三勢行工歌訣	"Do not neglect the thirteen postures." 十三總勢莫輕視
"Essentials of Sparring" 打手要言	"The commentary says: Circulate the *ch'i* with the mind." 解曰以心行氣 "The commentary says: Although the body moves." 解曰身雖動 "It is also said: First in the mind." 又曰先在心 "It is also said: If the opponent does not move." 又曰彼不動 "It is also said: With each movement." 又曰每一動
"Uncle Yü-hsiang's T'ai-chi Ch'üan Four-Character Secret Transmission" 禹襄母舅太極拳四字不傳秘訣	"Spread: Spread involves mobilizing the *ch'i* in your own body." 敷 敷者運氣于己身
"Song of Sparring" 打手歌	"Be conscientious in your practice of ward-off, roll-back, press, and push." 掤攦擠按須認眞
"Issuing Energy in Sparring" 打手撒放	"'P'eng' is rising tone." 掤上平
"Short Introduction to T'ai-chi Ch'üan" 太極拳小序	"I do not know who first created t'ai-chi ch'üan." 太極拳不知始自何人

TITLE	FIRST LINE
"Five-Character Transmission" 五字訣	"The first is stillness of the mind." 一曰心靜
"Secret of Issuing Energy" 撒放秘訣	"Raise, draw in, relax, repel." 擎引松放
"Essentials of the Practice of Sparring" 走架打手行工要言	"The ancients said, 'If you are able to draw the opponent in so that his energy lands on nothing.'" 昔人云能引進落空

TITLE	FIRST LINE
"An Explanation of the Name *T'ai-chi Ch'üan*" 太極拳釋名	"T'ai-chi Ch'üan is also called Long Boxing, or the Thirteen Postures." 太極拳一名長拳又名十三勢
"Body Techniques" 身法	"Relax the chest, raise the back." 涵胸拔背
"Wang Tsung-yüeh of Shanxi's Treatise on T'ai-chi Ch'üan" 山右王宗岳太極拳論	"T'ai-chi is born of the Infinite." 太極者無極而生 "Commentary: First in the mind." 解曰先在心 "It is also said: If the opponent does not move." 又曰彼不動
"Colloquial Song of the Postures" 各勢白話歌	"Lift the crown of the head, raise the crotch, suspend the heart." 提頂吊襠心中懸
"Song of the Practice of the Thirteen Postures" 十三勢行功歌	"Do not neglect the thirteen postures." 十三總勢莫輕視
"Song of Sparring" 打手歌	"Be conscientious in your practice of ward-off, roll-back, press, and push." 掤攦擠按須認眞
"Biography of My Late Grandfather, Lien-ch'üan" 先王父廉泉府君行略	"My late grandfather was named Ho-ch'ing." 先王父諱河清
"Explanation of T'ai-chi Ch'üan" 太極拳解	"Although the body moves, the mind is still." 身雖動心貴靜
"Summary of the Thirteen Postures" 十三勢說略	"With each movement." 每一動
"Four-Character Secret Transmission" 四字秘訣	"Spread: Spread involves mobilizing the *ch'i* in one's own body." 敷 敷者運氣于己身
Five-Character Transmission 五字訣	"We do not know who first created t'ai-chi ch'üan." 太極拳不知始自何人 "The first is stillness of the mind." 一曰心靜

TITLE	FIRST LINE
"Essentials of the Practice of Sparring" 走架打手行工要言	"The ancients said: 'If you can draw the opponent in so that his energy lands on nothing.'" 昔人雲能引進落空
"Exclamation of the Practice of the Thirteen Postures" 十三式行功要解	"Circulate the *ch'i* with the mind." 以心行氣
"Diagram of Left Empty, Right Full" 左虛右實之圖	"Fullness is not complete fullness." 實非全然站煞
"Secret of Issuing Energy" 撒放秘訣	"Raise: Raise the opponent's energy and borrow his strength." 擎 擎起彼勁借彼力
"Explanation of the Secret of the Word *Spread*" 敷字訣解	"'Spread' is like the expression 'To summarize in a word'." 敷所謂一言以蔽之也
"Issuing Energy in Sparring" 打手撒放	"'P'eng' is rising tone." 掤上平聲

TITLE	FIRST LINE
"Masters Chang San-feng and Wang Tsung-yüeh's Treatise on T'ai-chi Thirteen Postures" 先師張三豐王宗岳傳留太極十三勢論	"With each movement." 一舉動
"Master Wang Tsung-yüeh of Shanxi's Treatise on T'ai-chi Ch'üan" 山右王宗岳先師太極拳論	"T'ai-chi is born of the Infinite." 太極者無極而生 "Long Boxing." 長拳者
"Song of the Thirteen Postures" 十三勢歌	"Do not neglect the thirteen postures." 十三總勢莫輕視
"Mental Elucidation of the Practice of the Thirteen Postures" 十三勢行工心解	"Circulate the *ch'i* with the mind." 以心行氣
"Song of Sparring" 打手歌	"Be conscientious in the practice of ward-off, roll-back, press, and push." 掤攦擠按須認眞

TITLE	FIRST LINE
"Original Treatise of Master Lu-ch'an" 露禪師原文	"With each movement." 一舉動 "Long Boxing." 長拳者
"Song of the Thirteen Postures" 十三勢歌	"Do not neglect the thirteen postures." 十三勢來莫輕視
"Original Preface of Wang Ch'ung*[sic]*-yüeh" 王崇岳原序	"Circulate the ch'i with the mind." 以心行氣
"Original Treatise" 原文	"It is also said: If the opponent does not move." 又曰彼不動 "It is also said: First in the mind." 又曰先在心
"Wang Tsung-yüeh's Treatise on T'ai-chi Ch'üan" 王宗岳太極拳論	"T'ai-chi is born of the Infinite." 太極者無極而生
"Secrets of the Application of T'ai-chi Ch'üan" 太極用法秘訣	"Raise, Draw in, Relax, Release, Spread, Cover, Match, Swallow." 擎引鬆放 敷蓋對吞
"The Eight Gates and Five Steps" 八門五步 "The Application of the Eight Gates and Five Steps" 八門五步用功法 "Stick, Adhere, Connect, and Follow" 粘黏連隨 "Butting, Insufficiency, Separation, and Resistance" 頂匾丟抗 "Sparring Without Errors" 對待無病 "The Applications of Sparring, or Holding the Central Earth" 對待用功法守中土 "Body, Waist, and Crown of the Head" 身形腰頂 "The T'ai-chi Circle" 太極圈 "T'ai-chi Above and Below Are Called Heaven and Earth" 太極上下名天地	

Genealogy of the Wu Family of Yung-nien

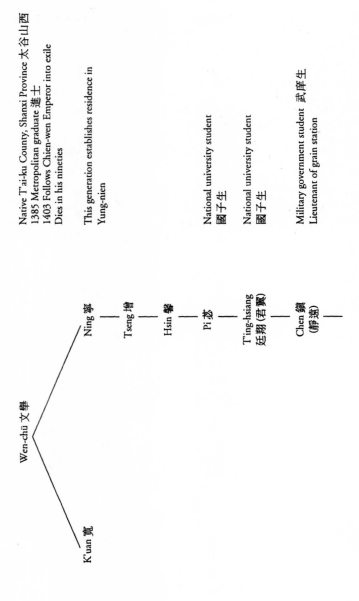

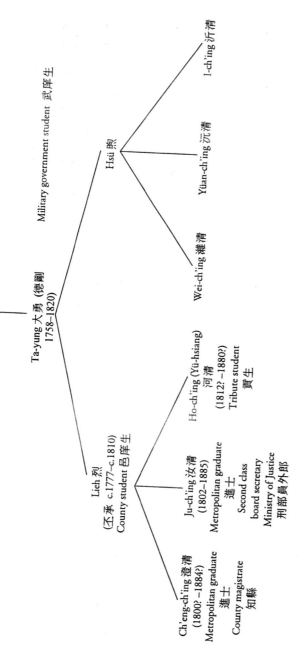

Note to Wu family genealogy and chronology:

1. All information presented in genealogy and chronology is gathered from *Yung-nien hsien-chih*, *Kuang-p'ing fu-chih*, *chi-fu t'ung-chih* and Hsü Shih-ch'ang's *Ta-ch'ing chi-fu shu-cheng* and *Ta-ch'ing chi-fu hsien-che chuan*.
2. Dates followed by "?" are those commonly cited without source in other accounts and whose accuracy is open to question.
3. Birth order of siblings in genealogy is arranged from left to right, eldest to youngest.
4. Information in chronology emphasizes dated events and official appointments cited in gazetteer and other biographies.

179

Chronology of Wu Family Members

NAME	STYLES	BIRTH	DEATH	PROVINCIAL DEGREE	METROPOLITAN DEGREE	EVENTS RECORDED
Wu Ta-yung 武大勇	Te-kang 德剛	1758	1820			– As boy gave up academics for riding and archery and at twenty entered local military academy; later refused to allow sons to study martial arts citing regrets for own choice. – Decline in family fortunes when young man; gave inheritance to uncles and struck out on own; became wealthy. – 1813 Led defense of neighboring Hua County 滑縣 in Shaanxi against "rebels."
Madam Wu née Chao 武母趙太夫人		c.1781	c.1876			– Married at 19 (c.1800); widowed at 29; died at ninety-five. Encouraged husband, Wu Lieh, to study outside county; in his absence Madame Wu tutored her sons in classics. – 1842 Awarded honorary plaque for exemplary virtue. – 1866 Endowed school for poor students which opened in 1873.
Wu Ch'eng Ch'ing 武澄清	Ch'i-yü 齊宇 Ch'iu-ying 秋瀛	1800?	1884?	1834	1852 (placed 92 of 128 passers in "3rd group" 第三甲 of "special exam" 恩科)	–1844 Chosen as instructor for school in Le-ting County, Hebei – 1852–55 Appointed magistrate for Wu-yang County 武陽, Henan; arrested local bandit, Li Chin 李進; arrested numerous Nien rebel leaders in neighboring Pi-yang County 泌陽; assisted Commander of Nan-yang 南陽, Henan, in bandit suppression; awarded "blue feather" and elevation of rank for meritorious service; when Wu-yang surrounded by one hundred thousand bandits under Sun K'ui-hsin 孫葵心

NAME	STYLES	BIRTH	DEATH	PROVINCIAL DEGREE	METROPOLITAN DEGREE	EVENTS RECORDED
						of Anhui, Ch'eng-ch'ing sallied forth at night with mounted troops and frightened bandits into fleeing; promoted to department head of Hsin-yang chou 信陽州, but declined on account of aged mother. – Returning to Yung-nien, participated in editing of local gazetteer, repairing city walls, establishing academy, and founding free school for poor scholars. – 1873 Wrote preface to Yen Pin's 閻斌 *Yün-ch'uang i-ts'ao* 芸窗易草 (Studio notes on the *I ching*). – Died at eighty-five
Wu Ju-ch'ing 武汝清	Cho-t'ang 酌堂	1802?	1885?	1825	1840 (placed 28 of 90 passers in 3rd group)	– 1840 Appointed to Ministry of Justice and served as examiner in Jiangsu, Shaanxi, and Yunnan; investigated abuses of prisoners. – 1843 Edited Shen Tuan-min's 申端愍 collected works in collaboration with Shen's seventh-generation grandson, Shen Lu-t'ang; praised Shen's self-sacrifice in resistance to Manchu conquest. – 1850 Promoted to second-class board secretary in Ministry of Justice for Sichuan; 1851 accompanies Sa Ying-a 薩迎阿 to Gansu where investigated case of false accusation; resisted Governor-general Ch'i Shan's 琦善 bribe and reported facts; praised by General Sa to Hanlin academician, Ho Tzu-chen 何子貞. Recommended in capital by Ho Tzu-chen and Shao Chi 邵基; enters court circles; slandered by Ch'i Shan, but defended by Tseng Kuo-fan 曾國藩 and praised by Emperor. – Returned to Yung-nien to care for aged mother.

181

(Chronology of Wu Family Members, continued)

NAME	STYLES	BIRTH	DEATH	PROVINCIAL DEGREE	METROPOLITAN DEGREE	EVENTS RECORDED
						– 1859 Participated in reconstruction of city gate tower in Kuang-ping Prefectural City. – 1860 Appointed by court to assist Sang Ch'un-jung 桑春榮 in organizing militia to suppress Nien rebels in region south of Beijing; Yung-nien officials requested that he remain home to strengthen local defenses, which were never breached by Taiping or Nien rebels. – 1868 Invited by Tso Tsung-t'ang 左宗棠 to join expedition to suppress Nien rebels, but declined because of mother's age; Tso Tsung-t'ang recommended that emperor grant him third rank 三品; granted honor of wearing peacock feathers. – 1869 Organized publication of fellow Yung-nien scholar Yen Pin's *Yün-ch'uang i-ts'ao*, Kuang-p'ing Prefectural City survives siege by "more than 100,000 Taiping and Nien rebels." – Kuang-p'ing Prefect Yang Yü-nan 楊毓相 invited him to manage the Ch'ing-hui Academy, where served for ten years; served thirty years as instructor at Tz'u-chou Academy. He repaired the Lotus Pavilion, dredged the city moat, and planted water lilies and willows. – 1885 Awarded second rank 二品; Died at age eighty-four.
Wu Ho-ch'ing 武河清	Yü-hsiang 禹襄	1812?	1880?			– Scholar recommended by prefectural officials to court 郡廪貢生. – Candidate for prefectural director of studies 廣文.

Place and Period of Wang Tsung-yüeh in Various Sources

Source		Publication Date	Native Place	Period
Ma T'ung-wen ms. 馬同文抄本		1867	Shanxi 山右 (山西)	None
Wu/Li ms. 武李抄本		1881	Shanxi 山右 (山西)	None
Kuan Pai-i 關百益	*T'ai-chi ch'üan ching* 太極拳經	1912	Shaanxi 關中 (陝西)	Disciple of Chang San-feng
Hsü Yü-sheng 許禹生	*T'ai-chi ch'üan shih t'u-chieh* 太極拳勢圖解	1921	Xian (capital of Shaanxi) 西安	Reign of Kublai Khan (1271–94)
Sun Lu-t'ang 孫祿堂	*T'ai-chi ch'üan hsüeh* 太極拳學	1924 Preface 1919	Shanxi 山右 (山西)	None
Ch'en Wei-ming 陳微明	*T'ai-chi ch'üan shu* 太極拳術	1925	Shanxi 山右 (山西)	Ch'ing (1644–1911)
Hsü Chih-i 徐志一	*T'ai-chi ch'üan ch'ien-shuo* 太極拳淺說	1927	Shanxi 山右 (山西)	Reign of Kublai Khan
Wu T'u-nan 吳圖南	*K'o-hsüeh hua te kuo-shu t'ai-chi ch'üan* 科學化的國術太極拳	1928	Xian 西安	None
Yang Ch'eng-fu 楊澄甫	*T'ai-chi ch'üan t'i-yung ch'üan-shu* 太極拳體用全書	1934	none	Ming (1368–1644)
Cheng Man-ch'ing 鄭曼青	*Cheng tzu t'ai-chi ch'üan shih-san p'ien* 鄭子太極拳十三篇	1950 Preface 1946	none	Ming

183

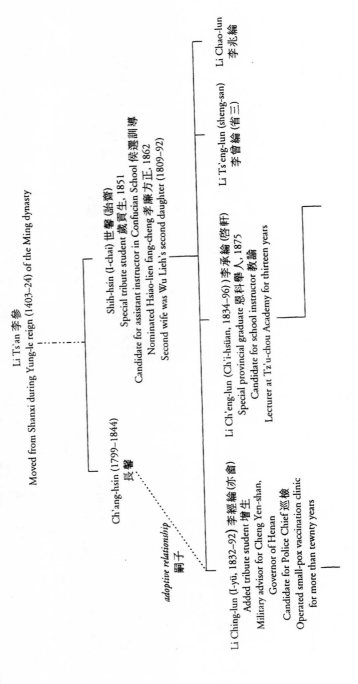

Genealogy of the Li Family of Yung-nien

Li Ts'an 李參
Moved from Shanxi during Yung-le reign (1403–24) of the Ming dynasty

Shih-hsin (I-chai) 世馨 (詒齋)
Special tribute student 歲貢生, 1851
Candidate for assistant instructor in Confucian School 候選訓導
Nominated Hsiao-lien fang-cheng 孝廉方正, 1862
Second wife was Wu Lieh's second daughter (1809–92)

Li Chao-lun 李兆綸

Li Ts'eng-lun (sheng-san) (僧三)
李曾綸 (僧三)

Li Ch'eng-lun (Ch'i-hsüan, 1834–96) 李承綸 (啟軒)
Special provincial graduate 恩科舉人, 1875
Candidate for school instructor 教諭
Lecturer at Tz'u-chou Academy for thirteen years

Ch'ang-hsin (1799–1844)
長馨

adoptive relationship
嗣子

Li Ching-lun (I-yü, 1832–92) 李經綸 (亦魚)
Added tribute student 增生
Military advisor for Cheng Yen-shan,
Governor of Henan
Candidate for Police Chief 巡檢
Operated small-pox vaccination clinic
for more than tewnty years

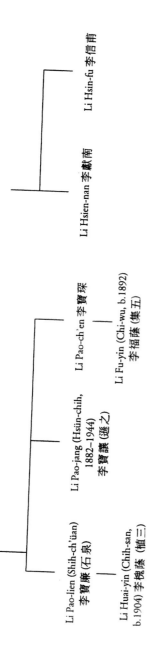

Li Pao-lien (Shih-ch'üan) 李寶廉 (石泉)

Li Huai-yin (Chih-san, b.1904) 李槐蔭 (植三)

Li Pao-jang (Hsün-chih, 1882–1944) 李寶讓 (遜之)

Li Pao-ch'en 李寶琛

Li Fu-yin (Chi-wu, b.1892) 李福蔭 (集五)

Li Hsien-nan 李獻南

Li Hsin-fu 李信甫

Note: Information for this chart from *Yung-nien Li-shih chih-p'u* 永年李氏支譜 and *TCCYC*, pp. 187–89.

185

Parallels between Ch'ang Nai-chou and the T'ai-chi Classics

Ch'ang Nai-chou	Page	T'ai-chi Classics	Text
"If the opponent does not move, I do not move; if the opponent seeks to move, I move first." 彼不動兮我不動 彼欲動兮我先動	55	"If the opponent does not move, I do not move; with the opponent's slightest movement, I move first." 彼不動己不動 彼微動己先動	"Essentials of Sparring" 打手要言
"Express spirit within and relaxation without." 內示精神 外示安逸	52	"Internally strengthen your spirit and externally express relaxation." 內固精神外示安逸	"Essentials of Sparring" 打手要言
"Do not bend or incline; be without excess or insufficiency." 不偏不倚　無過不及	4	"Do not lean or incline . . . be without excess or insufficiency." 不偏不倚 . . . 無過不及	"Treatise" 山右
"Allow the opponent to attack fiercely, for his *ch'i* will be unbalanced." 任他勇猛氣總偏	21	"Allow the opponent to attack with great force." 任他巨力來打我	"Song of Sparring" 打手歌
"Stick and connect without separating." 粘連不離	23,120	"Stick, connect, adhere, and follow." 沾連粘隨	"Song of Sparring" 打手歌
"Liveliness and suppleness overcome strength and hardness." 靈活催堅硬	124	"What hardness will not be smashed?" 何堅不摧	"Essentials of Sparring" 打手要言
"Move the *ch'i* like a windmill." 過氣如風輪	16	"As lively as a wheel." 活似車輪 "The *ch'i* is like a wheel." 氣如車輪	"Treatise" 山右 "Essentials of Sparring" 打手要言

Ch'ang Nai-chou	Page	T'ai-chi Classics	Text
"The lofty is *yang* and the lowly is *yin*; bending backward is *yang* and bending forward is *yin*." 故高者爲陽低者爲陰 仰者爲陽俯者爲陰	9	"Looking up, it is higher and higher; looking down it is deeper and deeper." 仰之則彌高俯之則彌深	"Treatise" 山右
"Before the *ch'i* moves, the mind moves first." 氣未動兮心先動	53	"First in the mind and then in the body." 先在心後在身	"Essentials of Sparring" 打手要言
"In spear and hand combat the spirit and *ch'i* are foremost and position and postures secondary." 槍拳要以神氣爲機勢先機勢次之	125		
"Borrow the opponent's *ch'i* to attack him." 借人之氣方行而打之	44	"I take the initiative and borrow strength from the opponent." 機由己發力從人借	"Essentials of Sparring" 打手要言
"When the opponent launches an attack that aproaches my body but has not yet made contact, I take this opportunity to launch my attack." 蓋彼之勢既發已近我身尚未落點我即趁此機會發我之勢	44–45	"When the opponent's energy approaches me, I wait in stillness, and as it makes contact, I immediately attack." 人勁已來我早靜待著身即發打去	"Commentary to the Original Treatise" 釋原論
"In closing, everything closes; in opening, everything opens." 合則無處不合開則無處不開	47	"In movement everything moves; in stillness all is still." 一動無有不動一靜無有不靜	"Essentials of Sparring" 打手要言
"The shoulders must be relaxed and not stiff; the elbows must be connected to our center and dropped downward and must not be extended outward in circles." 兩肩務要鬆活不可強硬 兩肘務要內連向下不可外圍	57	"Relax the shoulders and sink the elbows." 鬆肩沉肘	"Body Techniques" (Li Chi-hsüan version) 身法 (啓軒本)

187

(Parallels between Ch'ang Nai-chou and the T'ai-chi Classics, continued)

Ch'ang Nai-chou	Page	T'ai-chi Classics	Text
"You and the opponent are as one." 人己一元	120	"Give up yourself and follow the opponent." 舍己從人	"Treatise" 山右
"Slipping away means that we respond to hardness with softness and movement with turning." 滑脫 見硬而軟 見動而轉	120	"Being soft when the opponent is hard is known as neutralizing." 人剛我柔謂之走	"Treatise" 山右
"The *ch'i* flows smoothly without interruption." 氣之流利中無間斷也	10	"The whole body should be connected without the slightest interruption." 周身節節貫串 勿令絲毫間斷	"Essentials of Sparring" 打手要言
"If the opponent attacks my left side, I attack his right." 彼擊左兮吾擊右	54	"If the opponent puts pressure on my left side, I empty the left; if he puts pressure on the right, I empty the right." 左重則左虛 右重則右杳	"Treatise" 山右
"The crotch is protected." 襠亦護得住了	68	"Protect the crotch." 護襠	"Body Techniques" 身法
"Cause the *ch'i* above to return to the bottom." 使在上之氣盡歸于下	20	"Sink the *ch'i* to the *tan-t'ien*." 氣沉丹田	"Treatise" 山右
"Abandoning what is near and seeking what is far." 舍近就遠	24	"Abandoning what is near and seeking what is far." 舍近求遠	"Treatise" 山右

Texts in Ch'en Wei-ming's *T'ai-chi ch'üan shu*

TITLE	FIRST LINE
"Treatise on T'ai-chi Ch'üan" 太極拳論	"With each movement." 一舉動 "Long Boxing." 長手者 "T'ai-chi is born of the Infinite" 太極者無極而生
"Song of the Thirteen Postures" 十三勢歌	"Do not neglect the thirteen postures." 十三總勢莫輕視
"Mental Elucidation of the Practice of the Thirteen Postures" 十三勢行功心解	"Circulate the *ch'i* with the mind." 以心行氣
"Song of Sparring" 打手歌	"Be conscientious in your practice of ward-off, roll-back, press, and push" 掤攦擠按須認眞

Texts in Kuan Pai-i's *T'ai-chi ch'üan ching*

TITLE	FIRST LINE
"Treatise on T'ai-chi Ch'üan" 太極拳論	"T'ai-chi is born of the Infinite" 太極者無極而生
"An Explanation of T'ai-chi Ch'üan" 太極拳解	"Long Boxing" 長拳者
"Mental Elucidation of the Practice of the Thirteen Postures" 十三勢行工心解	"Circulate the *ch'i* with the mind." 以心行氣
"Song of Sparring" 打手歌	"Be conscientious in your practice of ward-off, roll-back, press, and push." 掤攦擠按須認眞
"Song of the Thirteen Postures" 十三勢歌	"Do not neglect the thirteen postures." 十三總勢莫輕視
"Comprehensive Treatise on T'ai-chi Thirteen Postures" 太極十三勢總論	"With each movement." 一舉動

Administrative Organization under the Ch'ing

EMPEROR

Council of State
(*chün-chi ch'u*)

Grand Secretariat
(*nei-ko*)

Six Ministries
(*liu pu*)

Governors-general
(*tsung-tu*)

Provincial governors
(*hsün-fu*)

Censorate
(*tu-ch'a yüan*)

Specialized administrative units

Imperial Household Department
(*nei-wu fu*)

Specialized service units

Banners
(*ch'i*)

Manchu generals
(*chiang-chün*)

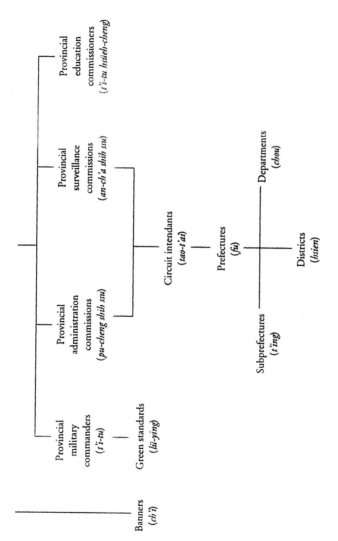

Provincial
military
commanders
(*t'i-tu*)

Provincial
administration
commissions
(*pu-cheng shih ssu*)

Provincial
surveillance
commissions
(*an-ch'a shih ssu*)

Provincial
education
commissioners
(*t'i-tu hsüeh-cheng*)

Green standards
(*lü-ying*)

Circuit intendants
(*tao-t'ai*)

Prefectures
(*fu*)

Subprefectures
(*t'ing*)

Departments
(*chou*)

Districts
(*hsien*)

Banners
(*ch'i*)

191

Civil Service Examination Degrees during the Ch'ing

METROPOLITAN GRADUATES進士

Note: Metropolitan examinations 會試 held every three years after provincial exams. After confirmatory palace exam 殿試, successful candidates ranked by excellence in groups 甲. During late Ch'ing, quota set at three hundred. Highest group appointed to Hanlin Academy. All metropolitan graduates eligible for high-level government positions.

↑

PROVINCIAL GRADUATES 舉人

Note: Provincial examinations 鄉試 held every three years. Quotas based on provincial population for candidates and passers. Graduates eligible for middle-level appointments.

↑

TRIBUTE STUDENT 貢生

Note: Receive state stipend; exempted from further itinerant Provincial Education Commission exams; entitled admission to National University 大學 as National University student 監生. Students admitted beyond quota include: Tribute by Grace student 恩貢生, Tribute for Excellence student 優貢生, and Tribute by Preeminence student 拔貢生. Eligible for low-level government posts.

↑

GOVERNMENT STUDENT 生員

Note: Every prefecture, subprefecture, department, and district was required to establish a Confucian School 儒學 with quotas of 70 to 120. Students admitted by entrance examination.

Texts in Yang Ch'eng-fu's *T'ai-chi ch'üan t'i-yung ch'üan-shu*

TITLE	FIRST LINE
"Treatise on T'ai-chi Ch'üan" 太極拳論	"With each movement." 一舉動 "Long Boxing." 長拳者
"Wang Tsung-yüeh of the Ming Dynasty's Treatise on T'ai-chi Ch'üan" 明王宗岳太極拳論	"T'ai-chi is born of the Infinite." 太極者無極而生
"Mental Elucidation of the Practice of the Thirteen Postures" 十三勢行功心解	"Circulate the *ch'i* with the mind." 以心行氣 "It is also said: If the opponent does not move." 又曰彼不動 "It is also said: First in the mind." 又曰先在心
"Song of the Thirteen Postures" 十三勢歌	"Do not neglect the thirteen postures." 十三勢來莫輕視
"Song of Sparring" 打手歌	"Be conscientious in your practice of ward-off, roll-back, press, and push." 掤攦擠按須認眞

Texts in Sun Lu-t'ang's *T'ai-chi ch'üan hsüeh*

TITLE	FIRST LINE
"Five-Character Secret Transmission" 五字訣	"If the mind is not still, it will not be concentrated." 心不靜則不專一
"Secret of Repelling" 撒放秘訣	"Raise, draw in, relax, and repel." 擎引鬆放
"Essentials of the Practice of Form and Sparring" 走架打手行工要言	"The ancients said: If you can draw the opponent in so that his energy lands on nothing." 昔人云能引進落空

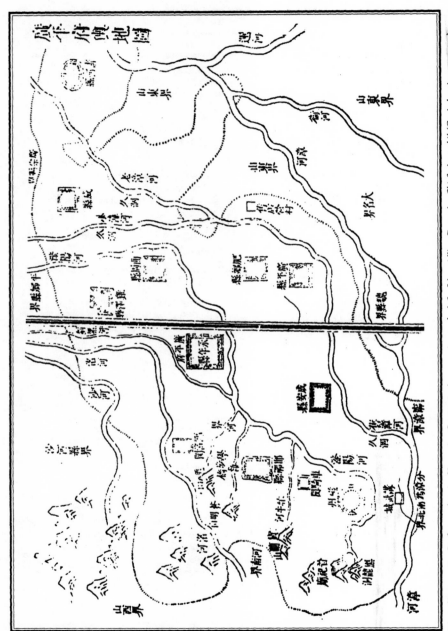

Map of Kuang-p'ing Prefecture showing Yung-nien County in the center just to the left of the midline. From the *Chi-fu t'ung-chih* (Capital region gazetteer).

NOTES

Works cited with high frequency in the notes are abbreviated as follows:

CSTCCTS *Ch'en-shih t'ai-chi ch'üan t'u-shuo*
陳氏太極拳圖說

CSWCS *Ch'ang-shih wu-chi shu*
萇氏武技書

SCWI *Shen-chou wu-i*
神州武藝

TCCCI *T'ai-chi ch'üan chiang-i*
太極拳講義

TCCCYC *T'ai-chi ch'üan chih yen-chiu*
太極拳之研究

TCCK *T'ai-chi ch'üan k'ao*
太極拳考

TCCS(C) *T'ai-chi ch'üan shu*, Ch'en Wei-ming
太極拳術

TCCS(K) *T'ai-chi ch'üan shu*, Ku Liu-hsin
太極拳術

TCCSTC *T'ai-chi ch'üan shih-t'u chieh*
太極拳勢圖解

TCCYC *T'ai-chi ch'üan yen-chiu*
太極拳研究

WTYTCCCYC *Wang Tsung-yüeh t'ai-chi ch'üan ching yen-chiu*
王宗岳太極拳經研究

Chapter I. Social and Historical Background of T'ai-chi chüan in the Nineteenth Century

1. Wu Wen-han, "Chin pai nien t'ai-chi ch'üan te fa-chan ho liu-p'ai te hsing-ch'eng." *Wu-tang*, 2 (1989), 35.

2. Chao Hsi-min, "T'ai-chi ch'üan shih-san shih chih yen-chiu," 90.

3. *Kuang-p'ing fu-chih, chüan* 51, 33.

4. Esherick, *The Origins of the Boxer Uprising*, 61.

5. *TCCYC*, 185; *TCCS(K)*, 364; *TCCK*, 120–2 (does not name Ch'en Te-hu).

6. Hao Yin-ju, "T'ai-chi ch'üan che-jen."

7. Hsüeh Nai-yin, "Wu-shih t'ai-chi chien-wen ch'ien-lu," *Wu-lin* 3 (1993), 44.

8. Chou Ming, "Wu-shih t'ai-chi ch'üan yüan-liu chi t'e-tien." *Wu-shu chien-shen* 4 (1991), 46–7.

9. Rankin, *Elite Activism and Political Transformation in China*, 101.

10. Esherick and Rankin, eds., *China Local Elites and Patterns of Dominance*, 311.

11. Rankin, *Elite Activism*, 7.

12. Ibid., 320.

13. In Johnson, ed., *Popular Culture in Imperial China*, 75–111.

14. Esherick and Rankin, eds., *China Local Elites*, 12.

15. Ibid., 168.

16. Ichisada Miyazaki, *China's Examination Hell*, 106.

17. In Johnson, ed., *Popular Culture in Imperial China*, 284.

18. Joseph Alter, "Celibacy, Sexuality, and Transformation of Gender into Nationalism in North India." *The Journal of Asian Studies* 53.1 (1995), 59.

19. Jonathan Benthall and Ted Polhemus, eds. *The Body As a Medium of Expression*, 10.

20. Roger Ames, "On the Body as Ritual Practice," 153.

21. Steven Tanaka, "Imaging History: Inscribing Belief in the Nation," *The Journal of Asian Studies* 53, 1 (1994), 25.

22. *TCCSTC*, 1.

Chapter II. Textual Tradition of the T'ai-chi Classics

1. *TCCSTC*, 1; Kuan's "Preface" states: "In the fall of 1911 I obtained a handwritten manuscript of the t'ai-chi ch'üan classics in Beijing" (In T'ang Hao, *Wang Tsung-yüeh t'ai-chi ch'üan ching*, 54).

2. Ch'en Kung, *T'ai-chi ch'üan tao chien kan san-shou ho-pien*, 210.

3. Tung Ying-chieh, *T'ai-chi ch'üan shih-i*, 34.

4. Wu Chih-ch'ing, *T'ai-chi cheng-tsung*, 202.

5. *TCCK*, 61–64, 66–68.

6. *TCCYC*, 161.

7. Ibid., 165.

8. Li's personal copy passed from Li Hsün-chih to Yao Chi-tsu 姚繼祖, who sent a photocopy to Ku Liu-hsin in 1964. The original "disappeared" during the Cultural Revolution (*TCCS(K)*, 376, 384–5).

Chapter III. Analysis and Translation of the New Texts

1. Wu Wen-han. "Wu-shih t'ai-chi ch'üan te t'ui-shou," 12.

2. The author's argument is also reminiscent of the "Great Learning's" 大學, "The ancients who wished clearly to exemplify illustrious virtue throughout the world would first set up good government in their states. Wishing to govern well their states, they would first regulate their families. Wishing to regulate their families, they would first cultivate their persons. Wishing to cultivate their persons, they would first rectify their minds . . . ." This leaves one wondering whether to start with the body or the mind.

3. *TCCS(K)*, 14.

4. *TCCYC*, 179.

5. It is interesting that the *Ch'üan-ching* 拳經 (Martial arts classics), an anthology of martial arts classics and lore published in 1918 in Shanghai contains nothing on t'ai-chi ch'üan.

6. *CSTCCTS*, 157.

7. 熟 in Wu Chien-ch'üan and Yang Chen-chi texts emended to 孰 in the Tung and Fang editions.

8. There is a discrepancy between the title of this text appearing in the Table of Contents and that which in the body precedes the text itself. The Contents title reads 太極補助氣力解, whereas the text title reads 太極補瀉氣力解. Since the latter reflects the actual content of the text, I have considered this version correct.

Chapter IV. Significance of the New Texts

1. Lines in Ch'en Hsin's *Ch'en-shih t'ai-chi ch'üan t'u-shuo* appearing under the heading "Secret Transmissions of the Shanxi Master received by Chiang Fa and Related by Tu Yü-wan" 杜育萬述蔣發受山西師

傳歌訣 (*CSTCCTS*, 495) that correspond with passages in the Wu/Li classics have convincingly been exposed by Hsü Chen (*TCCK*, 221–22) as having been copied from Yang sources.

2. *TCCS(K)*, 381.

3. *TCCK*, 205.

4. *TCCS(K)*, 381.

5. *TCCK*, 106.

6. *TCCK*, 200.

7. *TCCS(K)*, 381.

8. *TCCYC*, 149.

9. *TCCYC*, 149.

10. T.Y. Pang in his *On T'ai-chi Ch'üan*, 221,268, suggests that Wu Yü-hsiang forged the "Treatise" and added other texts under his own name so that they would " . . . then appear to be a continuation of an already established tradition." This is a serious thesis but presented more as an educated intuition than as a rigorous proof.

11. *TCCYC*, 153, 158.

12. Hsü Chen (*TCCK*, 138) points out that the Ch'en Hsin and Ch'en Tzu-ming versions of the four line "Song" vary slightly from the Liang-i Hall manuscript 兩儀堂本.

13. *TCCYC*, 169.

14. *TCCK*, 206.

15. *TCCK*, 385.

16. *TCCS(K)*, 376.

17. *TCCK*, 91; *TCCYC*, 157.

18. Yang Ch'eng-fu, *T'ai-chi ch'üan shih-yung fa*, 12–14.

19. *WTYTCCCYC*, 21,28; *TCCK*, 79.

20. *TCCK*, 109.

21. *TCCYC*, 101.

22. *TCCK*, 112–13,221.

23. *TCCYC*, 16.

24. *TCCYC*, 161–62.

25. Even Wu T'u-nan's 1984 *T'ai-chi ch'üan chih yen-chiu*, while strongly promoting the Chang San-feng connection, in recounting a 1917 research trip to Ch'en Village and interview with Ch'en Hsin makes no claim of hearing of Chang San-feng there.

26. Ch'i Chien-hai 戚建海, "Chao-pao t'ai-chi yü Ch'en-shih hsin-chia t'an-hsi," 10; Ch'i Chien-hai, "Chiang Fa t'ai-chi ch'üan ching-tien," 12–13.

27. Wang Te-ying 王德瑛, ed., *Wu-yang hsien-chih* 武陽縣志, *Chüan* 12, 1.

28. Li Hsi-yüeh's anthology of works attributed to Chang San-feng and anecdotes surrounding his "life" includes the passage from P'u Sung-ling's (1640–1715) *Strange Stories From a Chinese Studio* 聊齋志異 recounting Chang San-feng's creation of Internal Boxing (*San-feng ch'üan-chi, chüan* 4, 78.)

29. *TCCK*, 82, 107–11; *TCCYC*, 150–52.

30. *TCCCYC*, 29–30, 50. Wu never mentions either T'ang Hao or Hsü Chen by name, although the *TCCCYC* does contain a photograph of him with Hsü (49). Agreement between Hsü and Wu over the issue of t'ai-chi's importation into Ch'en Village does not extend to Wu's acceptance of the Sung Shu-ming account of t'ai-chi history that Hsü strongly condemned.

31. Ch'en Kung, *T'ai-chi ch'üan tao chien kan san-shou ho-pien*, 10; *TCCCYC*, 29.

32. *CSTCCTS*, 477; CSTCCJMTC, 1; *TCCK*, 118.

33. *TCCCYC*, 50.

34. Ch'en Wei-ming's 1925 *T'ai-chi ch'üan shu*, 3, deftly avoids the issue of succession by simply saying: "After several transmissions it reached C'hen Ch'ang-hsing and Chiang Fa of Henan."

35. *TCCYC*, 163.

36. *TCCK*, 86–87.

37. *TCCK*, 86–87, 118–199.

38. *SCWI*, 23.

39. *TCCYC*, 163.

40. *TCCK*, 118.

41. *TCCYC*. 7, 179; *TCCS(K)*, 350–52; *SCWI*, 50, 189.

42. *TCCK*, 80.

43. *SCWI*, 177–78.

44. *TCCCYC*, 30.

45. *TCCS(K)*, 387.

46. *TCCK*, 116–17; *CSTCCTS*, 478. Based on a note to the spear form in the Ch'en family *Wen-hsiu Hall* manuscript 文修堂本, Hsü Chen points out the interesting possibility of a transmission from Chang's teacher, Yü Jang 禹讓, to Ch'en Village. *TCCK*, 118–19.

47. *CSWCS*, 53,59.

48. Chiang Chia-chün 蔣家俊 "Ch'en Fa-k'e hsien-sheng ch'üan-chao chi" 陳發科先生拳照記 (Photographs of Ch'en Fa-k'e's form), *Wu-lin* 2 (1989), 13–14.

49. *CSTCCTS*, 478.

50. *CSWCS*, 58–59.

51. *TCCYC*, 153.

GLOSSARY

Bookstall Classics (*ch'ang pen* 廠本): Manuscript purchased by T'ang Hao in the Beijing used-book stalls in the 1930s containing the "Yin-fu Spear Manual," "Spring-Autumn Broadsword," "Preface to the Yin-fu Spear Manual," and version of the t'ai-chi classics nearly identical with Yang editions.

Ch'ang Nai-chou 萇乃周 (c.1700s): Scholar and martial arts master of Ssu-shui County, Henan; author of writings sharing many parallels with t'ai-chi classics.

Chao-pao Village 趙堡鎮: Village near Ch'en Village in Wen County, Henan, where Wu Yü-hsiang reportedly studied with Ch'en Ch'ing-p'ing; site of current t'ai-chi ch'üan revival claiming true transmission of Chang San-feng, Wang Tsung-yüeh, and Chiang Fa.

Chang San-feng 張三豐: Named by Huang Tsung-hsi as founder of the Internal School; named in 1867 Ma T'ung-wen manuscript and *in all Yang family writings* as creator of t'ai-chi ch'üan; placed by Sung Shu-ming and others in middle of transmission, beginning with Fu Hsi or Lao tzu, touching Hsü Hsüan-p'ing, and proceeding to the present age; connection with t'ai-chi ch'üan first denied by T'ang Hao and Hsü Chen in the 1930s; historicity questioned by Anna Seidel and Huang Chao-han.

Ch'en Ch'ing-p'ing 陳青萍 (1795–1868): Native of Chao-pao Village and teacher of Wu Yü-hsiang.

Ch'en Village (*Ch'en-chia kou* 陳家溝): Village in Wen County, northern Henan Province; native village of Ch'en family whose art was transmitted to Yang Lu-ch'an.

Ch'ing Dynasty 清朝: The Manchu dynasty founded in 1644 and overthrown in 1911.

"Epitaph for Wang Cheng-nan" (*Wang Cheng-nan mu-chih ming* 王征南墓志銘): Huang Tsung-hsi's description of the origins of the Internal School of Pugilism, founded by Chang San-feng and based on the principle of softness overcoming hardness; praises Wang's anti-Manchu stance.

Gazetteers 方志: Local histories written at the county (*hsien* 縣) and prefectural (*fu* 府) levels.

Hao Wei-chen 郝爲眞 (given name: Ho 和, 1849–1920): Student of Li I-yü and transmitter of Wu Yü-hsiang style of t'ai-chi ch'üan.

Hsü Chen 徐震 (1898–1967): Martial arts historian who challenged T'ang Hao, asserting that t'ai-chi ch'üan was brought to Ch'en Village by Wang Tsung-yüeh.

Li I-yü 李亦畬 (given name: Ching-lun 經綸, 1832–92): Nephew and student of Wu Yü-hsiang; compiler and preserver of Wu Yü-hsiang's writings and author of seminal t'ai-chi texts.

"Methods of the Internal School of Pugilism" (*Nei chia ch'üan-fa* 內家拳法): Huang Pai-chia's description of the technique and form of the Internal School.

"Postscript to the T'ai-chi Ch'üan Manuals" (*T'ai-chi ch'üan p'u pa* 太極拳譜跋): Postscript appended to Li I-yü's own copy of the "three old manuscripts"; earliest document claiming discovery of t'ai-chi ch'üan manuals in a salt shop in Wu-yang.

Republican Period 民國: The period from the founding of the Republic of China in 1912 to the founding of the People's Republic in 1949.

Salt Shop Manual (*yen-tien p'u* 鹽店譜): Writings of Wang Tsung-yüeh reportedly found by Wu Ch'eng-ch'ing in a salt shop in Wu-yang County, Henan.

Self-Strengthening Movement (*Tzu-chiang yün-tung* 自強運動): Late-nineteenth-century movement of Confucian elites to revive the nation by adopting Western technology while preserving Chinese cultural values.

"Short Preface" (*T'ai-ch'i ch'üan hsiao-hsü* 太極拳小序): Brief historical sketch of t'ai-chi ch'üan by Li I-yü beginning with Chang San-feng (Ma T'ung-wen manuscript) or Wang Tsung-yüeh ("three old manuscripts") and including Ch'en Ch'ing-p'ing, Yang Lu-ch'an, Wu Yü-hsiang, and Li himself.

Sun Lu-t'ang 孫祿堂 (given name: Fu-ch'üan 福全, 1861–1932): Student of Hao Wei-chen and founder of the Sun style of t'ai-chi ch'üan.

T'ang Hao 唐豪 (1897–1959): Prolific martial arts historian during the 1930s, 1940s, and 1950s; credits Ch'en Wang-t'ing of Ch'en Village with creating t'ai-chi ch'üan in the late seventeenth century; believes Wang Tsung-yüeh learned t'ai-chi ch'üan in Ch'en Village.

"Three Old Manuscripts" (*lao san-pen* 老三本): Three handwritten copies of Li I-yü's Wu/Li classics made in 1880 and 1881; one was given to brother Ch'i-hsüan, one to Hao Wei-chen, and one was retained in his own possessions; the Hao family copy was first shown to Hsü Chen in the 1930s.

Tseng Kuo-fan 曾國藩 (1811–72): Organized army in native Hunan active in suppression of Taiping Rebellion; admirer of Wu Ju-ch'ing.

Tso Tsung-t'ang 左宗堂 (1812–85): Regional governor and viceroy active in suppression of Taiping, Nien, and Muslim rebellions; admirer of Wu Ju-ch'ing.

Wang Tsung-yüeh 王宗岳: Putative transmitter of t'ai-chi ch'üan and author of early theoretical texts.

Wu Ch'eng-ch'ing 武澄清 (1800?–1884?): Oldest brother of Wu Yü-hsiang and magistrate in Wu-yang County, Henan, where Wang Tsung-yüeh manuals reportedly found.

Wu Chien-ch'üan 吳鑒泉 (1870–1942): Son of Yang Pan-hou's student, Chüan Yu, and standardizer of Wu style t'ai-chi ch'üan.

Wu Ju-ch'ing 武汝清 (1802–85): Second older brother of Wu Yü-hsiang.

Wu/Li Classics 武李本: Li I-yü's holographic manuscripts based on the writings of Wu Yü-hsiang together with Li's own compositions; differs in titles and distribution of language from Yang classics.

Wu-yang County 武陽縣: County in north-central Henan where Wu Ch'eng-ch'ing was posted as magistrate in 1852; site of salt shop where Li I-yü's "Postscript" claims Wang Tsung-yüeh manuals were found.

Wu Yü-hsiang 武禹襄 (given name: Ho-ch'ing 河清, 1812?–1880?): Compiler and editor of the t'ai-chi classics; student of Yang Lu-ch'an and Chen Ch'ing-p'ing; founder of the Wu (Hao) style of t'ai-chi ch'üan.

Yang Lu-ch'an 楊露禪 or 祿禪 (given name: Fu-k'ui 福魁, 1799–1872): Native of Yung-nien and student of Ch'en Ch'ang-hsing in Ch'en Village; founder of Yang lineage.

Yung-nien County 永年縣: One of nine counties belonging to Kuang-p'ing Prefecture in Southern Hebei Province during the Ch'ing dynasty; the seat of Kuang-p'ing Prefectural City; native county of the Wu, Li, Hao, and Yang families.

BIBLIOGRAPHY

Alter, Joseph. "The Body of One Color: Indian Wrestling, the Indian State and Utopian Somatics." *Cultural Anthropology* 1 (1993): 19–72.
———. "Celibacy, Sexuality, and the Transformation of Gender into Nationalism in North India." *Journal of Asian Studies* 1 (1994): 45–66.
———. "Hanuman and the Moral Physique of the Banarsi Wrestler." In *Living Banaras: Hindu Religion in Cultural Context*, edited by Bradley Hertel and Cynthia Humes, 127–44. Albany: State University of New York Press, 1993.
———. "The Sannyasi and the Indian Wrestler: The Anatomy of a Relationship." *American Ethologist* 2 (1994): 317–36.
———. *The Wrestler's Body: Identity and Ideology in North India.* Berkeley: University of California Press, 1992.
Ames, Roger. "The Meaning of the Body in Classical Chinese Thought." *International Philosophical Quarterly* 1 (1984). Also appears in *Self As Body in Asian Theory and Practice*, edited by Thomas Kasulis et al., 157–77. Albany: State University of New York Press, 1993.
———. "On the Body As Ritual Practice." In *Self As Body in Asian Theory and Practice*, edited by Thomas Kasulis et al., 149–56. Albany: State University of New York Press, 1993.
———, trans. *Sun-tzu: The Art of Warfare.* New York: Ballantine Books, 1993.
Benthall, J., and Ted Polhemus, eds. *The Body As a Medium of Expression.* London: Allen Lane, 1975.
Birdwhistell, Ray. *Kinesis and Context.* Philadephia: University of Pennsylvania Press, 1976.
Bissell, Greg. "Questions concerning the History of Taijiquan." *Journal of the Chen Style Taijiquan Research Association of Hawaii* 1, no. 5 (1993): 12–19.
———. "Traces of Zhang Sanfeng." *Journal of the Chen Style Taijiquan Research Association of Hawaii* 1, no. 3 (June 1993): 28–31.

Blacking, John, ed. *The Anthropology of the Body.* New York: Academic Press, 1977.

Brokaw, Cynthia. *The Ledgers of Merit and Demerit: Social Change and Moral Order in Late Imperial China.* Princeton: Princeton University Press, 1991.

Chang Chieh 張傑. "Hsien shen t'ai-chi ming ch'ui ch'ien-ku Chung-kuo chin-tai chu-ming t'ai-chi ch'üan chia Tu Yüan-hua" 獻身太極名垂千古中國近代著名太極拳家杜元化 (A life devoted to t'ai-chi: Famous modern t'ai-chi master Tu Yüan-hua). *Chung-hua wu-shu* 1 (1994): 39.

Chang Cho-hsing 張卓星. "K'ai-hu ho-hsi hai-shih ho-hu k'ai-hsi" 開呼合吸還是合呼開吸 (Exhale as you expand and inhale as you contract or contract as you exhale and inhale as you expand). *Wu-shu chien-shen* 1 (1987): 9. Also *Wu-lin* 3 (1987): 9.

———. "Tsen-yang li-chieh 'ch'i-ch'en tan-t'ien'" 怎樣理解氣沉丹田 (How should we interpret the phrase "sink the *ch'i* to the *tan-t'ien*"). *Wu-shu chien-shen* 1 (1985): 43–44.

Chang Chung-li. *The Chinese Gentry: Studies on Their Role in Nineteenth Century Chinese Society.* Seattle: University of Washington Press, 1955.

Ch'ang Nai-chou 萇乃周. *Ch'ang-shih wu-chi* 萇氏武技 (Ch'ang-style boxing), edited by Hsü Chen 徐震. Taiwan reprint n.p., n.d.; Hsü Chen's preface 1932, originally published 1936.

Chang Po-hsing 張伯行. *T'ai-chi t'u hsiang-chieh* 太極圖詳解 (Commentaries on [Chou Tun-i's] t'ai-chi symbol). Beijing: Hs'üeh-yüan ch'u-pan-she, 1990. First published as *Chou tzu ch'üan-shu* 周子全書, 1708.

Chang Shou-ch'ang 張守常. "T'ai-p'ing chün pei-fa jih-chih" 太平軍北伐日志 (Daily record of the T'ai-p'ing army's northern expedition). *T'ai-p'ing t'ien-kuo hsüeh-k'an* 3 (1987): 152–79.

Chang Tun-hsi 張敦熙. "T'ai-chi ch'üan fa-chan yü chu-shu" 太極拳發展與著述 (T'ai-chi ch'üan's development and writings). In *Chung-kuo wu-shu shih-liao chi-k'an*, vol. 2, 46–52. Taipei: Chiao-yü pu t'i-yü ssu, 1975.

———. "T'ai-chi ch'üan yüan-liu tsai t'an-t'ao" (A further examination of the origins of t'ai-chi ch'üan). In *Chung-kuo wu-shu shih-liao chi-k'an*, vol. 5, 40–64. Taipei: Chiao-yü pu t'i-yü ssu, 1980.

Chang Wei-chung 張唯中. *Kuo-shu t'ai-chi ch'üan shih-liao* 國術太極拳史料 (Historical materials on t'ai-chi ch'üan). In *Chung-kuo wu-shu shih-liao chi-k'an*, vol. 4, 72–105. Taipei: Chiao-yü pu t'i-yü ssu, 1979.

Chang Yü-ch'ing 張裕慶. "Wu-yen chi-chieh" 武諺集解 (Martial arts aphorisms collected and annotated). *Wu-lin* 6 (1986): 49–51.

Chao Hsi-min 趙錫民. "T'ai-chi ch'üan shih-san shih chih yen-chiu" 太極拳十三勢之研究 (A study of t'ai-chi ch'üan). In *Chung-kuo wu-shih shih-liao chi-k'an*, vol. 4, 85–105. Taipei: Chiao-yü pu t'i-yü ssu, 1979.

Chao Jen-ch'ing 趙任情. "Yung chieh-chi kuan-tien k'ao-ch'a t'ai-chi ch'üan te li-shih" 用階級觀點考察太極拳的歷史 (Use class analysis in the study of the history of t'ai-chi ch'üan). *Hsin t'i-yü* 5 (1965): 30–31.

Chen, Bill. "Taiji and Chang San-feng." *Internal Strength* 2 (1993): 5–7.

Ch'en Cheng 陳崢. "T'ai-chi ch'üan li-lun chung te 'shuang-chung'" 太極拳理論中的雙重 ("Double-weightedness" in t'ai-chi ch'üan theory). *Wu-shu chien-shen* 2 (1986): 34.

Ch'en Hsin 陳鑫. *Ch'en shih t'ai-chi ch'üan t'u shuo* 陳氏太極拳圖說 (Ch'en-style t'ai-chi ch'üan illustrated and explained). Hong Kong: Ch'en Hsiang-chi shu-chü, 1983. Reprint. Author's preface 1919; originally published 1933.

Ch'en Ku-an 陳固安. *Wu-shih t'ai-chi ch'üan hsin-chia* 武式太極拳新架 (Wu-style t'ai-chi ch'üan, new frame). Henan: Ho-nan k'o-hsüeh chi-shu ch'u-pan-she, 1988.

————. "Wu-shih t'ai-chi ch'üan t'ui-shou te t'e-tien" 武式太極拳推手的特點 (The characteristics of Wu yü-hsiang-style t'ai-chi ch'üan push-hands). *Wu-lin* 93 (1989): 9.

Ch'en Nai-ch'ien 陳乃乾. *Ch'ing-tai pei-chuan wen t'ung-chien* 清代碑傳文通檢 (Data from inscriptural biographies of the Ch'ing period). Shanghai: Chung-hua shu-chü, 1959.

Ch'en P'an-ling 陳泮嶺. "Ch'ang-chia ch'üan chih yüan-liu k'ao" 萇家拳之源流考 (A study of the origins of Ch'ang family boxing). *Kuo-shu chou-k'an*. (Photocopy of article in author's collection; year and issue unrecorded; c. 1934).

Ch'en Shao-tung 陳紹棟. "Lun kuan-yü t'ai-chi ch'üan yüan-liu te i-ke hsin shuo-fa" 論關于太極拳源流的一個新說法 (A critique of a new theory on the origins of t'ai-chi ch'üan). *Wu-lin* 12 (1992): 4–7. Also *Ch'i-kung yü t'i-yü* 5 (1992): 17–19.

Ch'en Wei-ming 陳微明. *T'ai-chi ch'üan shu* 太極拳術 (The art of t'ai-chi ch'üan). Hong Kong: Wu-shu ch'u-pan-she, reprint, n.d. Author's preface 1925.

Ch'en Kung 陳公. *T'ai-chi ch'üan tao chien kan san-shou ho-pien* 太極拳刀劍桿散手合編 (T'ai-chi ch'üan, broadsword, two-edged sword, staff, and sparring). Shanghai: Shang-hai ti-ch'an yen-chiu-so, 1943.

Ch'eng Ch'ing 澄清. "P'o-i 'ye-meng Hsüan-t'i shou ch'üan' shuo" 破譯夜夢玄帝授拳說 (Interpreting the phrase, "[Chang San-feng] received the art of pugilism from the god of war in a dream"). *Wu-tang* 2 (1994): 16–17.

Ch'eng Hsiao 程嘯. "Wan-ch'ing Chih-Lu mei-hua ch'üan-hui ch'ien-hsi" 晚清直魯梅花拳會淺析 (A study of the late Ch'ing Plum Blossom Boxing Sect in Hebei and Shandong provinces). *Ch'ing-shih yen-chiu t'ung-hsün* 1, 1988, 26–29.

Cheng Man-ch'ing 鄭曼青. *Cheng tzu t'ai-chi ch'üan shih-san p'ien*鄭子太極拳十三篇 (Master Cheng's thirteen chapters on t'ai-chi ch'üan). Taipei: Lan-hsi t'u-shu ch'u-pan-she, 1975. Reprint. Author's preface 1946. English translation, Douglas Wile. *Master Cheng's Thirteen Chapters on T'ai-chi Ch'üan*. New York: Sweet Ch'i Press, 1982. Revised ed. 1983.

Chesneaux, Jean. *Popular Movements and Secret Societies in China, 1840–1950*. Stanford, Calif.: Stanford University Press, 1972.

Ch'i Chiang-t'ao 戚江濤. "T'ai-chi ch'üan yüan-liu kuan-k'ui" 太極拳源流觀窺 (One view of t'ai-chi ch'üan's origins). In *T'ai-chi ch'üan yen-chiu chuan-chi*, 6, 7 (1967).

Ch'i Chien-hai 戚建海. "Chao-pao t'ai-chi yü Ch'en-shih hsin-chia t'an-hsi" 趙堡太極與陳式新架探析 (An examination of Chao-pao t'ai-chi and Ch'en family new style). *T'ai-chi ch'üan tsa-chih* 80, 81 (1992): 10–14, 11–13.

———. "Chiang Fa mi-ch'uan t'ai-chi ch'üan ching-tien" 蔣發秘傳經典 (Chiang Fa's secret t'ai-chi ch'üan classics). *Wu-tang* 6 (1990): 12–13.

———. "T'ai-chi ch'üan yü shih-san shih" 太極拳與十三勢 (T'ai-chi ch'üan and the Thirteen Postures). *Shao-lin yü t'ai-chi* 2 (1989), 41–42, 46.

———. "Wu-tang Chao-pao t'ai-chi ch'üan t'an-yüan" 武當趙堡太極拳探源 (An investigation into the origins of Wu-tang Chao-pao style t'ai-chi ch'üan). *Chung-hua wu-shu* 8 (1988): 18–20.

Chiang Jung-ch'iao 姜容樵. "Kuo-shu yüan-liu" 國術源流 (The origins of Chinese martial arts). *Kuo-shu chou-k'an* 79–115 (1932–34).

Chiang Pai-lung 江百龍, ed. *Wu-tang ch'üan chih yen-chiu* 武當拳之研究 (Study of the Wu-tang school of t'ai-chi ch'üan). Beijing: Pei-ching t'i-yü hsüeh-yüan ch'u-pan-she, 1992.

Chiang Po-yung 江波永. "'Yin-chin lo-k'ung ho chi ch'u' shih t-ai-chi ch'üan chi-chi te t'e-tien" 引進落空合即出是太極拳技擊

的特點 ("Draw the opponent in and when his energy lands on nothing, unite and issue" is the special characteristic of t'ai-chi self-defense). *Wu-tang* 4 (1990): 31.

Chiang Siang-tseh. *The Nien Rebellion.* Seattle: University of Washington Press, 1954.

Chiang Wei-ch'iao 蔣維喬. *Wu-i ch'üan-shu* 武藝全書 (Complete book of martial arts). Taipei: Hua-lien ch'u-pan-she, 1983. Reprint. Original n.p., n.d.; c. early Republican.

Chiao K'e-ch'iang 焦克強. "'T'ai-chi ch'üan lun' chu-shih" 太極拳論注釋 (Commentary to the "Treatise on Ta'i-chi ch'üan"). *T'i-yü shih-chieh* 5 (1983): 11–13.

Ch'iao Sung-mao 喬松茂. "Wu-shih t'ai-chi ch'üan te yüan-liu chi t'e-tien" 武式太極拳的源流及特點 (The origins and characteristics of Wu-style t'ai-chi ch'üan). *Chung-hua wu-shu* 4 (1994): 17.

Chin I-ming 金一明. "Kuo-shu shih-liao nei-jung lüeh-shu" 國術史料內容略述 (An introduction to the content of historical documents on Chinese martial arts). *Kuo-shu chou-k'an* 103 (1933): 4–6; 104 (1933): 3–4.

———. "Kuo-shu ying i ju-chia wei cheng-tsung" 國術應以儒家為正宗 (Confucianism should be the true philosophy of the martial arts). *Kuo-shu chou-k'an* 156–57 (1936).

Chin Min 晉敏. "T'ai-chi ch'üan wei-ho yu chiao shih-san shih" 太極拳為何又叫十三式 (Why is t'ai-chi ch'üan also called the Thirteen Postures). *Wu-lin* 19 (1987): 11.

Chou Chien-nan 周建南. "T'ai-chi ch'üan li-shih te yen-chiu" 太極拳歷史的研究 (Research in the history of t'ai-chi ch'üan). In *Chung-kuo wu-shu shih-liao chi-k'an*, 77–99. Taipei: Chiao-yü pu t'i-yü ssu, 1976.

Chou Hsi-k'uan 周西寬. "Sun Chung-shan yü t'i-yü" 孫中山與體育 (Sun Yat-sen and physical education). *Hsin t'i-yü* 10 (1981): 25–26.

Chou Lin-i 周林儀. "Lao tzu ssu-hsiang yü t'i-yü pen-chih" 老子思想與體育本質 (Lao tzu's thought and the nature of physical education). In *T'i-yü hsüeh-shu yen-t'ao hui chuan-k'an* (1975): 40–48.

Chou Ming 周明. "Wu-shih t'ai-chi ch'üan yüan-liu chi t'e-tien" 武式太極拳源流及特點 (The origins and characteristics of Wu-style t'ai-chi ch'üan). *Wu-shu chien-shen* 4 (1991): 46–47.

Chou Nien-feng 周稔豐. *T'ai-chi ch'üan ch'ang-shih* 太極拳常識 (Background on t'ai-chi ch'üan). Beijing: Jen-min t'i-yü ch'u-pan-she, 1978.

Chou Pao-chung 周寶忠. "Wang Wu i-wen" 王五軼聞 (Anecdotes on the life of Wang Five). *Chung-hua wu-shu* 8 (1985): 28–31.

Chu Chung-yü 朱仲玉. "Ch'i Chi-kuang ch'iang-shen pao-kuo" 戚繼

光強身保國 (Ch'i chi-kuang strengthened his body and defended the nation). *Hsin t'i-yü* 1(1963): 36.

Chu En-chia 朱恩嘉. "Yeh t'an 'han-hsiung pa-bei'" 也談含胸拔背 (A further discussion of "relax the chest and raise the back"). *Wushu chien-shen* 5 (1991): 11.

Ch'ü T'ung-tsu. *Local Government in China under the Ch'ing.* Cambridge: Harvard University Press, 1962.

Cohen, Kenneth. "A History of T'ai-chi ch'üan: The Oral Tradition." *Inside Kung Fu* (November 1981): 40–43.

Csikszentmihalyi, Mihalyi. *Beyond Boredom and Anxiety.* San Francisco: Jossey-Bass, 1975.

———. *Flow.* New York: Harper & Row, 1990.

DeMarco, Michael. "The Origin and Evolution of Taijiquan.*" Journal of Asian Martial Arts* 1 (1992): 9–25.

De Wachter, F. "The Symbolism of the Healthy Body: A Philosophical Analysis of the Sportive Imagery of Health." In *Philosophic Inquiry in Sport,* edited by W. J. Morgan and V. M. Klans. Champaign, Ill.: Human Kinetics, 1988.

Dennerline, Jerry. *The Chia-ting Loyalists: Confucian Leadership and Social Change in Seventeenth-Century China.* New Haven: Yale University Press, 1981.

Despeux, Catherine. *Taiji Quan: Art martial, technique de longue vie* (T'ai-chi ch'üan: Martial art and pro-longevity system). Paris: Guy Trédaniel, 1981. First published 1975.

Dissanayake, Wimal. "Body in Social Theory." In *Self As Body in Asian Theory and Practice,* edited by Thomas Kasulis et al., 21–36. Albany: State University of New York Press, 1993.

Donohue, John. "Dancing in the Danger Zone: The Martial Arts in America.*" Journal of Asian Martial Arts* 1 (1992): 87–99.

———. *The Forge of the Spirit: Structure, Motion, and Meaning in the Japanese Martial Tradition.* New York: Garland, 1991.

———. "Sword Magic: Belief, Form, and Function in the Japanese Martial Tradition." *Human Affairs* 14 (1988): 9–35.

———. "Wave People: The Martial Arts and the American Imagination.*" Journal of Asian Martial Arts* 1 (1994): 11–25.

Douglas, Mary. *Natural Symbols: Explorations in Cosmology.* London: Barrie & Rockliff, 1970.

Draeger, Donn. "The Martial-Civil Dicotomy in Asian Combatives." *Hoplos* (February 1981): 6–8.

Draeger, Donn, and Robert W. Smith. *Asian Fighting Arts.* Tokyo: Kodansha International, 1969.

Elman, Benjamin. *From Philosophy to Philology: Intellectual and Social Aspects of Change in Late Imperial China.* Harvard East Asian Monographs, no. 110. Cambridge: Harvard University, Council on East Asian Studies, 1984.

Elman, Benjamin, and Alexander Woodside. *Education and Society in Late Imperial China, 1600–1900.* Berkeley: University of California Press, 1994.

Elvin, Mark. "Tales of *Shen* and *Xin*: Body-Person and Heart-Mind in China during the Last 150 Years." In *Fragments for a History of the Human Body,* edited by Michel Feher. New York: Zone, 1989. Also in *Self As Body in Asian Theory and Practice,* edited by Thomas Kasulis et al. Albany: State University of New York Press, 1993.

Esherick, Joseph. *The Origins of the Boxer Uprising.* Berkeley: University of California Press, 1987.

Esherick, Joseph, and Mary Rankin. *Chinese Local Elites and Patterns of Dominance.* Berkeley: University of California Press, 1990.

Fan Cheng-chih 樊正治. "Chang San-feng shih te t'an-yüan" 張三豐史的探源 (In search of the history of Chang San-feng). In *Chung-kuo wu-shu shih-liao chi-k'an,* vol. 3, 100–105. Taipei: Chiao-yü pu t'i-yü ssu, 1976.

Fan Ching-wen 範景文. *Chao-tai wu-kung pien* 昭代武功編 (Military actions of the Ming and Ching periods). LC microfilm CBM, 21, no. 3: 294.

Feng Fu-ming 馮福明. "T'ai-chi ch'üan yüan-liu k'ao-cheng" 太極拳源流考證 (A study of the origins of t'ai-chi ch'üan). *T'i-yü wen-shih* 4 (1988): 30–34.

Fu Chen-lun 傅振倫. "Ts'ung wu-shu te li-shih fa-chan k'an wu-shu te she-hui tso-yung" 從武術的歷史發展看武術的社會作用 (Looking at the social function of the martial arts from the point of view of their historical development). *Ho-nan t'i-yü shih-liao* 3 (1983): 1–4.

Hao Shao-ju 郝少如. *Wu-shih t'ai-chi ch'üan* 武式太極拳 (Wu-style t'ai-chi ch'üan). Beijing: Jen-min t'i-yü ch'u-pan-she, 1963. Re-issued 1992.

Hao Wen 浩文. "Chou-i yü t'ai-chi ch'üan shu" 周易與太極拳術 (The *I ching* and t'ai-chi ch'üan). *Wu-lin* 19 (1987): 4–5.

Hao Yin-ju 郝吟如. "T'ai-chi che-jen: Chi-nien Wu Yü-hsiang tan-ch'en 180 chou-nien" 太極哲人紀念武禹襄誕辰180周年 (A sage of t'ai-chi: Commemorating the 180th anniversary of Wu Yü-hsiang's birth). *Chung-hua wu-shu* 8 (1992): 30.

Hay, John. "The Human Body As a Microcosmic Source of Macrocosmic

Values in Calligraphy." In *Theories of the Arts in China*, edited by Susan Bush and Christian Murck. Princeton: Princeton University Press, 1983. Also in *Self As Body in Asian Theory and Practice*, edited by Thomas Kasulis et al. Albany: State University of New York Press, 1993.

Ho Ping-sung 何炳松. *Chung-kuo li-tai t'ien-tsai jen-huo piao* 中國歷代天災人禍表 (Tables of natural and man-made disasters throughout Chinese history). Shanghai: Kuo-li chi-nan ta-hsüeh, 1939.

Ho Ping-ti. *The Ladder of Success in Imperial China.* New York: Columbia University Press, 1971.

Ho Shao-p'ing 和少平. "T'ai-chi ch'üan t'an-yüan" 太極拳探源 (An investigation into the origins of t'ai-chi ch'üan). *Wu-tang* 2 (1991): 21–22.

Hobshawn, Eric. *Primitive Rebels: Studies in Archaic Forms of Social Movement in the 19th and 20th Centuries.* New York: Norton, 1965.

Hsia T'ao 夏濤. "T'ai-chi ch'üan chi-chi che-li t'an" 太極拳技擊哲理探 (An examination of the philosophy of self-defense in t'ai-chi ch'üan). *Chung-hua wu-shu* 4 (1992): 38.

Hsiang Ling. "Fan-tui kuan-yü t'ai-chi ch'üan te shen-mi hua kuan-tien" 反對關于太極拳的神秘化觀點 (Oppose the tendency to mystification in t'ai-chi ch'üan). *Hsin t'i-yü* 5 (1965): 29–30.

Hsiao Chün 蕭軍. "Yu wen-shih che pi yu wu-pei" 有文事者必有武備 (Intellectuals should also practice martials arts). *Hsin t'i-yü* 12 (1979): 18–20.

Hsiao Ch'ung 肖沖. "Ch'ing-tai su-ch'uan p'eng-min kuo-lu pai-lien chiao chung te wu-i" 清代四川棚民國嚕白蓮中的武藝 (Martial arts among Szechuan refugees and White Lotus sectarians during the Ch'ing dynasty). *Ssu-ch'uan t'i-yü shih-liao* 1 (1987): 49–52.

Hsi Yün-t'ai 習雲太. *Chung-kuo wu-shu shih* 中國武術史 (History of Chinese martial arts). Beijing: Jen-min t'i-yü ch'u-pan-she, 1985.

Hsia I-yü 夏詒鈺, ed. *Yung-nien hsien-chih* 永年縣志 (Yung-nien County gazeteer), n.p., 1877.

Hsiao Yü. "T'ai-chi ch'üan ch'i-yüan tao-ti tsai na?" 太極拳起源到底在哪 (Where is the real birthplace of t'ai-chi ch'üan?). *Chung-hua wu-shu* 5 (1989): 19.

Hsü Chen 徐震. *Kuo-chi lun-lueh* 國技論略 (Summary of the Chinese martial arts). Shanghai: Commercial Press, 1930. Reprinted as *Kuo-shu lun-lueh* 國術論略, edited by Sung Keng-hsin 宋更新. Taipei: Hua-lien ch'u-pan-she, 1975.

———. "T'ai-chi ch'üan k'ao-hsin lu" 太極拳考信錄 (A study of the

truth of research on t'ai-chi history). In *T'ai-chi ch'üan k'ao*, edited by Teng Shih-hai. Hong Kong: Tung-ya t'u-shu kung-ssu, 1980. First published 1936.

———. "T'ai-chi ch'üan p'u li-tung pien-wei ho-pien" 太極拳譜理董辨僞合編 (Studies on the t'ai-chi ch'üan classics and spurious classics). In *T'ai-chi ch'üan k'ao*, edited by Teng Shih-hai. Hong Kong: Tung-ya t'u-shu kung-ssu, 1980. First published 1935.

Hsü Chih-i 徐致一. *T'ai-chi ch'üan chien-shuo* 太極拳淺說 (Introduction to t'ai-chi ch'üan). Shanghai: T'ai-chi ch'üan yen-chiu-she, 1927.

Hsü K'o 徐珂, ed. *Ch'ing-pai lei-ch'ao* 清稗類鈔 (Unofficial documents from the Ch'ing dynasty). Shanghai: Commercial Press, 1917.

Hsü Lung-hou 許籠厚 (Yü-sheng 禹生). *T'ai-chi ch'üan shih t'u-chieh* 太極拳勢圖解 (Introduction to t'ai-chi ch'üan). Taipei: Hua-lien ch'u-pan-she, 1982. First published 1921.

Hsü Shih-ch'ang 徐世昌. *Ta-ch'ing chi-fu hsien-che chuan* 大清畿輔先哲傳 (Biographies of famous scholars in the Beijing area during the Ch'ing dynasty). In *Ch'ing-tai ch'uan-chi ts'ung-k'an* 清代傳記叢刊 vol. 201, 78–80. Taipei: Ming-wen shu-chü, 1985.

———. *Ta-ch'ing chi-fu shu-cheng* 大清畿輔書徵 (Biographies from the Beijing area during the Ch'ing dynasty). Taipei: Kuang-wen shu-chü, n.d. Reprint, Preface 1969.

Hsü Yu-ken 許友根. "Wu-k'o k'ao-shih chung te i-wen ch'ü-shih" 武科考試中的軼聞趣事 (Some anecdotes from the old military examination system). *Chung-hua wu-shu* 1 (1994): 22–23.

Hsüeh Nai-yin 薛乃印. "Wu-shih t'ai-chi chien-wen ch'ien-lu" 武式太極見聞淺錄 (An account of Wu [Yü-hsiang]-style t'ai-chi ch'üan). *Wu-shu chien-shen* 2 (1993): 44. Also *Wu-lin* 3 (1993): 44.

Hu Chin-shan 胡金山. "Hao-men san-shih" 郝門三世 (Three generations of Hao stylists). *Wu-shu chien-shen* 6 (1992): 11–12.

Hu Feng-ming 胡風鳴. "Hao Wei-chen miao-hui fu mang-han" 郝爲眞廟會伏莽漢 (Hao Wei-chen humbles a ruffian at the temple fair). *Wu-shu chien-shen* 3 (1994): 55.

Hu, William C. C. "Ch'en Chung-sheng and the Problem of Sources." *Journal of the Chen Style Taijiquan Research Association of Hawaii* 1, no. 3 (June 1993): 7–12; no. 4 (August 1993): 4–16.

———. "Ch'en-shih chia-p'u: Translated with Commentaries." *Journal of the Chen Style Taijiquan Research Association of Hawaii* 1, no. 3 (June 1993): 1–6.

———. "The Origin of T'ai-chi ch'üan." *Black Belt* (September–October 1964): 20–23.

Huang Chao-han 黃兆漢. "Chang San-feng ch'ung-pai k'ao" 張三豐

崇拜考 (A Study of the Cult of Chang San-feng). *Wu-tang* 6 (1992): 17–19. Translation of a 1979 article that appeared in *Far Eastern Studies* 17: 1–2.

———. *Ming-tai tao-shih Chang San-feng k'ao* 明代道士長三豐考 (A study of the Ming dynasty Taoist, Chang San-feng). Taipei: Hsüeh-sheng shu-chü, 1989.

———. *Tao-chiao yen-chiu lun-wen chi* 道教研究論文集 (Studies of Taoism). Hong Kong: Chung-wen ta-hsüeh ch'u-pan-she, 1988.

Huang, Philip. *The Peasant Economy and Social Change in North China*. Stanford: Stanford University Press, 1985.

Huang Tso-chang 黃作章. "Li-ta wu-k'o ts'ung-t'an" 歷代武科叢談 (A discussion of the imperial military examination system). *Wu-lin* 2 (1994): 4–6.

Huang Tsung-hsi 黃宗羲. Nan-lei chi 南雷集 (Collected works of Huang Tsung-hsi). Shanghai: n.p., n.d. Photo reprint of edition preface dated 1680.

Hucker, Charles. *Dictionary of Official Titles in Imperial China*. Stanford: Stanford University Press, 1985.

Hummel, Arthur. *Eminent Chinese of the Ch'ing Period*. Washington, D.C.: U.S. Government Printing Office, 1943.

Johnson, D. H. *Body, Spirit, and Democracy*. Berkeley, Calif.: North Atlantic Books, 1994.

Johnson, David. "Communication, Class and Consciousness in Late Imperial China." In *Popular Culture in Late Imperial China*, edited by David Johnson, et al., 34–72. Berkeley: University of California Press, 1985.

Johnson, David, Andrew Nathan, and Evelyn Rawski, eds. *Popular Culture in Late Imperial China*. Berkeley: University of California Press, 1985.

Ju Jen 儒人. "Yang Pan-hou ch'uan t'ai-chi ch'üan chüeh" 楊班侯傳太極拳訣 (Yang Pan-hou's secret transmissions on t'ai-chi ch'üan). *T'i-yü wen-shih* 6 (1990): 39.

K'ang Ke-wu 康戈武. "T'an-so ch'üan-chung yüan-liu te fang-fa" 探索拳種源流的方法 (Methods in tracing the origins of martial arts styles). *Chung-hua wu-shu* 1 (1983): 43–44.

Kao Kuang-hsi 高廣西. "Ch'ien-t'an wu-shu ch'üan-yen te ssu-hsiang hsing ho k'o-hsüeh hsing" 淺談武術拳諺的思想性和科學性 (A brief discussion of the intellectual and scientific nature of martial arts aphorisms). *Shan-hsi t'i-yü k'o-chi* 3 (1986): 45–47.

———. "Wu-shu ch'üan-yen te i-shu hsing" 武術拳諺的藝術性 (The

artistic nature of martial arts aphorisms). *Shan-hsi t'i-yü k'o-chi* 4 (1986): 12–16.

Kasulis, Thomas, et al., eds. *Self As Body in Asian Theory and Practice*. Albany: State University of New York Press, 1993.

Kierman, Frank A. "Phases and Modes of Combat in China." In *Chinese Ways in Warfare*, edited by Frank Kierman and John Fairbank, 27–66. Cambrudge: Harvard University Press, 1973.

Kierman, Frank A., and John Fairbank, eds. *Chinese Ways in Warfare*. Cambridge: Harvard University Press, 1973.

Kilmer, Scott. "Sport As Ritual: A Theoretical Approach." In *The Anthropological Study of Play*, edited by David Lancy and B. Allan Tindall, 32–37. Cornwall, N.Y.: Leisure Press, 1976.

Knecht, Ted. "A New Look at Several Yang Style Postures." *T'ai Chi* 2 (1994): 22–24.

Kolatch, D. J. *Sports, Politics, and Ideology in China*. New York: Jonathan David, 1972.

Kraus, Richard. *Brushes with Power*. Berkeley: University of California Press, 1991.

Ku Liu-hsin 顧留馨. *P'ao-ch'ui: Ch'en-shih t'ai-chi ch'üan ti erh lu* 炮捶 陳式太極拳弟二路 (Cannon-hammer: Ch'en-style t'ai-chi ch'üan second form). Hong Kong: Hai-feng ch'u-pan-she, 1983.

———. *T'ai-chi ch'üan shu* 太極拳術 (The art of t'ai-chi ch'üan). Shanghai: Shang-hai chiao-yü ch'u-pan-she, 1982.

Ku Yüan-kuang 顧元光. "Kuo-shu t'an-yüan" 國術探源 (An investigation of the origins of Chinese martial arts). *Kuo-shu chou-k'an* 113 (1934): 3.

Kuhn, Philip. *Rebellion and Its Enemies in Late Imperial China: Militarization and Social Structure, 1796–1864*. Cambridge: Harvard University Press, 1970.

Kung K'o 龔克. "Wang Tsung-yüeh shih 't'ai-chi ch'üan p'u' te tso-che ma" 王宗岳是太極拳譜的作者嗎 (Is Wang Tsung-yüeh actually the author of the t'ai-chi classics?). *Chung-hua wu-shu* 12 (1992): 14.

Kuo Lien-yin 郭連蔭. *T'ai-chi ch'üan p'u* 太極拳譜 (The t'ai-chi ch'üan classics). Taipei: Kuang-hsin shu-chü, 1962.

Kuo-shu chou-k'an editors. "Kou-shu wen-hsien chi-ch'eng" 國術文獻 集成 (Historical documents for Chinese martial arts). *Kuo-shu chou-k'an* (1933): 95–102.

Larson, Gerald. "The Concept of Body in Ayurveda and the Hindu Philosophical Systems." In *Self As Body in Asian Theory and Practice*, edited by Thomas Kasulis et al., 103–21. Albany: State University of New York Press, 1993.

Lei Hai-tsung (1933)雷海宗. *Chung-kuo wen-hua yü Chung-kuo te ping* 中國文化與中國的兵 (Chinese culture and the Chinese military). Changsha: 1940.

Lei Hsiao-t'ien 雷曉天. "Chang San-feng, Wu-tang, t'ai-chi ch'üan" 張三豐武當太極拳 (Chang San-feng, Wu-tang, t'ai-chi ch'üan). In *T'ai-chi ch'üan yen-chiu chuan-chi* 26 (1969).

Lewis, Mark Edward. *Sanctioned Violence in Early China*. Albany: State University of New York Press, 1993.

Li Ching-wei 李晶偉. "Chou-i yü t'ai-chi ch'üan: T'ai-chi ch'üan yüan-li t'an-chen" 周易與太極拳太極拳原理探眞 (The *I Ching* and t'ai-chi ch'üan: A search for the philosophical principles of t'ai-chi ch'üan*)*. *Chung-hua wu-shu* 10 (1986): 12–13.

Li Ch'ang-yüan 李長源. "T'ai-chi k'ai-ho yü-han chi-chi miao-tao" 太極開合寓含技擊妙道 (The principle of opening and closing in t'ai-chi ch'üan contains the marvelous techniques of self-defense). *Wu-shu chien-shen* 2 (1994): 32–33.

Li Chien-fang 李劍方. "Wu-shih ch'uan-jen t'ai-chi ming-chia: Chi t'ai-chi ming-chia Yao Chi-tsu hsien-sheng" 武式傳人太極名家記太極名家姚繼祖先生 (A famous Wu-style t'ai-chi master: Remembering Master Yao Chi-tsu). *Wu-lin* 5 (1990): 27.

Li I-yü 李亦畬. "Ku-pen t'ai-chi ch'üan mi-ch'uan ko-chüeh" 古本太極拳秘傳歌訣 (Secret ancient transmissions on t'ai-chi ch'üan), edited by Chang Yao-chung 張耀忠. *Wu-hun* 5 (1989): 39–40.

Li Jung-nan 李榮南. "Tui 'Ssu-liang po ch'ien-chin' i-wen te ch'ien-i" 對四兩撥千斤一文的淺義 (A discussion of the article "With four ounces deflect a thousand pounds"). *Chung-hua wu-shu* 6 (1986): 16–17.

Li Pin 李賓. "Kuan-yü Ch'en Wang-t'ing yü Chiang Fa hua-hsiang te p'i-p'an" 關於陳王廷與蔣發畫像的批判 (Some critical thoughts on the painting of Ch'en Wang-t'ing and Chiang Fa). *Wu-tang* 5 (1990): 46–48.

Li Shang-ying 李尚英. "Pa-kua chiao te yüan-yüan, ting-ming chi-ch'i yü t'ien-li chiao te kuan-hsi" 八卦教的淵源定名及其與天理教的關系 (The origins and name of the Eight Trigrams Sect and its relation to the Heavenly Principles Sect). *Ch'ing-shih yen-chiu* 1 (1992): 50–55.

Li Shih-wei 李士偉, ed. *Yung-nien Li-shih chih-p'u* 永年李氏支譜 (Geneology of the Yung-nien branch of the Li family). n.p., 1921.

Li Yao-ch'en 李堯臣. "Piao-chü ch'un-ch'iu" 鏢局春秋 (The story of

China's former bodyguard associations). *Wu-hun* 3 (1994): 44–45; 4 (1994): 44–45; 5 (1994): 40–42.

Liang Ch'i-ch'ao 梁啓超. Chung-kuo chih wu-shih tao 中國之武士道 (The martial spirit in China). In *Yin-ping-shih ts'ung-shu*, vol. 7. Shanghai: Commercial Press, 1916.

Lin Ch'uan-chia 林傳甲. *Ta chung-hua chih-li sheng ti-li chih* 大中華直隸省地理志 (Geography of Chili Province). Beijing: Wu-hsüeh shu-kuan, 1920.

Ling Yüeh-hua 凌躍華. "Ch'ing-tai chiang-nan wu-chü yü Fu-yang wu-hsüeh" 清代江南武舉與富陽武學 (The military examination system and the Fu-yang Military Academy during the Ch'ing dynasty). *Wu-hun* 4 (1985): 25–26.

Lipman, Jonathan, and Stevan Harrell, eds. *Violence in China: Essays in Culture and Counterculture*. Albany: State University of New York Press, 1990.

Liu Ch'ang-lin 劉長林. "Chung-kuo ku-tai yin-yang shuo" 中國古代陰陽說 (The ancient Chinese theory of *yin* and *yang*). *Wu-hun* 4 (1987): 20–21.

Liu Chün-hsiang 劉峻驤. "Chung-hua min-tsu tu-t'e te jen-t'i wen-hua" 中國民族獨特的人體文化 (The unique physical culture of the Chinese people). *T'i-yü wen-shih* 1 (1986): 42–51.

Liu Hsiang-yang 劉向陽. "T'ai-chi ch'üan p'u yü hsiu-shen yang-hsing" 太極拳譜與修身養性 (The t'ai-chi ch'üan classics and Chinese health practices). *Wu-lin* 8 (1985): 3.

Liu Hui-chih 劉會峙, et al. "T'ai-chi ch'üan yüan-liu hsin-t'an" 太極拳源流新談 (A reexamination of the origins of t'ai-chi ch'üan). *Wu-tang* 3 (1992): 30–33.

Liu, K. C. "The Ch'ing Restoration." In *The Cambridge History of China*, edited by D. Twitchett and J. K. Fairbank, vol. 10, 409–90. London: Cambridge University Press.

Liu Kuo-chün 劉國鈞. "Ho-t'u Lo-shu yin-yang t'u yü nei-chia ch'üan" 河圖洛書陰陽圖與內家拳 (The relationship between the Yellow River Chart, Lo River Book, yin-yang symbol and the internal martial arts). *Wu-lin* 3 (1985): 5–6.

Liu Tien-chüeh (D.C. Lau) 劉殿爵. *Ping-shu ssu-chung chu-tzu suo-yin* 兵書四種逐字所引 (A concordance to the four military classics). Taipei: Commercial Press, 1992.

Liu Yü 劉宇. "'Han-hsiung pa-bei' yeh shih 'han-hsiung t'a-yao'" 含胸拔背也是含胸塌腰 ("Relax the chest and raise the back" is also "Relax the chest and release the waist). *Wu-lin* 12 (1988): 6–7.

Lu Chao-ming 陸兆明. "Wu-shu chung te yin-yang wu-hsing hsüeh-shuo" 武術中的陰陽五行學說 (Yin/yang and Five Phases theory in martial arts). *Chung-hua wu-shu* 4 (1987): 5–6.

Lu Ch'ung-shan 盧崇善. "Lun 'ye meng Yüan-ti shou-i ch'üan-fa'" 論夜夢元帝授以拳法 (A discussion of the phrase, "At night he (Chang San-feng) dreamt that the God of War taught him the art of pugilism"). *T'ai-chi ch'üan yen-chiu chuan-chi* 29 (1969): 28–29.

Lu Ta-chieh 陸達節. *Li-tai ping-shu mu-lu* 歷代兵書目錄 (Catalogue of works on military affairs for each dynasty). Taipei: n.p., 1969. Reprint. Originally published Shanghai: n.p., 1932.

Lu Ti-min 路迪民. "Yang Pan-hou t'ai-chi ch'üan chia hsi-lieh chi ch'i ch'uan-jen Chia Chih-hsiang" 楊班侯太極拳架系列及其傳人賈治祥 (Yang Pan-hou's various t'ai-chi forms and lineage successor Chia Chih-hsiang). *Wu-tang* 2 (1994): 20–23.

Ma Hung 馬虹. "T'ai-chi, t'ai-chi t'u, t'ai-chi ch'üan: chien-lun tao-chia ssu-hsiang tui t'ai-chi ch'üan te ying-hsiang" 太極太極圖太極拳兼論道家思想對太極拳的影響 (T'ai-chi, the t'ai-chi symbol, and t'ai-chi ch'üan, including the influence of Taoism on t'ai-chi ch'üan). *Wu-lin* 2 (1991): 20–22.

Ma Ming-ta 馬明達. "Ch'ing-tai te wu-chü chih-tu" 清代的武舉制度 (The military examination system during the Ch'ing period). *Chung-hua wu-shu* 5 (1986): 18–19.

Ma Yüan-nien 馬原年. "Shih-hsi 'shuang-chung'" 試析雙重 (An analysis of "double-weightedness"). *Wu-shu chien-shen* 3 (1991): 10–11.

Mai Chin-t'ung 麥進通. "Yang Pan-hou te 'chiu-chüeh' ho 'wu-yao'" 楊班侯的九訣和五要 (Yang Pan-hou's "Nine Secret Transmissions" and "Five Principles"). *Wu-lin* 119 (1991): 15.

Matsuda, Ryuchi 松田隆智. *Chung-kuo wu-shu shih-lüeh* 中國武術史略 (A brief history of Chinese martial arts). Chongqing: Ssu-ch'uan k'o-hsüeh chi-shu ch'u-pan-she, 1984.

Mccord, Edward. "Local Military Power and Elite Formation." In *Chinese Local Elites and Patterns of Dominance*, edited by Joseph Esherick and Mary Rankin. Berkeley: University of California Press, 1990.

Meng Nai-ch'ang 孟乃昌. "Chang San-feng k'ao" 張三豐考 (A study of Chang San-feng*). Wu-tang tsa-chih* [Special Tenth Anniversary Issue] (1991): 24–36.

——. "'T'ai-chi ch'ing-chung fu-ch'en' chu-shih" 太極經重浮沉注釋 (A commentary on the concept of "light, heavy, floating, and sinking"). *Chung-hua wu-shu* 2 (1987): 22–23.

——. "'Ta'i chi ch'üan lun' chiao-k'an chu-shih" 太極拳論校勘注

釋 (Commentary to the "Treatise on T'ai-chi ch'üan"). *Ch'i-kung* 2 (1984): 91–92; also *Wu-lin* 7 (1987): 40–41.

———. "'Ting pien tiu k'ang tui-tai wu-ping'" 頂匾丟抗對待無病 ("Butting, Insufficiency, Separation, and Resistance" and "Sparring Without Errors"). *Chung-hua wu-shu* 12 (1988): 14–15.

———. *T'ai-chi ch'üan p'u yü mi-p'u chiao-chu* 太極拳譜與秘譜校注 (The t'ai-chi ch'üan manuals and secret manuals with annotations). Hong Kong: Hai-feng ch'u-pan-she, 1993.

Meng Shih 夢時. "Ch'ing nin shen-chung shuo 'pu-hsing': Ts'ung 'Wang-shih t'ai-chi' shuo ch'i" 請您慎重說不行從王氏太極說起 (Please say sternly "This will not do": Reflections on "Wang-style t'ai-chi"). *Wu-hun* 5 (1994): 1.

Mo Ch'ao-mai 莫朝邁. "Ch'ing ch'ao wu-k'o shih-i" 清朝武科拾遺 (Anecdotes on the military examination system during the Ch'ing dynasty). *Wu-lin* 3 (1994): 56–57.

Morrison, Hedda. *A Photographer in Old Peking.* Hong Kong: Oxford University Press, 1985.

Miyazaki, Ichisada. *China's Examination Hell.* New Haven: Yale University Press, 1981.

Miura, Kunio. "The Revival of Qi: Qigong in Contemporary China." In *Taoist Meditation and Longevity Techniques,* edited by Livia Kohn, 331–62.

Myers, Ramon. *The Chinese Peasant Economy: Agricultural Development in Hopei and Shantung, 1890–1949.* Cambridge: Harvard University Press, 1970.

Naquin, Susan. *Shantung Rebellion: The Wang Lun Uprising of 1774.* New Haven: Yale University Press, 1981.

Naquin, Susan, and Evelyn Rawski. *Chinese Society in the Eighteenth Century.* New Haven: Yale University, 1987.

Neide, Joan. "Martial Arts and Japanese Nationalism." *Journal of Asian Martial Arts* 2 (1995): 35–41.

Nelson, Randy. *The Martial Arts: An Annotated Bibliography.* New York: Garland, 1988.

Pai Chao-jung 白昭榮. *Ch'üan-ching* 拳經 (Martial arts classics). Chifeng: Nei-meng-ku k'e-hsüeh chi-shu ch'u-pan-she, 1982.

Pai Yün-feng 白雲峰 and Liu Shih-chün 劉世君. "'Ching-shen neng t'i te ch'i' yü 'ch'i ch'en tan-t'ien'" 精神能提得起與氣沉丹田 ("Raising the spirit" and "sinking the *ch'i* to the *tan-t'ien*"). *Wu-shu chien-shen* 5 (1991): 11.

P'an Feng 潘鋒. "Wu-shu kai-nien chieh-kou mo-shih ch'u-t'an" 武術

概念結構模式初探 (A preliminary discussion of the structural model of martial arts concepts). *Chung-hua wu-shu* 6 (1986): 25.

P'an Tso-min 潘作民. *T'ai-chi ch'üan lun ch'an-wei* 太極拳論闡微 (A study of the t'ai-chi ch'üan classics). Taipei: Chung-hua wu-shu ch'u-pan-she, 1974.

Pang, T. Y. *On T'ai-chi Ch'üan.* Bellingham, Washington: Azalea Press, 1987.

P'ang Ta-ming 龐大明. "Yung-nien t'ai-ho t'ang yü t'ai-chi ch'üan" 永年太和堂與太極拳 (Yung-nien's T'ai-ho t'ang's Pharmacy and t'ai-chi ch'üan). *Shao-lin yü t'ai-chi* 6 (1994): 15–16.

Perry, Elizabeth. *Rebels and Revolutionaries in North China, 1845–1945.* Stanford, Calif.: Stanford University Press, 1980.

Pien Jen-chieh 卞人真. *Kuo-chi kai-lun* 國技概論 (Outline of the Chinese martial arts). Shanghai: Cheng-chung shu-chü, 1947; Taipei: Chen-shan-mei ch'u-pan-she, 1971; Taipei: Hua-lien ch'u-pan-she, 1972. Orginally published 1936.

Po Ch'i 伯奇. "Ch'ing-tai huang-ti te wu-kung" 清代皇帝的武功 (The Ch'ing dynasty emperor's practice of the martial arts). *Chung-hua wu-shu* 4 (1985): 15.

Polachek, James. *The Inner Opium War.* Cambridge: Harvard University, Council on Asian Studies, 1992.

Pomeranz, Kenneth. *The Making of a Hinterland: State, Society, and Economy in Inland North China, 1853–1937.* Berkeley: University of California Press, 1993.

Price, Maurice T. "Differentiating Myth, Legend and History in Ancient Chinese Culture." *American Anthropologist,* 48 (1946): 31–42.

Rankin, Mary. *Elite Activism and Political Transformation in China.* Stanford, Calif.: Stanford University, 1986.

Rawski, Evelyn. "Economic and Social Foundations of Late Imperial Culture." In *Popular Culture in Late Imperial China,* edited by David Johnson et al., 3–33. Berkeley: University of California Press, 1985.

Sawyer, Ralph. *The Seven Military Classics of Ancient China.* Boulder, Colo.: Westview Press, 1993.

Seidel, Anna. "A Taoist Immortal of the Ming Dynasty: Chang San-feng". In *Self and Society in Ming Thought,* edited by W. Theodore de Bary. New York: Columbia University Press, 1970.

Shaner, D. E. *The Bodymind Experience in Japanese Buddhism.* Albany: State University of New York Press, 1985.

Shang-hai ta-sheng shu-chü 上海大聲書局, ed. *Ch'üan-ching* 拳經 (Martial arts classics). Tianjin: Ku-chi shu-chü, 1987. Originally published 1918.

Shen Chia-chen 沈家楨. "T'ai-chi ch'üan shu-yü" 太極拳術語 (T'ai-chi ch'üan terminology). *Wu-lin ching-ts'ui* 1 (1984): 59.

Shen Shou 沈壽. *T'ai-chi ch'üan fa yen-chiu* 太極拳法研究 (Studies on t'ai-chi ch'üan). Fuzhou: Fu-chien jen-min ch'u-pan-she, 1984.

———. "T'ai-chi ch'üan 'shen-fa pa-yao' ch'ien-shih" 太極拳身法八要淺釋 (Some notes on t'ai-chi ch'üan's "eight body techniques"). *Chung-hua wu-shu* 4 (1987), 19–20.

———, ed. *T'ai-chi ch'üan p'u* 太極拳譜 (T'ai-chi ch'üan clasics). Beijing: Jen-min t'i-yü ch'u-pan-she, 1991.

———. "Wang Tsung-yüeh 'T'ai-chi ch'üan lun' ch'ien-shih" 王宗岳太極拳論淺釋 (Brief commentary to Wang Tsung-yüeh's "Treatise on Tai-chi ch'üan"). *Chung-chou wu-shu* 1/2 (1984): 7, 10.

———. "Wu Yü-hsiang 'Ssu-tzu mi chüeh' ch'ien-chieh" 武禹襄四字秘訣淺解 (Annotations to Wu Yü-hsiang's "Four-Character Secret Transmission"). *Wu-shu chien-shen* 3 (1994): 15–16.

Shih Tiao-mei 施調梅. *T'ai-chi ch'üan p'u nei-wei kung yen-chi lu* 太極拳譜内外功研幾錄 (A study of the internal and external practices in the t'ai-chi classics). Taipei: n.p., 1958.

Shu Chih 述之. "T'an-t'an t'ai-chi ch'üan te k'ai-ho" 談談太極拳的開合 (A discussion of opening and closing in t'ai-chi ch'üan). *Shao-lin wu-shu* 4 (1988): 17–18.

Staal, Frits. "Indian Bodies." In *Self As Body In Asian Theory and Practice*, edited by Thomas Kasulis, et al., 59–102. Albany: State University of New York Press, 1993.

Struve, Lynn. *Voices from the Ming-Qing Cataclysm.* New Haven: Yale University Press, 1993.

Su Ching-ts'un 蘇兢存. "Hsin-hai ke-ming ch'ien-hou te chün kuo-min chiao-yü te t'i-yü ssu-hsiang" 辛亥革命前後的軍國民教育的體育思想 (Thought on physical culture in military and civilian education immediately before and after the Republican Revolution of 1911). *T'i-yü wen-shih* 4 (1988): 19–22.

Su Hsiao ch'ing 蘇肖晴. "K'ang Yu-wei te t'i-yü ssu-hsiang chi ch'i ch'eng-yin" 康有爲的體育思想及其成因 (K'ang Yu-wei's views on physical culture). *T'i-yü wen-shih* 1 (1988): 49–52.

Su T'ung-feng 蘇桐鳳. "T'ai-chi ch'üan yüan-liu shu-yao" 太極拳源流述要 (Sketch of the origins of t'ai-chi ch'üan). In *Chung-kuo wu-shu shih-liao chi-k'an*, vol. 2. Taipei: Chiao-yü pu t'i-yü ssu, 1976.

Su Yün 蘇耘. "Wu-shih t'ai-chi lien-huan ch'ui" 武式太極連環捶 (Wu-style five punches sparring set). *Ching-wu* 3 (1989): 58–62.

Sun Fu-ch'üan (Lu-t'ang) 孫福全 (祿堂). *T'ai-chi ch'üan hsüeh* 太極

拳學 (The study of t'ai-chi ch'üan). Taipei: Chung-hua wu-shu ch'u-pan-she, 1973. Reprint. Author's preface 1919, first published 1924. Also Hong Kong: Wu-shu chu-p'an-she, n.d.

Sun Pao-yin 孫豹隱. "Wen-wu ch'üeh-i ch'i tao hu" 文武缺一豈道乎 (If the intellectual and martial are not combined, the *tao* is not complete). *Wu-shu chien-shen* 1 (1994): 49.

Sutton, Nigel. "Gongfu, Guoshu, and Wushu: State Appropriation of the Martial Arts in Modern China." *Journal of Asian Martial Arts* 3 (1993): 102–14.

Ta Tso-ken 答作根. "Shih 'hsiang-t'ui' hai-shih 'hsiang-t'ui'" 是詳推還是想推 (Are the two words in the t'ai-chi classics *hsiang-t'ui* or *hsiang-t'ui?*). *Wu-shu chien-shen* 6 (1992): 13.

Tanaka, Steven. "Imaging History: Inscribing Belief in the Nation." *Journal of Asian Studies* 1 (1994): 24–44.

T'ang Hao 唐豪. "Ch'ing-tai ya-p'o hsia te wu-shih chi-ch'i chu-tso" 清代壓迫下的武士及其著作 (Marital artists and their writings during the period of Manchu repression). *Kuo-shu chou-k'an* 161–69 (1936).

———. *Hsing-chien chai sui-pi* 行健齋隨筆 (Miscellaneous writings from the Hsing-chien Studio). Shanghai: Shanghai-shih kuo-shu kuan, 1937.

———. *Shen-chou wu-i* 神洲武藝 (China's martial arts). Kirin: Chi-lin wen-shih ch'u-pan-she, 1986 (Pp. 1–50 same as T'ang Hao, *Hsing-chien chai sui-pi*).

———. "T'ai-chi ch'üan ken-yüan" 太極拳根源 (The origins of t'ai-chi ch'üan), 1935. In *T'ai-chi ch'üan k'ao*, edited by Teng Shih-hai. Hong Kong: Tung-ya t'u-shu kung-ssu, 1980.

———. "Wang Tsung-yüeh k'ao 王宗岳考 (A study of Wang Tsung-yüeh), n.d. In *T'ai-chi ch'üan k'ao*, edited by Teng Shih-hai. Hong Kong: Tung-ya t'u-shu kung-ssu, 1980.

———. *Wang Tsung-yüeh t'ai-chi ch'üan ching yen-chiu* 王宗岳太極拳經研究 (Studies on Wang Tsung-yüeh's t'ai-chi ch'üan classics). Hong Kong: Ch'i-lin t'u-shu kung-ssu, 1969. Reprint. Originally published 1935.

T'ang Hao 唐豪 and Ku Liu-hsin 顧留馨. *T'ai-chi ch'üan yen-chiu* 太極拳研究 (Studies on t'ai-chi ch'üan). Hong Kong: Pai-ling ch'u-pan-she, 1963.

Teng Shih-hai 鄧時海, ed. *T'ai-chi ch'üan k'ao* 太極拳考 (Studies on t'ai-chi ch'üan). Hong Kong: Tung-ya t'u-shu kung-ssu, 1980.

Teng Ssu-yü. *The Nien Army and Their Guerrilla Warfare, 1851–1868*. Paris: Mouton, 1961.

Tou Hung-chi 竇洪基. "Shih-t'an t'ai-chi pa-fa" 試談太極八法 (A discussion of t'ai-chi's eight techniques). *Ching-wu* 4 (1988): 12–14.

Tseng Chao-jan 曾昭然. *T'ai-chi ch'üan ch'üan-shu* 太極拳全書 (The complete book of t'ai-chi ch'üan). Hong Kong: Yu-lien ch'u-pan-she, 1960.

T'u P'eng-nien 屠彭年. "Wu-shih t'ai-chi ch'üan shih i-hsiang chou-shen p'ing-heng te yün-tung" 武式太極拳是一項周身平衡的運動 (Wu Yü-hsiang-style t'ai-chi ch'üan is an exercise emphasizing whole body balance). *Wu-lin* 12 (1992): 35.

Tu Yüan-hua 杜元化. *T'ai-chi ch'üan cheng-tsung* 太極拳正宗 (Orthodox t'ai-chi ch'üan). K'ai-feng: n.p., 1935.

Tung Ying-chieh 董英傑. *T'ai-chi ch'üan shih-i* 太極拳釋義 (Principles of t'ai-chi ch'üan). Hong Kong: Chung-hua shu-chü, 1975. First published 1948.

Turner, Bryan. *The Body and Society*. Oxford: Basil Blackwell, 1984.

Wan I et al., comps. *Daily Life in the Forbidden City: The Qing Dynasty, 1644–1912*. Translated by Rosemary Scott and Erica Shipley. New York: Viking Press, 1988.

Wan Lai-p'ing 萬籟平. "Wu-tang t'ai-chi ch'üan yü ch'i-kung" 武當太極拳與氣功 (Wu-tang t'ai-chi ch'üan and *ch'i-kung*). *Wu-tang* 2 (1994): 7–8.

Wang Ch'ing-san 王慶三. "T'a-chi ch'üan te 'hsü-ling ting-chin" 太極拳的虛領頂勁 (The phrase "open the energy at the crown of the head" in t'ai-chi ch'üan). *Shao-lin wu-shu* 2 (1988): 19–20.

Wang Ch'uan-hao 王傳好. "Shih 'Shih-san shih hsing-kung ke-chüeh'" 釋十三勢行功歌訣 (Commentary to the "Song of the Practice of the Thirteen Postures"). *Wu-shu chien-shen* 5 (1990): 15–16.

Wang Chuang-fei 王壯飛. "Kuo-shu te yüan-liu" 國術的源流 (The origins of the Chinese martial arts). *Kuo-shu chou-k'an* 89 (1933): 2–3.

Wang Chung-han 王鍾翰, ed. *Ch'ing-shih lieh-chuan* 清史列傳 (Biographies from Ch'ing history). Peking: Chung-hua shu-chü, 1982.

Wang Chüeh-hsin 王玨鑫. "Kuo-shu li-shih chih ho-li t'an-chiu" 國術歷史之合理探求 (A rational approach to research in martial arts history). In *Chung-kuo wu-shu shih-liao chi-k'an*, vol. 3, 1–8. Taipei: Chiao-yü pu t'i-yü ssu, 1976.

Wan Hsin-nien 王新年. *T'ai-chi ch'üan fa ching-i* 太極拳法精義 (The essence of t'ai-chi ch'üan). Hong Kong: T'ai-p'ing shu-chü, 1962.

Wang Huai 王懷. "Tao-chiao yang-sheng-shu yü t'ai-chi ch'üan" 道教養生術與太極拳 (Taoist health practices and t'ai-chi ch'üan). *Wu-tang* 4 (1992): 23–24, 26.

Wang Jung-tse 王榮澤. "'Han-hsiung pa-pei' chih wo -chien" 含胸拔背之我見 (My view of "relax the chest and raise the back"). *Wu-shu chien-shen* 6 (1991): 16.

———. "'Hsi 'Yin-chin lo-k'ung ho chi ch'u'" 析引進落空合即出 (An analysis of the phrase "Draw the opponent in so that his energy lands on emptiness, unite, and issue energy"). *Wu-shu chien-shen* 3 (1992): 28.

———. "T'ai-chi ch'üan de 'po' yü 'fa'" 太極拳的撥與發 (T'ai-chi ch'üan "deflecting" and "issuing"). *Chung-hua wu-shu* 9 (1992): 5.

———. "'T'an 'k'e-k'e liu-hsin tsai yao-chien'" 談刻刻留心在腰間 (A discussion of the phrase "At all times pay attention to the waist"). *Wu-shu chien-shen* 2 (1992): 24.

———. "'Hsien ch'iu k'ai-chan, hou ch'iu chin-tsou' shih-i" 先求開展後求緊湊釋疑 (An explanation of the phrase, "First seek expansiveness and later seek compactness"). *Chung-hua wu-shu* 4 (1992): 46.

Wang K'ui-p'u 王魁溥. "'Ju-chia kung-li ch'ien-t'an" 儒家功理淺談 (Brief discussion of the principles of Confucian *ch'i-kung*). *Wu-hun* 1 (1994): 33.

Wang Shou-jen 王守仁. *Wang Yang-ming ch'üan-chi* 王陽明全集 (The complete works of Wang shou-jen). Shanghai: Sao-ye shan-fang, 1935.

Wang Te-ying 王德瑛, ed. *Wu-yang hsien-chih* 舞陽縣志 (Wu-yang County gazetteer). n.p. 1835.

Wang T'ieh-chih 王鐵志. "Hao Shao-ju t'an ch'üan shih-lu" 郝少如談拳實錄 (Hao Shao-ju's teachings on t'ai-chi ch'üan). *Wu-shu chien-shen* 2 (1992): 26.

Wang, Y. Q. *Yang-shih t'ai-chi ch'üan shu-chen* 楊式太極拳述眞 (Authentic Yang-style t'ai-chi ch'üan). Beijing: Jen-min t'i-yü ch'u-pan-she, 1990.

Wang Yung-ch'üan 汪永泉. "Jou-shou ching-i" 揉手精義 (The essentials of "rubbing-hands"). *Chung-hua wu-shu* 7 (1988): 17–18.

Wei Ch'ün-chieh 韋群傑. "T'ai-chi pa-fa te chin-li yü yung-fa" 太極八法的勁力與用法 (The power and application of t'ai-chi's eight techniques). *Chung-hua wu-shu* 5 (1987): 22–23.

Wei Ju-lin 魏汝霖 and Liu Chung-p'ing 劉仲平. *Chung-kuo chün-shih ssu-hsiang shih* 中國軍事思想史 (A history of Chinese military thought). Taipei: Li-ming wen-hua shih-yeh ku-fen yu-hsien kung-ssu, 1968.

Wen Tao 溫道, trans. "Wu-chi Liao-chai chih-i hsuan-i" 武技聊齋志

異 (Selections from the "Martial Exploits" chapter of [P'u Sung-ling's] *Strange Stories from a Chinese Studio*). *Chung-hua wu-shu* 4 (1992): 31.

Weng Wen-pin 翁文斌. "'Ssu tzu mi-chüeh' ch'ien shih" 四字秘訣淺釋 (Commentary to the "Four Character Secret Transmission"). *Wu-tang* 4 (1988): 7.

Wile, Douglas. *Cheng Man-ch'ing's Advanced T'ai-chi Form Instructions with Writings on Meditation, I ching, Medicine, and the Arts*. New York: Sweet Ch'i Press, 1985.

———. *T'ai-chi Touchstones: Yang Family Secret Transmissions*. New York: Sweet Ch'i Press, 1983. Revised ed. 1993.

———. *Art of the Bedchamber: The Chinese Sexual Yoga Classics, Including Women's Solo Meditation Texts*. Albany, New York: State University of New York Press, 1992.

Wile, Douglas, trans. *Master Cheng's Thirteen Chapters on T'ai-chi Ch'üan*. New York: Sweet Ch'i Press, 1982. Revised ed. 1983.

Wong, James I. *A Source Book in the Chinese Martial Arts*. Stockton, Calif.: Koinonia, 1978.

Wu Ch'eng-ch'ing 武澄清. "Wu-shih t'ai-chi ch'üan chiu-p'u i-wen ssu-p'ien" 武式太極拳舊譜佚文四篇 (Four lost Wu-style t'ai-chi texts), edited by Wu Wen-han 吳文翰. *Wu-tang* 1 (1993): 9, 45.

Wu Chien 武劍. "T'ai-chi i-ts'u tsui-tsao chien-yü I-ching ma?" 太極一詞最早見于易經嗎 (Does the term *t'ai-chi* first appear in the *I ching*?). *Wu-lin* 65 (1987): 13.

Wu Chih-ch'ing 吳志青. *Kuo-shu li-lun kai-yao* 國術理論概要 (Summary of Chinese martial arts theory), 1930. In *Kuo-min ts'ung-shu* 國民叢書 (National Library), series 1, vol. 50, 1989.

———. *T'ai-chi cheng-tsung* 太極正宗 (Orthodox t'ai-chi). Hong Kong: Chin-hua ch'u-pan-she, n.d.

Wu Chiu-lung 吳九龍 et al. *Sun tzu chiao-shih* 孫子校釋 (Commentaries on the *Sun tzu*). Beijing: Chün-shih k'o-hsüeh chu-pan-she, 1990.

Wu Chung-yen 吳中彥, ed. *Kuang-p'ing fu-chih* 廣平府志 (Kuang-p'ing Prefecture gazetteer), n.p., 1893.

Wu Ju-ch'ing 武汝清. "T'ai-chi ch'üan i-wen" 太極拳佚文 (Lost texts on t'ai-chi ch'üan), edited by Meng Cheng-yüan 孟正源. *Shao-lin wu-shu* 2 (1986): 33.

Wu Kung-tsao 吳公藻. *T'ai-chi ch'üan chiang-i* 太極拳講義 (Principles of t'ai-chi ch'üan). Shanghai: Shang-hai shu-tien, 1985. First published 1935.

Wu Meng-hsia 吳孟俠. *T'ai-chi ch'üan chiu chüeh chu-chieh* 太極拳九
訣註解 (Nine secret transmissions on t'ai-chi ch'üan with annotations). Hong Kong: T'ai-p'ing shu-chü, 1975.

Wu T'u-nan 吳圖南. *K'o-hsüeh hua te kuo-shu t'ai-chi ch'üan* 科學化的
國術太極拳 (Tai-chi ch'üan: A scientific martial art). Shanghai:
Commercial Press, 1934.

———. *T'ai-chi ch'üan* 太極拳 (T'ai-chi ch'üan). Hong Kong: Hsiang-
kang chin-hua ch'u-pan-she, n.d. Preface dated 1928.

———. *T'ai-chi ch'üan chih yen-chiu* 太極拳之研究 (A study on t'ai-
chi ch'üan). Hong Kong: Shang-wu yin-shu kuan, 1984.

Wu Wen-han 吳文翰. "Chin pai nien t'ai-chi ch'üan te fa-chan ho liu-
p'ai te hsing-ch'eng" 近百年太極拳的發展和流派的形
成 (The development of t'ai-chi ch'üan and the formation of the
styles during the past century). *Wu-tang* 2 (1989): 35–38.

———. "Ch'ing-tai te wu-ch'ang k'ao-shih" 清代的武場考試 (The
military examination system during the Ch'ing period). *Wu-shu
chien-shen* 5 (1990): 51–53.

———. "Hao Wei-chen chih-ch'eng te chen-ch'uan" 郝爲眞志誠得
眞傳 (Hao wei-chen was a dedicated student and received the
true transmission). *Wu-hun* 1 (1987): 4.

———. "T'ai-chi ch'üan hsiang Yung-nien hsing" 太極拳鄉永年行
(A trip to the land of t'ai-chi ch'üan, Yung-nien). *Wu-shu chien-
shen* 6 (1991): 4–6.

———. "Wu-shih t'ai-chi chiao-fa shu-yao" 武式太極教法述要 (Outline of teaching methods in Wu Yü-hsiang-style t'ai-chi ch'üan).
Wu-lin 6 (1989): 34–36.

———. "Wu-shih t'ai-chi ch'üan chih t'e-se" 武氏太極拳之特色
(The unique characteristics of Wu Yü-hsiang-style t'ai-chi ch'üan).
Shao-lin yü t'ai-chi 6 (1993): 40; 1 (1994): 43.

———. "Wu-shih t'ai-chi ch'üan te t'ui-shou" 武式太極拳的推手
(Wu style t'ai-chi ch'üan push-hands). *Shao-lin yü t'ai-chi* 5 (1994):
12–13.

[Wu] Wen-han 吳文翰. "Wu Yü-hsiang yen-hsiu t'ai-chi p'u" 武禹襄
研修太極譜 (Wu Yü-hsiang compiles the t'ai-chi classics.). *Wu-
shu chien-shen* 3 (1991): 52–53.

Yang Chen-chi 楊振基. *Yang Ch'eng-fu shih t'ai-chi ch'üan* 楊澄甫式太
極拳 (Yang Ch'eng-fu-style t'ai-chi ch'üan). Nan-ning kuang-
hsi min-tsu ch'u-pan-she, 1993.

Yang Ch'eng-fu 楊澄甫. *T'ai-chi ch'üan shih-yung fa* 太極拳使用法
(Self-defense applications of tai-chi ch'üan). Taipei: Chung-hua
wu-shu ch'u-pan-she, 1974. First published 1931.

————. *T'ai-chi ch'üan t'i-yung ch'üan-shu* 太極拳體用全書 (Complete principles and practice of t'ai-chi ch'üan). Taipei: Chunghua wu-shu ch'u-pan-she, 1975. First published 1934.

Yang Chih-ts'ai 楊志才. "'Ye meng Hsüan-ti shou chih ch'üan-fa' wo-chien" 夜夢玄帝授之拳法我見 (My view of the phrase "[Chang San-feng] received a martial art in a dream from the God of War"). *Wu-tang* 1 (1994): 15–16.

Yang Hung-lin 楊洪林. "Wu-tang su wu" 武當溯武 (Tracing the martial arts in the Wu-tang Mountains). *Wu-tang* 1 (1994): 13–15.

Yang Lien-chung, ed. *T'ai-chi ch'üan ch'uan-shuo* 太極拳傳說 (Legends concerning the history of t'ai-chi ch'üan). Wen County: Wen-hsien wen-hsüeh hsieh-hui, 1992.

Yang Ping-an 楊炳安. *Sun-tzu hui-chien* 孫子會箋 (Collected notes on the *Sun tzu*). Henan: Cheng-chou ku-chi, 1986.

Yang Shao-yü 楊紹虞. "Ch'uan-t'ung ch'üan-p'u ch'ü-ming shih-hsi" 傳統拳譜取名試析 (An analysis of terminology in traditional martial arts manuals). *Wu-lin* 2 (1993): 4.

Yen Han-hsiu 嚴翰秀. "Fang Yung-nien Wu-shih t'ai-chi ch'üan ch'uan-jen Li Chin-fan" 訪永年武式太極拳傳人李錦藩 (An interview with Yung-nien County Wu stylist, Li Chin-fan). *Wu-shu chien-shen* 2 (1992): 55.

————. "Yang Shou-chung erh-san shih" 楊守中二三事 (Some anecdotes concerning Yang Shou-chung). *Wu-shu chien-shen* 2 (1994): 54–55.

————. "'Yao-t'ui huan chin ying wan-tuan': Chi Wu-shih t'ai-chi ch'üan ch'uan-ren Yao Chi-tsu" 腰腿換勁應萬端記武式太極拳傳人姚繼祖 ("Shifting energy in the waist and legs, resond to ten thousand changes": Remembering Wu-style master, Yao Chi-tsu). *Wu-shu chien-shen* 5 (1991): 6–9.

Yü Chien-hua 于建華. "T'ai-chi ch'üan li-lun te che-hsüeh chi-ch'u ch'u-t'an" 太極拳理論的哲學基礎初探 (A preliminary discussion of the philosophical foundations of t'ai-chi ch'üan theory). *Che-chiang t'i-yü k'o-hsüeh* 3 (1986): 10–13.

Yü Shao-hua 于少華. "'Ssu tzu pu ch'uan mi-chüeh' chien-hsi" 四字不傳秘訣簡析 (An analysis of the "Four-Character Secret Transmission"). *Wu-lin* 121 (1991): 37.

Yü Shui-ch'ing 于水清. "Wu-shu chung te yen-yü ho k'ou-chueh" 武術中的諺語和口決 (Martial arts aphorisms and oral transsisions). *Hsin t'i-yü* 11 (1982): 28–29.

Yuasa Yasuo. *The Body: Toward an Eastern Mind-Body Theory*. Albany: State University of New York Press, 1987.

——— (Shigenori Nagamoto and Monte Hull, trans.). *The Body, Self-Cultivation, and Ki-Energy*. Albany, New York: State University of New York Press, 1993.

Yung Yang-jen 雍陽人. "T'ai-chi ch'üan yüan-liu chung te i-ke wen-t'i" 太極拳源流中的一個問題 (A problem in the origins of t'ai-chi ch'üan). *T'i-yü wen-shih* 5 (1989): 26–31.

———. "Li-p'ai t'ai-chi ch'üan p'u wen-hsien san-p'ien" 李派太極拳譜文獻三篇 (Three texts from the Li-style t'ai-chi ch'üan manuals). *Wu-tang* 5 (1994): 21–25.

———. "T'ai-chi ch'üan yüan-liu k'ao-cheng" 太極拳源流考證 (A study of the origins of t'ai-chi ch'üan). *T'i-yü wen-shih* 4 (1988): 21–27.

Zarrilli, Phillip. "Actualizing Power(s) and Crafting a Self in Kalarippayattu, A South Indian Martial Art and the Yoga and Ayurvedic Paradigms." *Journal of Asian Martial Arts* 3, no. 3 (1994): 11–51.

———. "Repositioning the Body: An Indian Martial Art and Its Modern Pan-Asian Publics." In *Modern Sites: Cultures and Contestation in a Postcolonial World*, edited by C. A. Breckenridge. Minneapolis: University of Minnesota Press, 1994.

———. "Three Bodies of Practice in a Traditional South Indian Martial Art." *Social Science and Medicine* 2 (1989): 1289–1309.

Zito, Angela, and Tani Barlow, eds. *Body, Subject and Power in China*. Chicago: University of Chicago Press, 1994.

INDEX

CPSIA information can be obtained at www.ICGtesting.com
Printed in the USA
LVOW11s1433260516

490109LV00001B/116/P